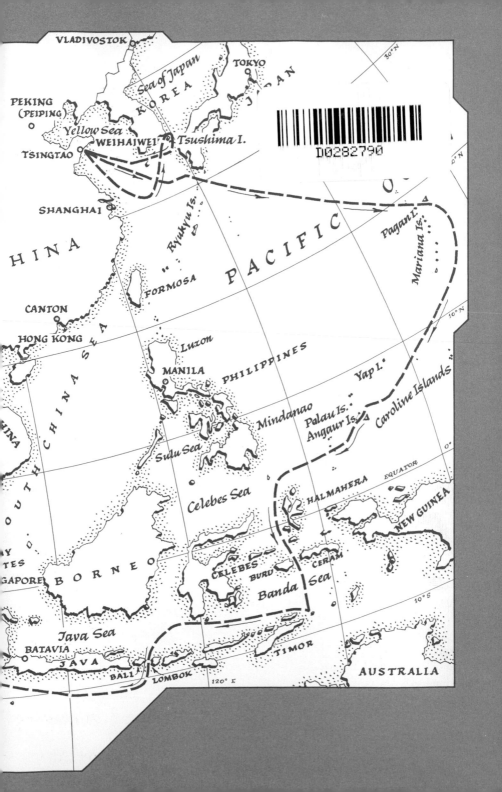

THE LAST CRUISE OF THE *EMDEN*

The Last Cruise
of the
EMDEN

~~~~~~

Edwin P. Hoyt

THE MACMILLAN COMPANY, NEW YORK

COLLIER-MACMILLAN, LTD., LONDON

Library of Congress Catalog Card Number: 66-16706

First Printing

The Macmillan Company, New York
Collier-Macmillan Canada Ltd., Toronto, Ontario

Printed in the United States of America

For Dinny,
who always did love a good adventure story.

CONTENTS

THE LAST CRUISE OF THE *EMDEN*

Chapter 1

TSINGTAO, 1914

ON ANY GIVEN DAY in the spring of 1914 a score of ships rode comfortably at anchor in Kiaochow Bay on the southern shore of China's Shantung peninsula, confident of their safety from any sudden storms that might arise in the choppy waters of the Yellow Sea. They rested thus safely through the courtesy of the Imperial German government, for Kiaochow was a German colony. Kaiser Wilhelm II's government held a ninety-nine-year lease on the territory thirty miles in every direction from the harbor. What had been the tiny fishing village of Tsingtao sixteen years earlier when the lease was granted at gunpoint was now the thriving city and capital of the German colony. It was connected by railway to the Chinese city of Tsinan and by cable to Shanghai. It was an important China port of call for passenger and cargo vessels cruising up and down the coast.

The harbor system was one of the finest in the Far East. It should have been, since the German government had spent two million dollars in developing the facilities since 1898. Three harbors were built in the bay, although only one concerned most Europeans; the others were a harbor for Chinese junks and a smaller harbor, complete with floating drydock, which was used for ship repairs.

The main harbor was enclosed by a long, semicircular jetty which formed two sides of the harbor, protecting the interior from the northwest winds that are prevalent in the bay. The third side was formed by the range of hills that projects between the city of Tsingtao and the eastern side of the peninsula that separates Kiaochow Bay from the open sea. Together with the fifteen thousand feet of breakwater formed by the jetty, the Germans then had as fine a harbor as existed in East Asia, man-made, yet quite comparable to Hong Kong.

The southern side of the harbor was given over to wharves. One, 2,400 feet long and 350 feet wide, was put at the service of merchant ships. Four warehouses, or godowns, were built on this wharf and three railroad tracks brought goods from the rail yards to the steamers.

Five hundred feet away stood a second dock, which was used by the German navy. It was only 1,600 feet long, but contained three godowns and four rail tracks.

The entire harbor was dredged, to allow entrance of vessels that drew as much as twenty-five feet of water. It was all completed by 1906, at a cost of twelve and a half million dollars.

Tsingtao was rebuilt by German engineers with the thoroughness that is the mark of their mentality. First they razed the Chinese fishing village. They settled the Chinese residents in the village of Taitungchen, across the hills of the peninsula. Then they laid out a planned European city. Sewage-disposal facilities and a water system were laid out underground before any building began. The streets, some forty feet wide with twenty-foot sidewalks for pedestrians, were laid out in an irregular manner, to prevent the cold northwest winds of winter from whistling through the city unhindered. Special tracks were laid out for wheelbarrows and carts, a Western concession to the main modes of transport of the Chinese. The hauling coolies were thus kept out of the center of the roadway, leaving it clear for carriages, automobiles, and rickshas.

The finest part of the city, running along the water side of the outer harbor, was reserved for homes of the wealthy and powerful and the government offices. The houses were European in design, mostly built of brick or native stone and covered with red and green tile roofs. The houses were very similar, because most of them were built by contractors under subsidy and supervision of the German government. The living rooms, the bedrooms, and the verandas of these houses were almost always on the south side. There they caught the winter sun. The kitchens and outbuildings, where the Chinese servants worked, were on the north side.

The outstanding man-made structure on the peninsula was the German garrison, located on a hillside overlooking the city. Not far away was the residence of the commander of the garrison. Down the hill, but still on the outer harbor, with a fine view, was the Tsingtao hospital, one of the most modern in Asia. It was equipped to serve both civil and military patients.

Eastward from the hospital was the bathing beach, surrounded by a hotel and summer cottages. The country club was not far away.

Originally this was desolate land. The hills had long been bare, their trees stripped by farmers and the poor fishermen of generations past. But the Germans did not allow such desolation to continue. They brought trees from Germany and planted them in rows along the streets and highways and in groves at propitious points. In a very few years after 1898 the trees were accepted as a part of the landscape of this enclave in Shantung province. They also served a useful purpose: Two of the highest hills were heavily forested, concealing the fortifications located below the trees. Iltis and Bismarck fortresses were located on these hills. They overlooked both the sea and the land, and if they were not built so strongly as Gibraltar, the German defensive strategy was quite different. The high command expected to defend Tsingtao from the sea. The fortresses and two water-level batteries were intended to provide temporary protection until the signal and wireless stations atop the hills could call down the might of the German Pacific Squadron to drive the attackers from the shores of the colony. The wireless station contained a transmitter quite strong enough to send messages freely to Yap, the German naval base in the Caroline Islands colony.

For the European in China, Tsingtao was the summer spa— the Newport of Asia. Its wide half-moon bathing beach was covered with fine light sand. The fresh winds from the sea blew inland steadily in the hot summer months, cooling the city and making it the most livable place in the East. Missionaries, businessmen and foreign officials tried to plan their affairs so they could spend a holiday each year at Tsingtao. There was plenty of entertainment: parties at the country club, at the hotels, at the military and naval clubs and the commercial clubs of the city; sailing in the bay; racing at the track outside the city. The governor of the colony, Kapitän-zur-See Meyer-Waldeck, was noted for his openhanded hospitality, and his generosity was matched by that of the residents of Tsingtao. It was a happy place. In the beginning, before the turn of the century, the Germans had oppressed the Chinese, but after settlement of the Boxer Rebellion, German policy changed. The railroads, the customs, the port authority and business were placed largely in Chinese hands. The Germans took the precaution of maintaining German officials at the tops of the heaps, but the Chinese had a major share in the running of affairs. There was a happy mingling of the races in the business and even the social world, much more so than in the other European colonies and spheres of influence in the Far East. The people, the Chinese people, of Kiaochow colony were happy and the colony was prosperous. It was a garden spot of the Far East.

At the country club in the spring there were occasional rumors of unpleasantness in Europe. In the noisy friendliness of the Dachsal restaurant the officers of the German ships often gathered around the big circular tables, drank beer, and discussed the unpleasant turn of events. And not just the Germans. There was a camaraderie among the Europeans in Asia that almost, if not quite, transcended nationality. A German, a Russian, and an Englishman might be found any sunny day lying together on the sand, taking the sun and discussing the problems of East Asia, not those of their homelands. Some Europeans, just out from home, warned solemnly of the coming of war in a few months. By and large the old China hands of all nations disregarded them. Life was too pleasant underneath the punkahs and lying in the sun to consider seriously problems that were eight thousand miles away. Who would worry about war when working beneath the arched balconies of the administration building in the morning hours and then descending the long sweeping staircase, summoning one's private ricksha man and heading for the club for a long and pleasant luncheon? War in Europe? Who could be concerned when there was a ball that night in the governor's great stone palace? The English and the French and the Russians talking about an Anglo-Russian naval alliance? What effect could that have on the gaiety of life in Tsingtao that summer? Particularly when thoughts were turned to a dinner to be held that night in one of the four-story houses that stood so proudly above the trees of Kuangsu Road.

And yet there were signs of the tension even in the Far East. The East Asia Cruiser Squadron of the Imperial German Navy was concentrated in Tsingtao. The admiral, the Graf von Spee, knew something of the tensions of the hour in Europe. There was no plan at the Reichsmarineamt for a battle role to be given the Imperial Navy, no plan at all. Yet the admiral knew what his role must be in case of war. The cruiser squadron in Asia would be of value if it could disrupt communications and supply movement between the colonies of the Triple Entente and the homelands. In Asia this meant largely the colonies of Great Britain, the important possessions at Hong Kong, and above all Australia and India. With more than the usual concern, then, the Graf von Spee awaited the arrival of the steamship that would bring the relief for his cruiser squadron. It was an annual affair, this relief of the squadron. The men and officers whose enlistments were running out or who were entitled to home leave would be replaced in May when the steamship from Wilhelms-haven brought the relief. This meant that for several months the cruiser squadron would be well below its standard as a fighting unit. The new men must be accommodated and trained to the East Asia Cruiser Squadron's way of doing things.

This year the relief came aboard the *Patricia*, a steamer of the Hamburg-Amerika line. One April day the *Patricia* entered Wilhelms-haven and tied up near the locks there. The loading of supplies and men began. For twenty-four hours the stevedores hauled slings of supplies into place and the whirring donkey engines above hoisted them up and then lowered them down into the holds of the ship. The squadron's contingent of officers and sailors boarded the ship, the flags, hundreds of them, were broken out from the ship and from shore installations, and the *Patricia* made ready to sail for Tsingtao.

It was peacetime. The girls came down to see their lovers off, listening to the promises and nostalgic words of parting.

They hung around the ship, and no one paid much attention, for this was peacetime. The changing of the guard in the East Asia Squadron was a relief from the monotony of the port. No one ex-pected trouble; no one in the lower echelons thought of war.

Sailing day was a Sunday, April 23. Early in the morning the departing navy men boarded the liner. The band of the Second Sea Battalion, under the famous music master Rhode, came to the quay and stationed itself beside the ship to play medley after medley of stirring marches and lively songs of departure. The scene was de-scribed by Boatswain's Mate Hermann Ottiger, one of those who was destined for Tsingtao and was eventually to join the light cruiser S.M.S. *Emden.*

On board the steamer it is as in a beehive. Everyone is free and happy since he has his place card in his hand, which promises him a cost-free sea voyage of six to seven weeks.

At first one is staggered to find himself in this colossus of a ship with its many decks, its passages and descending passages, quite as they ought not to be (for one used to a warship); as in a garden maze one runs around always in circles. I have the luck to share a cabin together with three comrades. Hundreds of sailors, all of the senior grades, rush around the decks and cluster in the outbuildings of the wharf, bringing armloads of their belongings with them, stopping for one last earnest chat with friends. Some climb the rigging, and a few sit above the ship on the mast. But these are only the seniors; division after division comes with drums beating, and each passes away in the bowels of the ship. . . .

Finally, the carnival atmosphere was reduced to order. The *Patricia* began to blow her mighty whistle. Lines were loosed and dropped from ship to pier. Some were hauled up to the deck of the ship. The waving of those on deck and those on shore increased in tempo as the ship's engines began to throb. With one last mighty blast of the whistle she began to move and was away. The men destined for the East Asia Squadron moved out to sea and to the final sight of a peaceful homeland.

As the weeks of the voyage slipped by, the tensions in Europe increased. When the *Patricia* reached the Far East, nearly seven weeks after her departure from Wilhelmshaven, the fears and rumors were fully developed. Among the Germans of the military caste, of course, there was no fear but an eagerness for the war to begin. This eagerness, not so much a Prussian characteristic in 1914 as a pan-German one, was stated in detail, along with justification for the war effort by Kapitänleutnant Hellmuth von Mücke, first officer of the *Emden*, who was to play a role in the last cruise of the *Emden* and in the war that other Germans termed the most miraculous of the century.

Von Mücke was a professional navy man. At this time he was in his early thirties, and except for minor schooling in Germany before puberty he had not known any real life outside the navy. The navy was his training ground and his moral teacher. He was a slim hawk-nosed man, diffident in a way although regarded as a disciplinarian (which a first officer must be in a proper German naval vessel). He had large ears and deep, piercing eyes, set beneath heavy brows. His hair was thick and parted neatly on the left, receding slightly at the temples but with a widow's peak. He was muscular and lithe, and he wore the wing collar and dark formal uniform of his navy with assurance and pride. Not having known command himself he had not enjoyed the luxury of questioning his superiors in their judgment or action. He never questioned an order.

So the first officer of the *Emden* was loquacious and positive that spring in his statements that war was coming soon. He said, of course, that it was the fault of Germany's enemies. They were ringing her in.

He spoke of the "persistent cries for revenge" of France and Russia, but his real hatred was reserved for England and "English greed for wealth and power." Inch by inch, he told his juniors, England's power was being given up to Germany. England found herself unable to compete successfully with Germany in peace, so England would soon resort to her old trick: "Sink, burn, destroy!"

How England would do this was yet to be determined. Would she entangle others and let them fight her battles, as she had so often in the past? Von Mücke did not know, he said. She might do so. She might fight. "Lack of a sufficient reason has never deterred England," he wrote, "when a desired end was to be obtained."

Von Mücke raged against England, true to the traditions of the German military mind. He recalled the ignominies suffered by Spain at England's bloody hands; those of Holland ("drained by the English vampire"); Denmark, whose fleet was attacked by the English "at a time when the two countries were absolutely at peace"; China, "Overrun with war because the Chinese refused to buy opium of the English merchants"; Egypt, which was forced to plant cotton instead of grain, thus reducing her to vassalage to help England; India, where "the blessings of English culture" included what von Mücke termed an annual tribute of one and a half billion pounds; the Boer states, subjugated because of England's lust for diamonds and gold; Turkey; France; Russia; Portugal; even America—"England made the attempt to forbid the construction and fortification of the Panama Canal." He worked himself into a fine passion, then declared to his listeners that Germany's turn had come. He purported to quote from an English publication of 1907, which said "England's prosperity could not be assured until Germany has been destroyed."

Thus matters stood, in the eyes of Hellmuth von Mücke and others of the German military mind, in the late spring when the *Patricia* arrived, bringing the annual replacement of crews for the cruiser squadron.

The first sight of the men of the *Patricia* was the land of Cape

Jatan, where the steamer made a sharp turn to port, heading past many small rocky islands into Kiaochow Bay. Before them, rising out of the Lauchan mountains, still covered with snow, lay the peak of Lanting, highest mountain in the eastern Shantung range. A few minutes later the bay widened and those aboard the *Patricia* had their first view of Tsingtao, pearl of Germany's overseas colonies.

The *Patricia* moved slowly into harbor, circled now by a dozen small motorboats and deluged with greetings from the signal tower atop the hill behind the city. As the steamer drew close to the city and its mole, the passengers could make out the individual ships of the East Asia Squadron: the ironclad cruisers *Scharnhorst* and *Gneisenau*, the smaller *Emden* and *Leipzig*, their tenders, and the destroyers and gunboats that made up the rest of the naval fleet in port.

It was a holiday in Tsingtao; every relief day was a holiday in the city, and the Europeans flocked to the quay to see the arrival of the steamer from the fatherland. From the signal stations of the warships came blinker messages shining in the sunlight. Aboard the *Scharnhorst* and the *Gneisenau* the crews stood in ranks on the upper deck as for a divisional review. The admiral, the Graf von Spee, was aboard the *Scharnhorst*, on his bridge, standing with his staff officers. Next to him were two young lieutenants: his sons.

The admiral, his heart-shaped face abeam above the Vandyke and mustache, raised his hand in salute as the *Patricia* pulled into the grand harbor. The band aboard the *Scharnhorst* struck up the German national anthem, then followed it with the Prussian anthem. The men aboard the naval vessels, at a signal, unleashed three lusty cheers that could be heard plainly on the merchant ship by every man. Then three times the *Patricia* dipped her ensign to the naval flags, the cross and eagle flags, that flew at the sterns of the warships, all the while edging her way into the pier. As the *Patricia* moved forward the new arrivals could see into the repair harbor with its floating drydock. One naval vessel, they did not know which, was undergoing repairs at that moment, and of all the Germans in Tsingtao, perhaps only these repairmen were so occupied that they could not take time out to watch the coming of the relief ship. From the drydock came the earsplitting sounds of riveting and hammering and the flash of torches. Now the land was close enough to see the azaleas in bloom on the hillsides and the brown of the distant hills and mountains. Were it not for the lusty voices of the warriors in the harbor, it would have been as peaceful a setting as a visitor might wish to see.

~~~~~~

Chapter 2

THE SHIP

SEINE MAJISTÄTS SCHIFFE *Emden,* His Majesty's Ship, was one of those German cruisers envisioned and launched in the warmth of the high command's hopes for domination of the seven seas. Chancellor von Bismarck had warned against a German attempt to compete with England on the oceans of the world, but Chancellor von Bülow had no such sagacity. He would rather antagonize England than ally himself with her, and so around the turn of the century the Germans began to build their naval war machine and plan for the war of the future, which would make them supreme in Europe and formidable in all the rest of the world.

Before World War I very few of the world's naval leaders had much confidence in the powers of the submarine to wreak damage on warships. Nor was the concept of unrestricted naval warfare of any kind yet invented. War was a relatively leisurely matter, particularly on the high seas. There were rules to govern it, developed in a series of international conferences. It was proper to sink a vessel that belonged to the enemy, of course. This was accomplished by the warship's overtaking the enemy, calling on her to stop, even firing a shot across her bow. The enemy merchantman, having stopped, would then be boarded, and the boarding officer would present his compliments to the captain of the enemy merchant ship, then inform him as to the fate of his vessel. It might be towed into a port belonging to the attacker or to a neutral port. Its cargo might be transferred to the warship or to one of her retinue of coalers. (No warship, in these days before the Diesel engine, could hope to travel long without coaling.) The enemy merchantman might be sunk. Usually this was accomplished by opening the sea cocks of the vessel and allowing her to go down, aided perhaps by a few small explosive charges placed strategically in the bottom. Sometimes, if the attacker was in a hurry or wished to give his crew some gun practice, the merchantman was made into a target. But all this was done after the crew and the passengers had been safely removed from the scene of action. They were not usually abandoned to their fate in lifeboats; the finest traditions of naval warfare called for the protection of the crew and passengers and the guarantee of their safety by the attacker. Consequently, those who wished to practice warfare in the grand tradition used the first ship they might capture in their train of suppliers as what the French called a *chiffonier* and the Germans a *Lumpensammler*. Both words mean junkman in English. The *Lumpensammler* was the ship saved to house prisoners. When it became an overloaded ark, it was dispatched from the train with orders to seek a neutral port and deliver the human cargo safe and sound.

A neutral vessel, under the carefully wrought rules of naval warfare, might be stopped on the high seas and searched. (The Americans in particular objected to this practice very strenuously.) If it was found to be carrying contraband, it too might be captured. Contraband was to become very broadly defined, and seizures were to be handled most ineptly by the belligerents, contributing to the swift breakdown of the rules of civilized warfare in the early days of World War I. But in the *Emden's* day warfare was a civilized matter, with the fighting to be conducted between men matched as nearly as possible, and with civilians and noncombatants to be protected even at the cost of the lives of the fighters.

Since the submarine did not seriously enter the calculations of the naval leaders in the first decade of the twentieth century, they devised other plans for the harassment of the supply lines of their

potential enemies. The raider was considered to be their major
weapon for this use. The raider was the successor to the privateer of
the days of the American Revolution. Governments could afford to
commission and operate their own raiders, so the spoils of war were
no longer turned to private profit, but the principle was the same. A
raider might be a fast converted merchantman armed with only one
or two pieces of naval artillery. Even one gun capable of piercing
holes beneath the water line of a merchant ship would make a raider
effective against unarmed merchantmen. These converted merchantmen were called auxiliary cruisers. They came in all sizes and varieties.
It was enough that they be able to sport some kind of gun to terrorize
and if necessary to sink enemy ships.

The Germans led all other nations in the development of a
special naval vessel designed for this purpose. This was the *kleiner
ungepanzerfer Kreuzer*—the small unarmored cruiser. Such was
S.M.S. *Emden*, built in Danzig in 1907 and 1908 as the *Ersatz Pfiel*
(*Artificial Arrow*). During the course of her building someone in the
Berlin government had the idea that it would be useful and binding
in a patriotic way to name this series of cruisers after various German
cities. So Emden, a port on the Ems River and once, under the
Brandenburgs, a leader in the development of the German maritime
industry, was chosen to sponsor this particular little cruiser. The
mayor of the city journeyed to Danzig on May 26, 1908, and in the
name of the Emperor Wilhelm II he christened the new ship.

She was to remind the people of Emden of the power of their
emperor and of the new growth of Germany. With the opening of
the Dortmund-Ems Canal, Emden was to become again an ocean-
oriented port, and the naming of the cruiser for the town was to
remind the citizens also of their stake in the expansion of German
Empire. The emperor, on the exalted day of the ship's christening,
sent a message to the citizens of Emden noting that the Imperial
German government had so named the vessel "in recognition of the
rise and growth of the harbor of Emden." At Danzig the mayor spoke
of the Brandenburgs and Frederick the Great, who had brought
Emden under the Prussian crown. He noted the connection of Emden with the East Asia company and the development of German
trade with China under the Brandenburg flag. He reported the pleasure it gave Emden's businessmen to furnish the ship. Thus the sleepy
little town on the edge of the Dutch border, more Dutch than Ger-

man in its orientation around the turn of the century (according to Baedeker), was converted into a bastion of German nationalism and empire building.

The *Emden* displaced 3,650 tons. Her two steam-driven engines, fired by coal, could attain a speed of 24.5 knots. If she was operated at reduced speed and handled carefully, she could travel as far as six thousand miles without recoaling. This, at the time of her launching, was regarded as a major breakthrough in the logistics of naval warfare. She was armed with ten guns of 10.5 centimeters, which were capable of rapid fire. These were not large for naval guns; a British light cruiser, for example, might mount guns of more than fifteen centimeters in size; but the *Emden* was not built to fight other cruisers. She was built to be the twentieth-century equivalent of the privateer. The French had a word for this class of cruiser: they called it the *corsaire*.

On commissioning, the *Emden* carried a force of seventeen officers and 361 men under a captain who, in the tradition of the German navy, also commanded one of the two watches that alternated in the routine operation of the vessel. Her trial runs were held between July and September 1909, and she functioned as nearly perfectly as the admiralty had any right to expect. For a time she was kept in home waters. On April 1, 1910, she became officially a part of the Imperial German Navy in a ceremony in which her flag was raised amid streamers and the hoots of the whistles of accompanying vessels. Captain Vollerthun sat down that day and wrote to the authorities of the city of Emden, describing the performance of the ship and her mission in the world, and with due patriotic ceremony the message was received and publicized. And a month later the *Emden* was off around the world to begin her mission: the strengthening of Germany's bonds of empire.

Captain Vollerthun took her first to Buenos Aires and up the Chilean coast, to honor the centennial of Argentine and Chilean independence. She then made a name for herself in naval circles when she steamed from Takahuano, Chile, to Apia in the Pacific islands, without recoaling—a distance of 4,200 sea miles in nineteen days. Apia was in Western Samoa, where the German Empire had been extended after arguments with the United States and Britain.

In Apia the *Emden* joined Germany's East Asia Cruiser Squadron, led by the armored cruiser *Scharnhorst*, with her sister ship, the

Gneisenau. Now she wore the colors she would bear until war came. Her hull was silver gray, very nearly white, and her three tall funnels and superstructure were darker gray.

In the fashion of the steel warships of the period, the *Emden* was long, low and rakish in design. The breakwater of her bow projected farther forward at the water line than at the level of the main deck—a hangover from the days of ramming and the use of ironclads as ships of all work.

Dark round portholes dotted her hull forward and aft. Most of her living and working space was below the main-deck level. The superstructure was dominated by two tall masts which served as radio towers, lookout stations and signaling posts, by the three towering stacks, and by the bridge superstructure, which stood some three decks high, about halfway up the smokestack level. She sported two torpedo tubes in addition to her other armament, and her turrets, inconspicuous as they might appear in the overall view, made her a formidable weapon to any vessel but a larger cruiser or a battleship.

She was armored, although she was not called an armored cruiser because the steel plating that protected her was relatively light. Her armor deck was only between two and five centimeters thick. The command tower was more heavily armored, however, since it projected above the ship; here and also at the vulnerable water line the armor was six to ten centimeters thick. Altogether, with her length of 118 meters and width of fourteen meters, she was a slim and graceful ship. In the Far East she was known among German navy men as the Swan of the East.

In September 1910, the *Emden* arrived in Tsingtao, headquarters of the East Asia Squadron, and there she remained for three months. In December she was called to Ponape, one of the South Sea Islands in which the Germans had established colonial power, but where the natives were not ready to accept the new rule. She landed fighting men with arms on that trip and her first blood was shed there. Several men were killed in the punitive action against the natives, including one of the ship's officers.

By March 1911, the political and military affairs of Ponape were stable enough so that the *Emden* could be returned to her station. Later she traveled to and from Samoa several times, and in the middle of November 1911, she was on hand in Shanghai harbor to protect the German citizens there during the revolution that overthrew the Manchus and established the Republic of China. During that revolution the command of the *Emden* changed. On January 5, 1912, Captain von Restorff assumed command of the cruiser.

Von Restorff's tenure lasted just over a year. When the relief of the East Asia Squadron arrived in Tsingtao in May 1913, it brought Korvettenkapitän Karl von Müller from a workroom in the Reichsmarineamt in Berlin to fulfill a personal dream: command of a small cruiser.

In the East Asia Squadron it was considered necessary for a ship and its captain to have three months following the relief of the squadron in the spring for drill and training of his crew before the ship could be brought to its fighting peak. In 1913 there was no such leisure, for a month after his arrival in Tsingtao, Captain von Müller was ordered to take the *Emden* to the South Seas again to meet a threat of disorder. He sailed on his birthday, June 16. All that day the *Emden* had sat in the harbor at the naval pier, loading supplies and taking on coal. Coaling was an indescribably filthy job. At the end of it every nook and cranny of the ship was covered with black dust, the men coughed dust for days, and their eyes were red and running from the irritation. There was no easy way to coal; it was one of the harsh necessities of naval life.

The *Emden*, preparing for a long trip, became a floating farmyard, too. She took on live calves, cows, and oxen, which were led to stalls built on the deck. Three pigs were brought aboard and placed in a sty the carpenters had built for them, not far from the cages where a hundred hens clucked and beat their wings.

As evening descended on the harbor with its calm the *Emden* was ready for her voyage south, her funnels pouring forth smoke and the heavy load pushing her down at the water line. At five o'clock the engine room reported steam up in all boilers, and an hour later the ship threaded her way around the mole, past the two points and out into Kiaochow Bay. She passed the opposing point of the Haihsi peninsula at the mouth of the bay, steamed between Chuchatao island and Taikingtao, and set her course through the Yellow Sea for the Pacific island group of Yap.

It was the monsoon season in the Orient, and at the outset the weather was cold and damp. They ran through fog for several hours and only gradually emerged from the cold as they headed southward. Then the weather changed completely. The men had been freezing, now they steamed in the hot sleeping quarters below decks. Von Müller took pity on them and allowed his crew to move their sleeping hammocks onto the main deck, where they could rest in the cool night breezes.

Across the thousands of miles to Yap they did not see a single sail or a trace of smoke, so lonely was the Pacific. Finally a lookout announced the appearance of land dead ahead. Outside the harbor they took aboard a pilot, and then they were inside the reef, surrounded by dugout canoes carrying red or black mat sails.

The *Emden* was received with joy and thanksgiving by the German inhabitants, who had little news or contact with their homeland except for the coming of a ship. They remained at Yap for several days, anchored in the open water of the bay. They entertained the islanders and the German residents in the wardroom and the commander's cabin. They went ashore to visit the new wireless station and to attend native feasts and dances. Life was quiet enough at the coastal settlement of Citapé, but ten miles inland it was worth a man's life to travel alone.

Since life was quiet at Yap, the *Emden* was summoned to Kaiser-Wilhelmsland by wireless message from the squadron, and then, on arrival at Rabaul, she was directed back to Tsingtao. They arrived at the squadron's home port again in July, in the middle of the summer bathing season, and as they sailed inside the harbor they could see the people tumbling in the surf along the white sandy beach.

There was little leisure for the crew of the *Emden* that year, little time to enjoy the pleasures of beach and mountain or the company of friendly civilians in Tsingtao. In August the cruiser was ordered to the Yangtze to protect the lives of Germans and join with other European naval contingents in a show of force that would preserve the foreign extraterritorial position in China. China was now a republic, but not a peaceful one. Along the shores of the Yangtze a new revolution raged, partly led by communists, partly by warlords. The *Emden* sped to the Yangtze and anchored in that river near the English cruiser H.M.S. *Hampshire*, not far from an American cruiser and one from the empire of Japan. Along the shore of the river the guns spoke loudly and often. Sometimes the shells fell near the ships, raising gouts of water mast-high.

A few hours after the *Emden*'s arrival, when Captain von Müller was just emerging from a bath he had taken to try to cool off in the Yangtze summer heat, the German consul came aboard.

He bore two letters, he said, from Ho Hai-ming, both addressed to the captain of the *Emden*. The Chinese general, commander of the rebellious forces along the Yangtze, claimed that a German ship had fired on his troops in Fort Lowenberg, which they had occupied, and threatened that he intended to take countermeasures. The consul apparently believed that the Chinese general's information was correct and had come aboard, uncertainly, to attempt to persuade the captain against seizing the forts.

Instead of giving an apology for an act he had not committed, the commander of the *Emden* drafted a letter to the Chinese general demanding an apology. The consul, who knew his Chinese, opposed the brusque tone, but Captain von Müller, unwise in the ways of the East, found the reversal amusing. He was not so unwise in the ways of men, however, that he failed to make the ship ready for action just in case of trouble.

The dispute continued. In the afternoon another Chinese boat came alongside the *Emden,* bearing an emissary who charged specifically that four Germans had fired on the fort and had destroyed a gun carriage. Von Müller protested again and demanded proof. Finally he secured an apology from General Ho Hai-ming and the matter seemed to be ended. Only later did von Müller discover that there was some truth in the Chinese charge.

About two weeks later, when the *Emden* was nearly ready to leave the vicinity, Captain von Müller noticed a Chinese gunboat in the river, Chinese but flying the German naval ensign. He ordered the gunboat to heave to and explain, but the smaller vessel hauled down its flag and ran. The rebels, or some rebels, had taken to using the German flag, perhaps in revenge against the *Emden*'s demands for apology. Not long after this incident a transport loaded with rebel troops came by. This too bore the German flag, and the captain had the gall to salute the *Emden* with it. The squadron flagship, the *Scharnhorst*, had joined the *Emden* on the Yangtze, and von Müller radioed the information along the river. The transport was seized and the flag removed.

On the way down river, in her movement out of the Yangtze, the *Emden* came to a point where the shores of the Yangtze are close together and both shores were commanded by forts. It was near evening as the cruiser reached this point, and although the fort on the left seemed clear of rebel forces, the captain could not be sure of the fort on the southern side of the river, so he anchored for the night rather than run the risk of a night engagement in narrow, treacherous waters.

In the morning, all hands were called to battle stations, and cautiously the *Emden* made her way through the narrow passage. Captain von Müller wanted to be sure he did not give the rebels the slightest cause for action if they still occupied the fort on the right bank of the river. The artillery spotters were in their places atop the masts and the artillery officers were in the turrets, but the captain ordered them to keep the guns trained straight ahead, so no offense would be given nor any excuse for the rebels to open fire on the cruiser.

As the *Emden* came through the channel Captain von Müller was on the bridge, looking to left and right. On the left the fort was deserted, but on the right, behind field artillery pieces, stood Chinese gunners of the rebel army. They needed no provocation, it seemed, for at six o'clock in the morning, as the *Emden* drew to a point about 1,500 yards from the batteries, the Chinese opened fire. The Germans heard a bugle—obviously a signal of some kind—and at the same time the water in front of the bow of the cruiser spewed up in three fountains.

The captain spoke to his adjutant.

"Gaede," he said, "they shoot very badly. We will show them how one shoots."

The cruiser came to a stop in the center of the river and von Müller gave the order to his gunners to open fire. Two salvos were fired. The Chinese answered. But while the Chinese shells exploded harmlessly in the water about the *Emden,* a shower of dust and stones arose from the embrasures of the fort. Two more salvos and the Chinese guns were quiet. The captain signaled from the bridge and the *Emden* again began to steam ahead. Later that day another rebel post on the river fired at them. This artillery, too, was silenced after three salvos.

When the cruiser reached the port city of Wuhu, von Müller went ashore and protested sharply against the action of the rebels. No German consul was in residence at Wuhu, but there was an English representative there, and he was pleased to carry the letter of protest for the German commander.

The *Emden* then made her way to Shanghai. The news of her action had preceded her there, and she was greeted as a conquering hero. English and French ships had also been fired on by the rebels, but their commanders had not returned the fire. Von Müller was not sure what he might expect from his squadron commander, Vice-Admiral the Graf von Spee, for his action might precipitate an international incident. But the Graf von Spee was pleased with the forthright behavior of his commander.

"I am content," he wrote to von Müller, "with the determined and energetic action in the settlement of the incident of the bombardment of the *Emden,* in every way."

And so the *Emden* was blooded and returned to Shanghai from the Nanking area as the most celebrated foreign ship on the river. At home in Germany the news of her action was received with cheers. She had comported herself in a manner quite fitting for a daughter of the German empire. Partly on the success of this action, von Müller was promoted a few months later to the rank of Fregattenkapitän, the full four-stripe rank of captains the world around.

The *Emden* and her proud crew returned to the East Asia Squadron's base at Tsingtao, the most famous naval contingent in the Orient.

Chapter 3

THE MEN OF THE *EMDEN*

THE CREW THAT HAD MADE HISTORY by returning the rebel fire on the Yangtze was broken up by the relief changes in the spring of 1914, but the tradition remained. The *Emden* was a proud and happy ship. Emil Ludwig attributed the successes of the *Emden* and its crew to the temperament of its leaders: "Perhaps it is the old law that the courageous attract the courageous, the noble attract the noble, the pure attract the pure," he wrote. There was another quality for which the *Emden* and its crew became famous, not nearly so flamboyant as the qualities given the men of the *Emden* by Ludwig but much more important in time of war: Throughout the odyssey of the *Emden* its officers and men were distinguished for their loyalty and responsibility above all. This latter quality certainly came to the men of the *Emden* through their captain, Karl von Müller.

Von Müller represented all that was best in the Prussian officer class. That was his background and his tradition; his was an officer family for as far back as anyone could remember. Both his grandfathers were officers in the army. His father was a colonel in the Prussian army and then in the German army. On his mother's side the military tradition was strengthened by a political tradition. His mother was born Charlotte Bennigsen. Her brother, Rudolf von Bennigsen, was a leader of the German nationalist movement early in the century.

There was no question about Karl von Müller's future in life even on the day he was born, June 16, 1873. He would be a German officer. His older brother became a German officer before Karl and later served as the German general staff's chief of the reserve corps. It was something of a shock that Karl chose the navy rather than the Prussian army that had so firm a grip on the family's sentiments, but in 1891, when the young Karl's choice was made, times were changing. Germany was to have a navy, said the masters in Berlin, that would not dip its flag to any nation anywhere in the seven seas save out of courtesy. So the boy's wishes were respected and he left the academy at Kiel where his father and brother had gone before him to become a cadet in the Imperial Navy. His service was typical of the training of young German officers, first in the cadet corps at Plon, then to Berlin and Lichtenfeld for schooling and the discipline of military life. His first school ship was the *Stosch*, his next was the famous cruiser *Gneisenau*, aboard which he traveled to South America and the United States on training cruises. Even then his most noteworthy characteristic was emerging. Kapitän-zur-See Persius of the *Gneisenau* singled him out for commendation in his reports to Berlin for his orderliness and "painful conscientiousness." On this service von Müller came to know Meyer-Waldeck very well; later they would renew acquaintance when von Müller took the *Emden* and Meyer-Waldeck served as the last governor of Kiaochow.

Promotions came regularly for the earnest young officer. In the autumn of 1894 he was promoted to Leutnant-zur-See, three years later to Oberleutnant-zur-See, in 1903 to Kapitänleutnant, in 1908 to Korvettenkapitän, the rank he held when he came to the *Emden*. His experience was broad and his knowledge was extensive by 1913. He had been signal officer on the old ship-of-the-line *Moltke*, officer of the guard on the cruiser *Geflon*. He had served aboard the torpedo school ship *Blucher*, on the flagship *Blitz*, and on the armored coastal cruiser *Agir*. He had been to minesweeping school and torpedo school, and he had served for two years on the light cruiser *Schwalbe* in colonial waters. Most of the time the *Schwalbe* was stationed on the coast of East Africa.

For two years he was adjutant of the First Naval Division, stationed at Kiel. Then in 1902 he became artillery officer on the battleship *Kaiser Wilhelm I*. He had served as a staff officer at sea and at the admiralty. He had served royalty, as aide to Prince Heinrich, grand admiral and commander of the flagship *Deutschland*. Finally, he had sat at the knee of the great von Tirpitz in the Reichsmarineamt in Berlin, and there he had applied for command of a light cruiser, to receive the *Emden*.

Von Müller had been decorated several times for service and bravery. He held the Red Order of the German Eagle, fourth class with a crown, which signified its second presentation. He held the Imperial Crown Order, third class, with swords to increase its honor. The swords came following the incident on the Yangtze.

Von Müller's men, while with one exception not so distinguished as himself, were competent representatives of His Majesty's Imperial Navy. Kapitänleutnant von Mücke, second in command, was the tall blond Saxon who might well be mistaken for a Prussian. He was correct and nearly as disciplined in his manners as von Müller. Kapitänleutnant Ernst Gaede, the gunnery officer, was a Prussian like his captain, the son of a Hanover judge and the graduate of Bromberg's gymnasium and the grammar school at Königsberg before he became a professional member of the naval officer corps. Gaede had directed the guns that silenced the rebels on the Yangtze. He was twenty-nine years old that year.

Kapitänleutnant Gropius, the ship's navigator, was thirty-one years old, a gay young bachelor who was noted for his personal bravery. He had been saber ensign on the *Weissenberg* in 1904 and during maneuvers had saved the life of a seaman, exposing himself to great danger to do so.

The *Emden* was signally honored by the royal family in 1914, for aboard her was the Kaiser's nephew, Prince Franz Joseph von Hohenzollern, serving as second torpedo officer. The prince was a young bachelor, too, as were most of the officers. He put on no princely airs among his fellows but was as ready to stand his turn at paying for the beer as von Mücke or the others. His companion, assigned to him by the naval authorities, was Leutnant Ernst von Levetzow, a nephew of another of Germany's naval heroes. He was about the same age as the prince, in his late twenties.

One of the favorites with the crew and even with the quiet, stern captain, who played no favorites, was Leutnant Albert Bernhard Maria von Guerard, son of one of Düsseldorf's finest families. His grandfather was one of Germany's best-known eye surgeons, the Professor Doktor Mooren. His father was Theo von Guerard, a career naval officer. He was the jolliest of them all, a slender young man with pleasant manners and a bright eye. Von Müller regarded him as potentially the finest officer aboard his ship, and yet his disposition was so pleasant and his friendliness so puppylike that not one of the other officers resented von Guerard's favored position. He was the youngest of the group who had the captain's ear; he was only twenty-one years old and would not celebrate his twenty-second birthday until after the war began. Young as he was, Leutnant von Guerard was serving that summer as adjutant of the ship. He was the man responsible for the relations of the *Emden* with the ever correct, ever watchful, ever demanding division commanders of the squadron and the fleet.

Youth, love of good food and good wine and good music and girls marked the officers of the *Emden*, but so did sharp eyes for military precision and good seamanship. First Officer von Mücke was an accomplished musician who could perform on half a dozen instruments and often amused his companions late at night as they sat in some Tsingtao beer hall or clubroom, steins in hand. He could also knife a seaman with a glance for leaving an oily handle or a paint stain on the deck.

Except for a handful of older petty officers and specialists, the enlisted men of the *Emden* were surprisingly young. Most of them were under twenty-one. They were single, boisterous and good-natured. They were aware of their extreme good fortune in being assigned duty in East Asia rather than in the rough North Sea, where training exercises were conducted summer and winter under the eyes of the high command and nothing was ever good enough. Their two complaints were that they did not have enough money and that the Chinese girls were not very friendly. As for the money, they were paid in the Mexican silver dollars that were currency at Tsingtao, and their money was in fact worth about twice as much in purchasing power as back in Germany. As for the girls, one sailor put it this way:

". . . they are deprived of many things, especially of a bride for each. Chinese girls are not adapted for this purpose, for, first of all, the language difference nips advances in the bud, and second, as everyone knows, love enters through the stomach. . . ."

Few of the Germans bothered to learn more Chinese than it took to negotiate passage in a ricksha. Like soldiers and sailors everywhere they expected a native to be fluent in their language. Fewer acquired any taste for Chinese cooking as a staple diet. So love came seldom to the men of the East Asia Squadron in Tsingtao.

With the arrival of the steamer *Patricia* in Tsingtao harbor and her departure in June, taking the happy men home to be discharged into the reserves or given long leaves before reenlistment, life settled down a bit and some planning was done by Admiral von Spee for the future months.

The admiral's command was a huge one, speaking geographically. He was responsible for everything in the Pacific, including the Indian Ocean, as far as the Cape of Good Hope and the Red Sea on one side and the coast of Mexico on the other side, north to the end of the world, and south to the waters of Australia. The squadron of half a dozen cruisers and smaller supporting vessels represented German might in this area. One small cruiser, in recent years, had been detailed semi-annually to serve in Mexican waters, to make trips to South America as diplomacy demanded and to show the flag where it would help. There had been talk of this year sending the *Emden* to Mexico, but in the end it was decided that the *Nürnberg* would go there, and she had gone at the first of the year. It was time to relieve her. Again the *Emden* was mentioned, but again the admiral made other plans. The light cruiser *Leipzig* was at that moment to be engaged in a state visit in the waters of Japan. The international situation had continued to be so undecided all spring that Admiral Spee was looking to his coal supplies. Japan was a thousand miles closer to Mexico than Tsingtao, and by leaving from Tokyo Bay the *Leipzig* could beg her coal supply from the Japanese. Thus the coal dumps in Tsingtao, replenished at great trouble and expense by ship each month, could be saved so much fuel for whatever needs might come.

In June the cruiser squadron lay at anchor in Tsingtao, and the new men were taught the rules of their ships. Every day was given over to drills and inspections. The ship was burnished down watch on watch, the crews were trained to run out the ten guns, to use the depth charges she carried at the taffrail, to play the hoses for damage control. The stokers were taught how to keep the fires burning brightly without smoking overmuch. The torpedo men were taught to use their weapons. Youngsters were given doses of discipline for thoughtless infractions, and old sailors were reminded that the East Asia Squadron demanded as much spit and polish as did the ships in Helgoland.

There was practice in gunnery, with the squadron steaming majestically out of harbor into the Yellow Sea, one cruiser towing the targets for another, or a gunboat put to service for the task. The admiral wanted to be sure that his ships were all ready for any action that might develop, and he had very little time in which to make ready. For the next three months the squadron would be scattered, because the *Scharnhorst* and *Gneisenau* were destined to make a journey of state to the South Seas and the *Emden* was to go to Shanghai for a few weeks.

During the training there were embarrassing incidents. One day the admiral came aboard the *Emden* to observe the progress of Captain von Müller's replacements. His launch was drawn alongside and he was piped with proper ceremony aboard the ship, as the deck crew stood at attention in their summer whites and the captain gave the admiral the bridge.

Steam was up and von Müller gave the order for slow ahead and navigated the long silvery ship out of the harbor and into the bay. Half speed was rung down and registered in the engine room, and then full speed. The foamy tops of the waves of open water sped by at more than twenty knots. Then and only then did anyone notice the admiral's launch, bouncing merrily against the side of the *Emden* to which she was so neatly tied, beating a merry tattoo with her lap-strake hull against the armor plating.

The admiral was not amused. Captain von Müller, that disciple of naval perfection, was chagrined and upset by the laxness of his crew in attending to a normal, routine matter. (The admiral's boat crew was not without fault either, but this did not matter, nor was it ever considered as an excuse by von Müller.) A lesser captain might have had someone's head for the error. Von Müller took the blame upon himself, and except for ordering the ship stopped and the launch disengaged and hoisted aboard, he never mentioned the matter to his subordinates. He did not need to shout. Such was the respect in which he was held by all his men that the incident served to strengthen morale aboard the *Emden* and to prove to every doubter what a great captain they had.

A few days after this incident the *Emden* moved out of the main harbor and into the repair harbor, where she went into drydock for repair of damage she had suffered to the propeller of her port screw. This meant only a minimum crew would be needed aboard the *Emden* for a week, so Adjutant von Guerard was kept busy figuring the shore leave coming to the officers and men, furloughs and extra passes, and arrangements were made for a virtual vacation from duty for most of the crew for the week. The other ships had extra duty that week, for the German navy was playing host to the British. Vice-Admiral Jerram, commander of the cruisers in China waters, brought his flagship, the *H.M.S. Minotaur*, for a state visit. This meant a round of balls and dinners and entertainments for the officers and beer halls and football games and rowing contests for the men.

Before the English came, the *Leipzig* was ordered to Japan. There were rumors that she would never return to Far Eastern waters, because after her stay in Japan and Mexico she would be sent home to Germany, to be replaced in this region with a new light cruiser.

So for several days before the *Leipzig* sailed for her state visit there was a round of parties. The men of the *Emden* did their share, entertaining their friends from the other cruiser. So did all Tsingtao, it seemed, and on the Sunday that the *Leipzig* left one would think that everyone in the city came down to Pier II as on a pilgrimage to say goodbye to the ship that had been stationed there for so long.

It was that way among the ships of the East Asia Squadron in those days before the war. Much was made of each arrival and departure, not so much because life on station was boring as because the seas were broad and one never knew when one would run into an old shipmate again.

For three days civilians, sailors, and Chinese had been collecting around the pier in front of the ship or on the ship. Flags and banners flew all around the city, and peddlers brought their carts with sweetmeats and soups to the edge of the harbor to serve the crowds. It was a rich, steamy, sweaty-smelling crowd, happy and busy doing what the people liked best, which was enjoying themselves in an air of good fellowship.

On Sunday the admiral brought his staff and every captain brought his officers to the *Leipzig* to pay a farewell visit. The band of the *Scharnhorst* appeared shortly after lunch and gave a concert aboard the ship for the crew and the watchers on the pier.

Governor Meyer-Waldeck came aboard with his staff of military and naval men, and there was much handshaking all around. Just before two o'clock the decks of the *Leipzig* were cleared of outsiders and the distinguished guests came down the gangplank. It was hauled abroad the ship. The band assembled again at the edge of the pier and played more tunes, some of them sprightly and military, and some of them nostalgic even in their brassiness.

The crews of the other warships in the harbor were in attendance, and they stood in orderly lines, instructed by their officers. As the lines were drawn in and the *Leipzig* began to get under way the men on shore gave three cheers for the *Leipzig*, and the men on the *Leipzig* responded with three cheers of their own. The band struck up *Muss i Denn*, and the cruiser moved majestically out of the harbor. There was hardly a dry eye as she left.

Then came preparations for the visit of the English naval contingent. Admiral von Spee and Governor Meyer-Waldeck outdid each other in planning entertainments for the visitors. The governor gave a ball at the stone palace. The admiral gave a gala open house aboard the *Scharnhorst*.

During the daylight hours the crews of German and British vessels moved to the sports arena ashore or to the area marked out in the harbor for water games. There were competitions of every sort, races, boat races, football matches, artillery shoots, track and field events. The English won the football match, but the score was close enough to please everyone. So it went with the other competitions;

the English and the Germans were very nearly evenly matched in every division of sport and skill. The Germans were especially pleased with a tug of war between the sailors of the *Scharnhorst* and those of the *Minotaur*. The *Scharnhorst* crew looked inferior in every way to the big and burly Englishmen, but when the signal was given the *Scharnhorst's* sailors picked up the hawser, put it over their shoulders, and began to walk away with the English crew. They never stopped. The English never got their footing and it was a quick and clean victory for the Germans. That made up for the football match. When the prizes were handed out they were divided equally enough for the happiness of all. There were many occasions for mixing of the two crews in shore restaurants and beer halls, but there were no unpleasant incidents. The Germans and the English got on amazingly well, considering the atmosphere that existed during those June days between their governments. They played tennis together and golf together and swam together on the half-moon beach during their free hours. As an exhibition in international amity the visit of the *Minotaur* could not have been a more striking success.

The stay of the *Minotaur* lasted four days. By the time she was sent out of the harbor, band playing a busy march and flags flying, the damage to the *Emden* was repaired and she was fit for sea.

She was ready, then, to perform her duties of hospitality and social responsibility when the *Scharnhorst* and *Gneisenau* set forth on their visit to the South Seas, which would take them away from Tsingtao all during the summer months and might extend deep into autumn.

The men of the *Emden* would train here in Tsingtao for the next few weeks, using one of the gunboats to tow targets and simulate attacks. Then, toward the end of July, the *Emden* was to steam to Shanghai, for her own visit of state. Not a man aboard the ship looked forward with any pleasure to this duty. To change the cool air and bright skies of Tsingtao in August for the steaming stink of Shanghai, and to exchange the bright clean water of the bay for the muddy filth of the Whangpoo, was real sacrifice. It meant extra duty for the crews, extra heat and sweat, extra hard work in keeping the ship fit and clean. After wasting the rest of the summer in Shanghai they could not even come home for the lovely autumn of Kiaochow, but must wriggle up the Yangtze to Hankow for another few weeks.

Shanghai and Hankow duty were not so bad in the winter, although the men of the *Emden* preferred Tsingtao in any season, but southern duty in the summer was not welcomed, and there was quiet grumbling among the men of the ship about their misfortune. They were glad not to be going to the American station, but they wished they had been allowed to remain on duty in Tsingtao.

After the departure of the admiral for the south, the officers and men of the *Emden* were able to relax a little. Discipline did not give way, but the absence of the commanding officer of the flotilla removed a certain extra strain that was always present when he was in harbor.

Captain von Müller worried less, for one thing, although the men of his ship would hardly know that, for he seldom saw them except in line of duty, and then he nearly always seemed abstracted. The men loved and respected von Müller for his fairness and his good nature, but there was no close bond of affection between captain and crew. He always seemed to have his nose in a book, a naval book of some kind. He was soft-spoken and quiet. They really did not know him at all, or know that at home he was jolly and much loved by his family, and that his sister, who was extremely close to him because he remained a bachelor, always called him Charlie. The character of Fregattenkapitän Karl von Müller, Prussian officer of His Majesty's Kleinkreuzer *Emden*, scarcely conformed to the popular idea of a man called Charlie, but that was not so much a reflection on sister Elfriede's use of the nickname as on the artificial character assumed by so many captains of vessels. They live in godlike splendor. For the sake of discipline they must adopt character that they do not own. And added to the need for awe were Captain von Müller's own feelings of insecurity and incompetence. The "painful conscientiousness" had never disappeared from his makeup. He was determined that he would be the best captain of the best light cruiser in German service, and to accomplish this he did not relax for so much as a minute.

On the departure of the *Scharnhorst* and the *Gneisenau*, von Müller gave the days over to gunnery, practicing mine laying and recovery, practice of explosion of mines, and seamanship. Kapitänleutnant von Mücke had two great enthusiasms, and von Müller allowed him to indulge them. Von Mücke felt the men of the German navy did not normally have enough practice and were thus slow and incompetent in the actual manning of the guns. So the crew of the *Emden* spent an hour or so every day in practice, far more than they were used to on other ships.

Von Mücke's other enthusiasm was swimming. He wanted every man aboard the *Emden* to be able to swim and to swim well. This was not so much because of the possibility of the ship's crew saving itself by swimming en masse from their sinking vessel in time of disaster but to eliminate accidents and to keep the men physically fit and to increase their endurance. So he went to the captain with his ideas, filled with bright, blond vigor and the zeal of a promoter, and von Müller was amused and indulged him. While other men of the German navy sat in the afternoons, the men of the *Emden* swam. Von Mücke supervised them, and so did Kapitänleutnant Gaede and Marine Engineer Stoffer, who had been converted in much conversation in the late hours of parties to von Mücke's enthusiastic point of view.

Hellmuth von Mücke had one other quirk, or so his seamen thought at that time. He said the men of the ship must be able to take care of themselves. In Tsingtao, as in so many other ports of the Far East, the actual loading of the ship was done by Chinese coolies. They brought in the coal. They brought in the provisions. They packed and stacked these supplies and the guns and arms and even some of the ammunition. The life of the seaman was easy; except on the high seas his manual labor was concerned with his specialty, as a rule. In port the coolies did the work. Von Mücke did not like this one bit. He kept after the captain to allow him to use the men for the work, and the captain agreed that the slovenly practices of Europeans in the Far East would be changed in the case of the *Emden*. So the first officer won another argument that he felt was peculiarly important, and the men of the *Emden* became proficient at supplying and actually loading their own ship in fast time. Von Mücke had a reason for this beyond the naval officer's love of a tight ship and a ready crew. He was certain that in a very short time, the *Emden* was going to need these skills. He was the principal reader of newspapers and magazines and the student of international affairs aboard the *Emden*. He studied politics as well as naval guides. He was certain that Germany was going to war, even perhaps with the men of the British *Minotaur* with whom they had become so friendly a few weeks before, but certainly with the Russians and possibly with the French. He was also sure that the *Emden* was going to war before summer was over that year.

~~~~~~

Chapter 4

THE *EMDEN* GOES TO WAR

KAPITÄNLEUTNANT VON MÜCKE was not the only man in Tsingtao to feel that war was coming to the world very soon, although from a glance around the city on any given day it would have been hard to find notable evidence of fears or preparations. Life went on almost as usual. There was polo at the country club and riding for those officers who had the time. There was entertainment at the officers' club ashore and at the Tsingtao Club, and there were the big public restaurants, the Bude and the Dachsal, where officers and civilians met to talk. The talk was the key.

One night, sitting at a table at the Dachsal, officers from the *Emden* got to talking with Captain Julius Lauterbach, commander of the North German line steamer *Staatssekretär Kraetke*. Lauterbach was a huge bull of a man. He weighed 255 pounds, by his own statement, and he was prone to announce that he had no intention of losing a pound of it, then downing another stein of beer. The men of the *Emden* could not have asked for a better intelligence agent.

Lauterbach knew everyone on the China coast and everyone knew him: the big fat jolly German skipper of the mail boat.

On this night Lauterbach asked one of the senior officers present at the table if he could not begin serving his reserve officer's annual stint of two months immediately. It came out then that Lauterbach was expecting war within the next two months. He had just come into port from Dalny, or Talien, the eastern terminus of the Trans-Siberian Railroad. It was part of his normal run from Vladivostok to Hong Kong; he would pick up passengers at Dalny who were destined for various points in the Far East.

On this occasion Captain Lauterbach had chatted for a while with an old acquaintance, a Dutch bishop who was returning to his mission in China after home leave. The bishop told the captain to expect war very soon. He had seen one troop train after another as they moved across the single-track railroad coming East, he said. Seen them? The eastbound train had been held up time after time on sidings as the westbound troop trains thundered past. There had been no general mobilization, no incident, and no apparent reason for such a callup of Siberian troops to the west. But the only real reason could be to emplant these troops on the borders of Germany and the Austro-Hungarian Empire. Everywhere in Europe, the bishop said, the talk of war was in the air.

So Captain Lauterbach, on his way south, made it a point to stop in for a talk with the senior officers of the East Asia Squadron and apply for his reserve service to begin immediately. It was decided that he would serve on the *Emden*, for the *Emden* was to be left as station ship in Tsingtao while the remainder of the squadron went off about its routine duties. Admiral von Spee did not believe Lauterbach when he reported his news of the troop movements and the feeling of recent passengers on the Trans-Siberian that war was coming. He had just come back from an outing with Admiral Jerram of the *Minotaur*. They had gone snipe shooting together. The admiral led the laughter when the big fat captain talked seriously of war. And so, seeing that he was not believed, Captain Lauterbach shrugged, joined in the laughter, and ordered another stein of beer.

He came back to Tsingtao for duty a little later and boarded the *Emden* on June 15. As an Oberleutnant-zur-See he was to join the other senior lieutenants as a watch officer. He soon had von

Mücke even more convinced that war was coming, and the others began to listen to his tales.

Two weeks later came the news of the assassination of Archduke Francis Ferdinand and his consort at Sarajevo. This was the incident the big powers of Europe had been simultaneously seeking and dreading. In Austria-Hungary and in Germany the leaders of the armies had the ear of the heads of government, and there was a definite predilection in these circles for war. At Tsingtao the news of the assassination came to the men of the *Emden* by cable, but that was all they had. It was two weeks before the details were known; all during the crisis the people of the Orient were living two weeks behind events.

The next event came the day after the assassination. The Austro-Hungarian foreign minister, the Graf von Berchtold, told the chief of the general staff that the time had come to settle with Serbia once and for all, even though there was no indication of Serbian government complicity in the attack. The general staff chief was delighted. So were the Germans, who had been urging the Austro-Hungarians forward in their conflict with the Serbian government, which the Russians were bound by treaty and inclination to support and protect. The Austro-Hungarian leaders set forth to discover demands for an ultimatum that would be wholly impossible for the Serbians to accept. They wanted war.

In Tsingtao most of the people lived on in the blissful quiet of superior beings who dwelt above and not with the people of the land. Chinese dock coolies continued to load the ships, Chinese ricksha coolies hauled their burdens of humanity and goods across the city. Chinese cooks prepared the meals that Chinese houseboys served, and Chinese amahs cared for the European children until they were old enough to be sent to European school. The talk in the clubs and restaurants was about servants and the latest social scandal. It was exciting and interesting to read of events in Berlin and Vienna and Moscow, but there was a relaxed certainty of belief that the crisis would evaporate as so many crises had before.

Aboard the *Emden* only because of von Mücke's fervor was the pace of training increased. Even so, the pace would have been relatively swift, for this was training time. And so Oberleutnant Lauterbach joined the ship and its watches, and Kapitänleutnant

Gaede began working the fat off him and the others in intensive exercises in gunnery and seamanship. No one minded. The exercise was offset by long cool evenings of storytelling and laughter.

The crew of the *Emden* was sharply divided on one point alone. The newcomers, which meant most of the younger officers and the seamen, were eager to move down to Shanghai to see the sights. The old hands told them they were crazy to want to stir from Tsingtao in the heat of summer. That dissidence was quelled on July 7 when orders came from Admiral von Spee in the south to remain on duty in Tsingtao. This change was unwelcome to all, for it impressed on the captain and crew the seriousness with which Berlin regarded the political situation in Vienna.

As tension increased, the training continued.

On July 24 the Austro-Hungarian cruiser *Kaiserin Elizabeth* steamed into Tsingtao. The habits of peacetime were still strong, so the newcomers were greeted by the royal welcome the Imperial Navy could give its friends. There were contests and games again, and the officers took the Austrians on motoring trips to the Lauchan mountains and gave musical dinner parties to amuse them. Those who concerned themselves with basic matters reasoned that the obsolete *Kaiserin Elizabeth* had more than hospitality on her mind when she sought the safety of Tsingtao's landlocked bay. The tension increased.

Now it became known on the *Emden* that Captain von Müller and Adjutant von Guerard were in constant wireless communication with the squadron—and, more important, and most unusual, with the Reichsmarineamt in Berlin. The *Emden* was, in effect, the listening post for the absent cruiser squadron and its connection with higher authority.

By July 29, when Berlin announced that Austria-Hungary had declared war on Serbia, the tension was almost unbearable. Captain von Müller began mobilizing all the resources of Germany in the China area. This was his duty as senior officer of the station. He called in the gunboats from the Yangtze and other points along the coast. He ordered the supply steamers for the squadron to load supplies. He ordered the mail steamers to come into port, or, if they could not reach the German colony, to find their way to neutral ports and stay there. This meant to get out of Russian and English waters. The mail steamers would be equipped if possible and sent out as auxiliary cruisers if war came, with the mission of disrupting enemy shipping. The freighters would become part of the supply train of the cruiser squadron.

The next day Captain von Müller called a meeting of all commanders of vessels on the *Emden*. When the vessel commanders arrived they found the *Emden* on a war footing. Early in the morning von Mücke had called the officers together and given them the order: *auspacken,* which meant prepare the ship for action. Only the officers were given this blunt order. Captain von Müller instructed his first officer to tell the crew to make ready for maneuvers, but few of the crew believed the captain really expected to go on training maneuvers.

Later, the captain assembled his officers in his cabin and told them about the political situation. War was expected with Russia at any moment.

The group that assembled in his cabin later that day included the commanders of three gunboats and one torpedo boat. Other gunboats were on their way, one from Shanghai, one from its station up the Yangtze, but it would be several days before they would arrive. One of the gunboats, the *Kormoran,* was badly in need of repairs. It was decided that she would be put into drydock immediately. The collier *Elsbeth* was to be dispatched with coal to the squadron as soon as she could be loaded. The various gunboats were assigned war duty: either to be at the disposal of the commander of the garrison at Tsingtao or to go off on special duty as escorts for auxiliary cruisers.

Aboard the *Emden,* preparations had been made swiftly to go on a war footing. This meant the officers and men had to unload all their purchases. Civilian clothes went ashore. So did all surplus belongings. The ship was to be reduced to the minimum as called for in Paragraph A of the naval regulations pertaining to war duty.

There was no leisure now for long evenings at the officers' club or days spent playing tennis or lolling on the beach. A detail was sent to the post office and another to the telegraph office in Tsingtao to await any messages that might come for the *Emden* or Captain von Müller and to rush them to the ship so they would arrive without delay.

One last shore leave was granted on the night of July 30 so the men and officers could tidy up their affairs. The next day in Berlin the German government sent ultimatums to Russia and to France warning against mobilization. Aboard the *Emden* the tension of the past few days was replaced by frenzied activity. Gunnery Officer

Gaede took as many men as von Mücke would allow him to load ammunition from the dump nearby. The captain ordered the removal of all the paneling that the officers had installed in the wardroom and in their quarters. It would be dangerous in case of action, he said, because the wood might splinter and burn. So von Mücke had to assign men to that task. Still others were occupied with exchange and the securing of new torpedoes from the mine depot. At six o'clock they would begin coaling, which meant an all-night job for some of the crew and several of the officers, even though the actual loading was done by Chinese coolies.

That day came a cable from Berlin which announced that a serious state of tension existed between the Central Powers and the Triple Entente of Russia, France and Britain. A few hours later a message arrived from the admiralty notifying von Müller that ten thousand tons of coal had been shipped to Tsingtao for the use of the cruiser squadron. (It would never arrive for the use of the squadron.)

The *Kaiserin Elizabeth* came up alongside the *Emden* that day at Mole No. 1 and began landing all the peacetime luxuries her crew had acquired too, but it was a futile gesture. The *Kaiserin Elizabeth* was absolutely useless as a ship of war, and it would have been suicidal for her to move out into action with any French, British, or Russian cruiser in Far Eastern waters. Even a modern destroyer could run circles around her, then blow her out of the water without fear of the Austrian ship's returning fire.

The *Elsbeth* moved to the coaling station that day, preparing to leave to supply the cruiser squadron in the south, which was bound to be short of coal, moving so far from home in waters where native coal did not exist. Couriers brought the sacks of mail for the squadron to the *Elsbeth*, and Captain von Müller prepared dispatches and papers that would be sent to the admiral aboard this ship.

There were a hundred details to be managed in a few hours. Transport had to be sent to the Tsingtao Naval Hospital to bring back the crewmen of the *Emden* who were suffering only from minor illness and could be expected to return to duty shortly. Kapitänleutnant Gaede was dispatched to make a round of the German shipping companies in the city and warn them to wireless all their merchant ships and tell them to seek neutral ports at once.

Steam was raised in the boilers of the *Emden* and live ammunition was brought forward for the guns. The torpedoes were fitted with warheads and the dummy practice heads were sent ashore.

All this activity was leading to a point. By evening the point was reached. Captain von Müller ordered the ship to prepare to leave port. In his indefatigable reading of naval history and tactics he had come across the story of the Russian warships *Warjag* and *Korejetz* during the Russo-Japanese war of 1905. They had been in harbor at Chemulpo (now Inchon) when the war began and had remained so long inside that they were blockaded by the Japanese before they could escape and were trapped like rats. Von Müller did not intend to be trapped in the landlocked harbor of Tsingtao by an English or French warship. He intended to get outside and fight if war was declared.

He had conferred with Governor Meyer-Waldeck before taking such action. It was eminently sensible action, for the *Emden*, with its light guns and light armor, could not hope to defend the harbor in case of siege, but would be lost quickly without a chance to do her job as a raider of the seas. That was the reason for the haste that drove First Officer von Mücke to the breaking point and caused him to snap at his fellows.

At seven o'clock that night the order was given and the *Emden* began to move out of the coaling dock and then into Kiaochow bay. The *Elsbeth* tagged behind her.

The passage outward was as always, for the mine fields had not yet been laid to protect the harbor from the enemy. Actually there was no enemy at this moment, although there would be one within hours. Von Müller's movement was precautionary, but made with the certainty that war was coming momentarily. So much had been made clear in the dispatches of the last few hours from Berlin.

As the ship steamed toward the bay entrance the crew were informed that they would go on a war-watch basis. In peacetime the watches were split into four parts, and a man stood watch only four hours in twenty-four when at sea. But with the war watch the ship was divided into two watches, one commanded by the captain and the other by the first officer, and it was four hours on and four hours off, with the men of the watch always at battle stations.

Outside the harbor the drum and bugle suddenly blared with the call to clear the ship for action. The surprised officers and crew rushed to comply. When an hour passed they relaxed. The men continued to stand at their guns, at the searchlights, in the torpedo room, on the command bridge and in the high lookout towers on the masts, but they saw nothing and heard nothing. It grew oppressively hot within the ship; the portholes were closed to extinguish all lights, and the blower system was shut down. It was particularly hot below decks, where the ship's hospital was located. Some relief came when the *Emden* ran into a storm and the captain ordered the portholes opened in the cover of the rain and clouds. Still the blowers remained off until the alert was ended and normal duty stations were in order.

The *Emden* set her course southeast, toward the Pacific Islands where the squadron lay, and steamed in that direction until eleven o'clock that night. She was providing escort and company for the *Elsbeth*, hoping to set her on her way to safety. At eleven, or 2300 hours, the *Emden* turned away, wishing the *Elsbeth* godspeed. Captain von Müller laid the course for Quelpart (now Chejus) island, just off the normal steamer lanes. He intended to stay out on cruise until the political situation in Europe was resolved. Every few minutes messages were flashed back and forth between the ship and the wireless station atop the hill back in Tsingtao, but the crisis was not resolved on this night of July 31. The next day, August 1, the *Emden* lurked on the edge of the steamer routes, keeping sharp lookout, but not ready yet to attack any vessel she might see. The lookout under these conditions was all in the hands of officers. They climbed the masts and took charge of the stations. Other officers and men stood at every high point on the ship, their eyes trained on the horizon, looking for telltale smoke or sail. But on August 1, while the wireless buzzed with messages, none were conclusive, and in the calm glassy sea there was nothing to see, not even one of the tiny fishing junks that usually sailed so far out to sea in good weather.

Everyone aboard the *Emden* was growing edgy. The tension of the previous days in Tsingtao was as nothing compared to this, which could mean life or death to the ship and its crew, for if the *Emden* did not get the news, and war was declared, and she was sighted by a belligerent she did not see, her end might come at any time. She must know if Germany was at war and with whom Germany was at war. The radiomen of the *Emden* faithfully carried each message to the captain as it was received, but this was not enough. First Officer von Mücke took to dropping into the radio shack and

waiting as the messages were coming in. At about three o'clock in the
afternoon he came in again.

"Any strange traffic?" he asked, and he picked up the receiver
himself. From the receiver came a loud crackling, and the first officer
jerked the instrument from his ear. The English dogs were so close
that their radioing nearly broke his eardrums, he said, and reminding
the radiomen to report anything immediately to the bridge he strode
off to inform the captain.

English warships were very near, he told the captain. He was
quite right, as they saw not long afterward. In the calm waters of the
sea they discovered what they called *Kielwasser*, the lingering wake
of ships, and the *Kielwasser* they saw indicated that one large ship
and a number of torpedo boats had just passed. Later they discovered
that ships of the English East Asia Squadron had been lying in Weihaiwei, above Tsingtao, and that they had been called to Hong Kong
by order of Winston Churchill, First Lord of the Admiralty. At that
moment the *Emden* lay almost on the steamer route between Weihaiwei and Hong Kong.

Had the English commander been left to his own devices the
career of the *Emden* might have come to an end at the beginning of
the conflict between England and Germany. The English admiral
had announced that he intended to take his heavy cruisers from
Weihaiwei down to Tsingtao and steam about the entrance to the
German port, capturing ships as they came in and out. Churchill,
however, planned a more pointed activity than casual belligerence
for the British fleet in Asiatic waters. So the *Emden's* most dangerous
enemies moved out of nearby waters.

Late that afternoon the wireless crackled and the operators
became excited. One of them rushed to the captain on the bridge to
deliver the message that Berlin had ordered the mobilization of the
army and the fleet. Physically, this meant very little to the men of
the *Emden*, who were as completely mobilized as the men of a warship can be, but some realized that now war was certain. Among
these was Prince Franz Joseph, the Kaiser's nephew, who had spent
a trying four hours in the crow's-nest aft, where he had had the
"stokers" in his face. These tiny flakes of soot got under the collar
and into the eyes and nose, and after four hours at the aftermasthead
it was well that he was relieved, because he could hardly see. There

was no complaint from the prince, however. He accepted his lot with grace and good cheer.

The following day was Sunday, and thus the day for divine worship conducted by the captain. The men appeared in their dirty work clothes this Sunday, because they were arming ammunition and there was no time for niceties any more. At the end of the service all hands were called aft. The officers and men came to the afterdeck. It was just past two o'clock in the afternoon. Captain von Müller appeared on the poop, holding a message slip in his hand. Germany was at war with Russia. War with France and England seemed inevitable, he said. Like Germany, the *Emden* had not sought war, he said, but now he was going to head the ship in the direction of Vladivostok, for here his intelligence reports told him was the greatest concentration of Russian and French naval vessels in the Pacific region. Here they might expect to meet the enemy. "Our first duty," he said, "is to raid the commerce of the enemy."

Of the major French and Russian warships the only one the *Emden* might really wish to meet was the *Yemtschuk*, the Russian light cruiser stationed in Vladivostok. She was a fair match for the *Emden*. The Russian heavy cruiser *Askold* could blow the *Emden* out of the water quickly enough, and so could the French heavy cruisers *Montcalm* and *Dupleix*, which were known to be somewhere in Asian waters—probably in Vladivostok. Von Müller would fight another warship if he had to, but his orders were to avoid a fight and concentrate on enemy shipping. He did not say so much to his crew. Since the Russians and French were in the area, he said, "It is therefore probable that we shall encounter them. In that event, I feel confident that I can rely upon my men."

It was a low-keyed statement, typical of the man. It brought three lusty cheers from the crew for the Kaiser.

So war came to the *Emden*. The afternoon was quiet, and the men, now that they knew where they were going and what they were doing, lay down in their hammocks when they were off watch, contented and ready for sleep. The past few days had brought little sleep for anyone aboard the ship.

Von Müller now conferred with Oberleutnant Lauterbach, who, a steamer captain in civil life, was an expert on the movement of steamer traffic in the region. Lauterbach suggested that they move into the Tsushima straits between Japan and Korea, to intercept Russian ships bound between Vladivostok and Shanghai. This move brought a certain amount of danger, because the *Emden* still did not know what part the Japanese intended to play in this war. They suspected that the Japanese intended to attack Tsingtao, but they did not know for sure, and they could not act against the Japanese until war came.

The other great unknown was England. But by moving northward von Müller decreased his chances of running into any English vessels.

At a steady cruising speed of fifteen knots the *Emden* moved north and east, through the straits, and then due north. The night was moonless and black. The *Emden* ran dark, her smoke control in effect, and the only sign of her presence was the throbbing of the engines and the churning of the phosphorescent water of her bow wave and her wake.

At midnight the captain lay down for a little sleep and the port war watch took over. First Officer von Mücke made his first tour of inspection, then settled down on the bridge in the blackness to peer into the night.

Nothing.

At four o'clock the captain was awakened and took his post on the bridge, while von Mücke went below to his cabin. He had just gotten to sleep when the alarm bells began to shrill. It was a false alarm, only a cloud, which they could not attack. Later they heard strange wireless conversations. It might have been a warship of some kind, but they did not move close enough to find out.

The weather turned rough and the sea began to run high.

Von Müller decided to head south again, hoping to find good weather. It was difficult enough to take a green crew into action, to capture and board a merchantman, without trying in heavy seas. On August 3, the *Emden* moved into the west channel of the straits, off the Korean coast. At about two o'clock on the morning of August 4, during a squall, the lookouts spotted the stern light of a vessel. Then the weather closed in and no more could be seen. Four hours later the lookouts saw the masts and stern of a ship ahead. At the same time the other ship spotted the *Emden* and turned away, beginning to make a dense cloud of smoke. The captain ordered more speed and began the chase.

"Action stations!" was the order.

"Oberleutnant Lauterbach to the bridge."

As the steamer came in view Lauterbach took the glass. She had two golden funnels. As she turned it became apparent that she was heading inland toward Tsushima island. If she could reach the three-mile limit she would be in Japanese territorial waters and immune from attack, protected by the laws of war concerning neutral regions.

Lauterbach recognized her immediately. He had visited on her bridge a dozen times. She was the Russian mail steamer *Rjasan*, an almost new ship of 3,500 tons, equipped with wireless. She was very fast. At nineteen knots the *Emden* was drawing near, but the *Rjasan* was coming closer to safety. The *Emden* might not overhaul her in time.

Von Müller ordered a shot to be fired across the *Rjasan*'s bows. One of the 10.5-centimeter guns sent a shell well ahead of her. The *Rjasan* disregarded it. The signal "stop at once" was run up the fore-mast, but this brought no more response. Von Müller ordered Lieu-tenant Gaede to begin firing across her bow, bringing each shell closer than the one before. Several rounds were fired before one came so close that the Russian captain turned and stopped his ship. Twelve shots had been fired at her.

Von Müller assigned Oberleutnant Lauterbach to lead a board-ing crew to take the prize, and Lauterbach ordered his men into a boat. Then, von Mücke reported that the Russian was trying to send out an S.O.S. by wireless. The signal "do not radio" was run up the *Emden*'s foremast. It made no difference. The *Emden*'s cutter was over the side with Lauterbach and twenty-two men, twenty of them armed and ready for action. The small boat sped across the choppy water to the Russian, now about 150 yards away. The Russians dropped a rope ladder, but on going alongside in the rough sea the cutter was nearly stove against the steel plates of the steamer, the ladder flapping free above. Von Müller considered the situation so dangerous that he dispatched another boat to the rescue of his cutter, but as the boat went over the side, the men on the *Emden* saw the burly Lauterbach grasp the swinging ladder and pull himself up hand over hand, moving wildly back and forth in the air, an involuntary trapeze artist. Even stopped, von Müller could scarcely see 150 meters through the glass, the weather was so foul. Earlier Gaede's firing had been much hampered by the rolling and bucking of the ship, and no one knew which shot had persuaded the Russian to stop.

Lauterbach helped his men board, and then first of all the armed crew took possession of the wireless station. The frantic tapping of the operator suddenly stopped, and aboard the *Emden* nothing more could be heard.

Lauterbach left Wireless Operator Wille in charge of the station, then moved to the bridge, where Captain Austin stood.

"I am awfully sorry, Captain," he said in German, "but it is my duty to make your ship a prize of war."

"I don't know what you're saying," Captain Austin replied in English. "I do not speak German."

"Well," said Lauterbach, shrugging his big shoulders, "you have forgotten a lot. You knew German well enough a fortnight ago when we were drinking beer together in the club at Tsingtao."

Austin laughed. It was impossible even for an enemy to dislike Lauterbach.

Lauterbach took the ship's papers and after a few minutes of conversation went to the wireless station to report back to the *Emden*. The *Rjasan* was carrying the Russian mail and a very little cargo. Mostly she was under ballast. But she had some eighty passengers aboard. What was to be done with her?

Von Müller thought about it for a little bit. The cargo was of little value. The passengers could be put into lifeboats and the ship sunk, but the sea was very rough, and the lifeboats might not survive. Further, the *Rjasan* was new and big and nearly as fast as the *Emden*. She would make a good raider. The guns from the ailing gunboat *Kormoran* could be put aboard her and she could be converted into an auxiliary cruiser.

That is what he decided to do with the Russian ship, and he ordered Lauterbach to remain aboard with twelve men and keep control. They would steam into Tsingtao.

The weather grew worse, and soon both ships were pitching in the heavy gray seas. It was a typhoon. The *Emden*'s prize crew probably would have been unable to board the *Rjasan* an hour later than they did. Lauterbach ordered the lifeboats loosened and made ready for instant use. He ran the German war flag up her taffrail pole and informed Captain Austin that he was ordered to sink the passenger ship immediately in case of approach by enemy warships or other trouble.

Captain Austin protested. He said that his ship was a peaceful merchantman and that her seizure was a violation of international law. They had seized the ship in Japanese waters, he said. By radio von Müller said this was nonsense, the *Rjasan* had been taken at 35° 5′ North Longitude, 19° 39′ East, well out of Japanese waters.

Von Müller steered a course slightly south, which would bring him fairly close to Nagasaki, from which the *Rjasan* had come on her way to Vladivostok. By wireless, Captain Austin protested again. He had a right to be taken directly to Tsingtao, if that was where they were going. Von Müller grew annoyed and told the captain of the Russian ship that he was now under German martial law and that if he did not obey he would be placed in irons.

Aboard the *Rjasan*, Prize Officer Lauterbach looked over the log of the ship and saw that the Russian had been in communication with several French ships during the chase. He informed Captain von Müller, who repeated that he should be ready for action and ready to sink the prize. Lauterbach also learned that it was the tenth shot from the *Emden* which had made Captain Austin heave to. That shell had landed just five yards off the *Rjasan*'s bow.

Poor Lauterbach during the voyage back to port had little or no sleep. Most of the passengers aboard the *Rjasan* were women, and they undertook to protest singly and in groups and berate the good-natured prize officer for interrupting their journey to Russia. He had to stay awake, be sure that the Russian was keeping her speed of fifteen knots and her course, just about 1,200 yards ahead of the *Emden* as ordered, keep the captain and crew of the Russian from signaling other vessels, and placate the women passengers.

Late that afternoon, having passed a Japanese fishing boat earlier, the *Emden* and her prize saw smoke off the starboard bow. There were five wispy plumes. The masts were in sight from the crow's-nest on the foremast when von Müller turned away to the east. The *Emden* was south of the Tsushima islands, and these ships, he was sure, included the French heavy cruisers *Montcalm* and *Dupleix*, which had passed through the straits on the other side of the islands and were now steaming to Shanghai. Only after darkness fell did he turn back to the northwest toward Tsingtao.

When night came, Oberleutnant Lauterbach was still to have no rest. The *Rjasan*'s blackout precautions were faulty and all night long the signal lamps of the *Emden* were flashing, instructing the prize officer to douse this light or that. It was the frightened lady passengers.

The next day again all were on the alert, for the *Emden* and her prize passed two big Japanese steamers which dipped their flags. Lauterbach had finally solved the problem of the frightened ladies by stopping all the generators on the ship except those needed to operate it. He did not stop the protests of the ladies, who were certain, it seemed, that they would all be sold into white slavery by the barbarous Germans immediately on their arrival at Tsingtao.

Von Müller was doubly on the alert after passing the Japanese ships, for on the evening of August 5 he learned that England had declared war against Germany. He was standing on the bridge when the message came to him. Young von Guerard, the adjutant, came up to him and asked if there was any news. Von Müller said England had declared war.

The boy's wide eyes lit up and he said, "Now we know what we can do and how."

"We can do our duty, Guerard," von Müller said gravely, taking the boy's hand.

Now at least nearly every ship they would meet except the Japanese could be regarded as enemy and plans could be made on sighting. And if the news that Germany had so many enemies was disheartening, it was also encouraging to know that they would find plenty of targets, because English shipping was the most plentiful in the Far East.

Von Müller's immediate concern was the whereabouts of the English heavy cruisers, which might be lying in wait for him just off Tsingtao. He was pleased when the wireless operators on the *Emden* intercepted a Reuter news report which stated that the *Emden* had been sunk. He had a good laugh over that. It decreased the chances that the English would be looking for him at that moment.

He double-checked that day by asking if any enemy warships had been sighted by the gunboats or shore stations in Tsingtao. None had. So he continued a straightforward course for his home port. It was necessary to make speed. He was due in five days at the South Seas rendezvous of the cruiser squadron. There was no time to waste in cruising northern waters, either hiding or searching for more prizes.

Until the two ships came near Tsingtao, the *Rjasan* preceded and the watchful *Emden* followed. But as they neared the port, von Müller took no chances. There just might be enemy warships about, and in case of action, Lauterbach must be given a chance to run for it and make the safety of the harbor while he fought the enemy. He changed the order, and Lauterbach in his prize followed the *Emden* by 1,200 yards.

As the cruiser came within an hour of land, von Müller gave the order for action stations. The wireless began snapping and crackling. It was code, which meant the enemy, and the strength of the signals indicated that the enemy was very close.

There was nothing to be done save run into port, no matter how close the enemy might be, so von Müller set the course for the Chalientao lighthouse, which stood on an island outside the bay, and then for Cape Yatau. At three o'clock on the morning of August 6 a bright light was sighted and the men, already at action stations for hours, grew nervous in the renewed suspense. Suddenly the cry of "alarm" rang out, and then again. It was the signal that an enemy ship had been sighted. But in a moment it became clear that there were no enemy ships; the *Emden* had come upon and through a fleet of Chinese junks.

At dawn the *Emden* reached the entrance to the mine field and the harbor and joined the *C. S. Leiss*, which was waiting for the escort patrol to come out and bring it safely through the newly laid mines. Tsingtao, which could always be seen from the lip of the harbor, was totally dark. Not a light gleamed in the streets.

The *Emden* was expected, for she had been in wireless contact with the shore station for several hours, and near the island of Matau she blinked a signal, which was answered immediately by the entry gun, shot off to warn of the coming ship to the patrol vessels. She was greeted by the gunboat *Jaguar* in a few moments, and the captain and a pilot came aboard to bring the cruiser safely through the mine field. The *Emden* entered harbor at six o'clock in the morning, and the crew could sigh with relief.

Poor Lauterbach, aboard the *Rjasan*, had to sit unprotected outside the mine field for several more hours, his Russian women yammering at him, and even when the *Rjasan* was escorted into harbor he was to have no relief. He returned to the *Emden* after the prize was made fast and went to his cabin to try to get his first sleep in three days.

Broad daylight or not he fell sound asleep the moment his plump stomach hit the bunk. He was awakened a moment later by prize-court justice Richter Lehmann, who felt it was imperative to discuss prize protocol.

Lehmann left in an hour. Lauterbach stroked his brown beard, lay down, and sighed gratefully. He closed his eyes. Soft hands seemed to be stroking his shoulder. Then suddenly they were not soft hands at all, but the rude hands of the captain of the *Kormoran*, who was standing there grinning at him, surrounded by his officers, demanding to know all about the *Rjasan* and how suitable she was for conversion to an auxiliary cruiser.

Lauterbach gave up and went to breakfast. At breakfast he was told that he must appear in government court that morning to settle the question of the *Rjasan's* status as a prize. He escaped the court at lunchtime and appeared at the Tsingtao club, and there he was greeted at the bar by what seemed to be all his old friends of the merchant trade.

"Good day, Lauterbach," said one old acquaintance, a merchant captain now in the uniform of a sergeant major. "How was it outside?"

Lauterbach, the genial clown of the China seas, looked him up and down.

"You should say 'Herr Oberleutnant' when you speak to me," he said. "It's a good thing that you come under military discipline now, young man, very good for you. High time. Stand up, if you please, when you are talking to your superior officer."

For Lauterbach, now one of the men of the *Emden*, had already been to war.

Chapter 5

TO THE SOUTH SEAS

THE BAMBOO TELEGRAPH is as effective as any system in the world. Long before the *Emden* and her prize returned to the harbor the news of the capture of the *Rjasan* had spread across Tsingtao. The city and the colony were under wartime restrictions, but as the *Emden* returned to port a little army of soldiers, civilians, sailors and Chinese clustered about Mole No. 1 to greet the conquering heroes. They wanted to see how their ship had come through its first engagement. They also wanted to discover how badly the *Emden* was hurt, because the bamboo telegraph, although lively, is not always totally accurate, and the word was out that the *Emden* had engaged in battle with the Russian heavy cruiser *Askold* in order to secure her prize.

The rumor of damage was so strong that the surgeon general of the naval hospital had already reserved most of his beds for the scores of wounded who were reported coming back on the limping ship.

The *Emden* glided into harbor and pulled straight to the coaling pier. The lines were made fast to the quay, and the coaling coolies began to line up, each carrying his filled coal trough. The gangplank that led below into the bunkers was made secure and the coolies were aboard, beginning their dirty task before the screws of the *Emden* had stopped churning.

Captain von Müller secured his ship and left von Mücke in charge of the loading of munitions and the coaling. They were to take on every shell and every ounce of coal they could carry, for no one knew when they would have another chance to supply themselves. Von Mücke put part of his crew to coaling, following his conviction that they must learn to do it quickly because in the future they would be doing it alone.

That morning von Müller found time for a meeting with the commanders of the ships in the harbor to discuss the political situation. He was senior naval officer in the harbor, with the absence of the admiral and the captains of the larger cruisers, and as such it was his responsibility to lead the discussions of plans and tactics. There was little he could do, however, except sanction the conversion of the *Rjasan*, which would take the *Kormoran's* guns and its name, advise the gunboat commanders to take their orders from the governor, and indicate that the *Kaiserin Elizabeth* would be wise to refrain from action. (She was later scuttled in the bay outside the harbor.)

Tsingtao was already making ready for a war that would have to be waged without the protection of her cruiser squadron. That had always been considered to be the first line of defense of Kiaochow colony, but now the strategy was changed. Von Müller went to the governor's palace after lunch to inform His Excellency of the orders he had received while on the high seas: He would report immediately to the Marianas Islands, where Admiral von Spee lay in harbor awaiting the *Emden* and the *Nürnberg*.

So the entire day of August 6 was spent in furious preparations for the long journey to the harbor at Pagan in the Marianas. The *Emden's* boats were all put over the side, and crews scurried about the harbor begging and bartering for the luxuries they wanted to carry with them. There was no time to draw from stores any more than the necessities, and no one knew when Tsingtao would receive more soap, cigarettes and liquor for its own use. Governor Meyer-Waldeck did not know what to expect. His total resources must be used to protect the colony. Already the mine field had been laid outside the bay, and on the cape, piers were built up for better defense and placement of more guns. Antiaircraft guns were brought into station around the inner harbor.

A number of German merchantmen had come into harbor to place themselves at the disposal of their country now that war had begun. Some would be sent out, after guns were put on their decks, to raid enemy shipping. Two were selected to follow the *Emden* south. Captain von Müller went aboard the 9,000-ton passenger ship *Prinz Eitel Friedrich* and told her captain to be ready to sail with him. The *Eitel Friedrich* was just installing the deck guns. She would become a raider. Von Müller also informed the captain of the collier *Markomannia* that he was to become the supplier and shadow of the *Emden*.

All that night the coaling continued and the *Emden's* officers argued with the supply men ashore about their needs. Captain von Müller consulted with the governor and the other senior naval officers about the defense of the harbor. It was decided finally that the *Kaiserin Elizabeth* would be loaded with rocks and scuttled near the entrance to the harbor to prevent enemy ships from making their way in to bombard the town and the port. Some of the older gunboats, the *Iltis, Jaguar,* and *Tiger,* would also be scuttled. Governor Meyer-Waldeck was becoming certain that an attack would soon be launched by Japan. The bamboo telegraph had it much earlier. Just before war was declared the British coastal steamers *Kanschow* and *Ningpo* had arrived in Tsingtao, to be filled immediately by Chinese refugees who came to the pier, lugging children on their backs and pushing two-wheeled carts laden to the top with their belongings. One seaman who later joined the *Emden* asked several Chinese why they were leaving.

"Master, Japan, Tsingtao soon much boom-boom," was the answer in Pidgin. The word was out that Japan was marching, and even after the harbor was closed to foreign shipping the refugees continued to desert the city, overland by rail and road.

On August 7 Governor Meyer-Waldeck learned that the bamboo telegraph can be surprisingly accurate, too. The naval attaché in Tokyo, Korvettenkapitän von Knorr, cabled Berlin that the German consul in Mukden had learned of the movement of Japanese troops who were headed toward Tsingtao with the firm intention of attacking. The Japanese war plan was in motion.

On August 7 the *Emden* embarked more men; added to those she had taken on before sailing to the Tsushima straits, she now had three new officers, one new deck officer, seventeen new seamen and thirteen new technicians. A Catholic chaplain came aboard now that the ship was definitely heading for war and gave the sacraments to the Catholics aboard, plus a general absolution.

Von Müller was engaged again in meetings all day long. Dozens of officers from land and other ships came aboard to pay what might be their last respects to the *Emden* and her men. Captain Fahss of the *Markomannia* came aboard for discussions, and so did Korvettenkapitän Thierichens, commander of the *Prinz Eitel Friedrich,* which would accompany the cruiser southward.

Around five-thirty an exhausted First Officer von Mücke could report that the coaling was complete—the *Emden* had taken on an additional 950 tons—and that all supplies which could be obtained had come aboard and were stowed. The ship was ready to sail.

All that day, as the *Emden* coaled, the crews of the *Markomannia* and the *Prinz Eitel Friedrich* had been hard at work to resolve problems of their own. The *Markomannia* completed her coaling and the crew gave her the markings of an English Blue Funnel liner, just to increase her chances of going unrecognized in waters that were certain to be scoured by British ships. The job of concealing the identity of the *Prinz Eitel Friedrich* was more difficult but also more important, since she was to be a fighting ship. The crew spent the entire day repainting the ship and giving her the markings of the British P & O line.

The Catholic mass was just finished when von Mücke made his report to the captain. One last quick trip ashore to pay a final duty call on the governor at the palace, and Captain von Müller was as ready as he ever would be to leave Tsingtao. He called von Mücke in to give the orders, and shortly before 6 P.M. the Swan of the East was ready for her departure, fully laden with the goods of war and steam up.

She was the Swan of the East no longer. In their haste the coolies and the men of the *Emden* had tracked more soot than usual through the ship, and in the emergency of the hour there was no time to hose down the ship or worry about such niceties as her appearance. Her lines were fuddled by the piles of coal heaped on her decks. Coal stood in heaps on the main deck, on the middle deck, and on the poop. Everywhere that extra coal could be carried it was loaded.

At six o'clock Captain von Müller walked out onto the bridge deck and gave a signal. A boatswain piped the maneuvering whistle and the members of the deck crew moved to their stations. The ship's band moved to the poop deck and stood in formation. The engines began to tremble a little and the screws of the *Emden* began to turn.

Captain von Müller signaled to cast off. The hawsers from the quay slapped as they hit the water. The wireless began to clatter —already they were receiving signals from the Tsingtao wireless station. The telegraph from bridge to engine room squeaked a little as the signal for more speed was rung down. Obviously in the grip of strong emotion, the commander made a short speech to those staring from the shore, which nearly no one heard above the gathering noises of departure. He was cut off by the beginning of three cheers from the crew of the *Kaiserin Elizabeth*, cheers joined by the hundreds standing on the pier to see their warship go.

"Eyes to starboard," came the shout above the last of the cheers, and turning, the crew could see his excellency the governor, resplendent in his formal naval uniform with medals, passing by in his motor launch, accompanied by his staff. He waved goodbye and his staff all raised their hats. Then they were gone, moving on to pay final respects to the *Prinz Eitel Friedrich*.

The *Emden* gathered speed and began to move away from the mole. The band on the poop deck struck up "Hail to thee, laurel-crowned victor," and the crew sang lustily as they went about their duties. "*Deutschland, Deutschland über alles, über alles in der Welt* . . ." The songs became more martial: "*Es braust ein Ruf wie Donnerall, wie Schwertgeklirr und Wogenprall* . . ." ("There roars a call, a thunderous sound, like swords clashing, waving round . . .")

The procession began, moving outward from the harbor, as on shore hundreds of people, Germans and Chinese, men, women and children, waved and shouted words of farewell to their cruiser, bound outward to seek the enemy and battle. The sun was sinking low in the northern sky and the water of the harbor was still in the evening calm.

S-90, the old German torpedo boat, led the way and would lead the convoy through the mine field. The *Emden* was next, then the *Markomannia* and the *Prinz Eitel Friedrich*. As the *Emden* slipped away from the pier, the continued shouts and cheers of those on shore faded. The band struck up "*Die Wacht am Rhine*," and the sailors sang louder than ever. Now the other noises were half drowned by the growing sound of the engines, but from the mast tops and rigging of the ships in the harbor could be seen sailors, caps in hand, waving and cheering the convoy on its way.

Outside the harbor the convoy anchored, and Captain von Müller took the ship's cutter over to the *Markomannia* for a conference to establish their steaming procedure on the route south. Very early in the morning, as the sun was rising, the convoy steamed out through the outer roads and into the steamship lane between Yokohama and Shanghai. Captain von Müller was not wasting any time. If there were prizes to be taken he would take them on his way south to join the squadron.

Hardly were they under way when the alarm bells rang and the cry for action stations echoed through the ship. The order came for the gunners to load their guns and the searchlight men to be ready to beam their fore and aft lights. The lookouts strained their eyes to see what the captain had discovered, but there was nothing. The ship steamed on in silence. They passed a Chinese junk, and then another, but no enemy came in sight. Ten minutes went by, then came the order from the bridge to unload the guns and stand at ease. It was a practice alarm. Kapitänleutnant Gaede was taking no chances. He wanted to see just how long it would take the *Emden's* gun crews to come to readiness for battle. The practice alert was repeated on the other watch.

When the ships left the inner harbor the torpedo boat S-90 preceded them. She went out to Cape Yunnuisan to see if enemy warships were lurking outside the harbor in wait for the convoy. But there was no blockade, and at the cape the end of the piloted journey came. The pilot descended into his boat, last farewells rang out across the water, and the ships set out, each in her separate direction, alone. The *Prinz Eitel Friedrich* was to adopt one course and steam alone. The *Markomannia* would go ahead, and the *Emden* would join her at the Ryukyu Islands. This left the *Emden* free to maneuver and take prizes if she could.

Only after the pilot boat had left did the officer of the *Emden* discover that a deserter had gone with it. The officers' Chinese orderly, whom they had christened Joseph, had stowed away somewhere in the pilot boat or the S-90 and made his way back to Tsingtao. Earlier he had protested that he wanted nothing more than to accompany his masters into battle. Something had changed his mind. The officers, not yet irritated by war, laughed derisively at the cowardice of the Chinese. The S-90 accompanied them from Yunnuisan as far as Cape Yatau, and then the *Emden* was alone.

For several days she made her way slowly southward, through the China sea, traveling toward the rendezvous but also looking out for enemy vessels. Several times she hopefully gave chase to wisps of smoke that appeared on the horizon, but in each case the ship turned out to be a German or a neutral. Several were Japanese, and as far as the *Emden* knew the Japanese were neutrals. They had not yet attacked Tsingtao.

On August 8 the wireless operators picked up messages that told of German victories on land and sea in Europe, and the crew cheered when the messages were read to them. That evening they intercepted a message for the English ships at sea which rang the alarm: The *Emden* was at sea, said the message, accompanied by two captured merchantmen. Captain von Müller chuckled. He knew who he had to thank for that message. On the night of their departure they had been trailed through the mine field by a small Japanese steamer.

August 9 was Sunday. The *Emden* had made contact with the *Markomannia* at the Ryukyus. Since it was Sunday, even though the ship was at war every effort was made to make it as much a day of relaxation as possible. Religious services were held in the morning, and afterward the crew were given the freedom of the decks to gossip and play cards. After the service Captain von Müller joined the officers in the wardroom for a cocktail; it was the invariable custom of the ship to serve cocktails in the wardroom after church—one of the few times during the week that the captain mingled with his officers. For the most part he ate alone in his cabin, occupied by charts or a book. Once in a while he appeared at mess, but he seldom ate anything, and from time to time he would ask one of the officers with whom he wished to confer to come to the cabin and join him in a meal, but then he ate a scrap of meat or half a potato and pushed the rest away.

Sunday, August 9, marked the last day of the wardroom as an oasis in the warship. The captain noted absently that day that there was still too much wood paneling about and too much upholstered furniture. He decreed that the next day it would have to be torn down and burned. In case of battle it endangered the ship.

The next day enough coal had been burned out of the bunkers to clear off the deck loads and clean up the ship, and some of the time of the men on watch was spent in this pleasant task. Starting with that Sunday, and regularly thereafter, First Officer von Mücke conducted an orientation course for the crew. Every Sunday he held a session in which he gave a chalk talk with a map, showing the men the trend and movements as reported from Europe. The news was all good, and his narrow features brightened as he told of the victories over the French and English on land and sea. He was particularly proud to report on the successful trip of the warships *Goeben* and *Breslau*, which had run right through the English fleet on the eve of war and made their way safely to Turkey.

This was the day the wardroom was torn apart. The curtains had to go. So did the overstuffed furniture and the paneling. The temporary wall between the wardroom and the after battery was torn out, and the carpets were lifted. Every last bit of it went into the furnaces, to speed the *Emden* on and eliminate a fire hazard. Then the wardroom's bare walls were covered with a green paint that the officers could describe only as "poisonous." There was some relief. Prince Franz Joseph was a caricaturist of sorts, and he amused his fellow officers by drawing their pictures on the walls as they were deciding what color to paint the mess. These, too, were covered in the end by the green paint.

This day was August 10. The *Emden* met the *Prinz Eitel Friedrich* as planned and spent several hours acting as target tug for the raider as her crew practiced their shooting. The *Markomannia* was supposed to appear but did not, nor did she appear on August 11. The *Emden* called her repeatedly in code and finally in clear. Late on August 11 the wireless room received a message which purported to come from the *Markomannia*.

"Am at the rendezvous," said the message. "Give your position."

Von Müller read the message and suspected it to be a trap. The wording was vague (what rendezvous?), and the request for position was so innocently audacious that it had all the earmarks of the request of an enemy warship. The *Emden* did not respond. The *Markomannia* had no business knowing the *Emden's* position even if it was she.

He radioed the squadron, asking for information about the *Markomannia,* but received only the snappish reply, "Do not use your wireless." It was all the more incomprehensible (and it never was satisfactorily explained) because the wireless operator swore that the station that sent this second message was the same station that had asked the *Emden* for her position. As it turned out, the *Scharnhorst* had sent the second message. Later, von Müller learned that the *Markomannia* could not have sent either message because her wireless was out of order.

On August 12, the *Emden* made her landfall in the Marianas. The crew had not been told before where they were going; Captain von Müller had kept this information to himself and a handful of trusted officers. Around noon she approached Pagan, whose volcano crown was so distinctive a geographic feature that many of the men knew the island by sight. The *Emden* skirted the island's coast, seeking the harbor, until a ship detached itself from the horizon and steamed forward to investigate this intruder. It was the *Titania*, the squadron's repair and supply ship. She was flying the commandant flag, too, which meant that a ranking naval officer was aboard and the incomer was to obey his instructions. Admiral von Spee had sent the *Titania* out to greet the *Emden* and show her the way to the squadron. A little later, turning into the bay of Pagan, the *Emden* came upon the *Scharnhorst*, the *Gneisenau* and the *Nürnberg*, all at anchor, surrounded by a crowd of merchant ships.

As the *Emden* came into the harbor a volley of cheers came from the throats of the men of the cruiser squadron aboard the other ships. A few days before they had heard the radio broadcast the news that the *Emden* had been sunk by the Russian heavy cruiser *Askold*. The admiral and his staff knew this was not true, but they had not enlightened the crews of the squadron ships, so the actual sight of the *Emden* was the first good news the men had had.

The *Emden* threaded her way slowly past the other ships and found an anchorage between the rocky shore and the *Scharnhorst*. She had every right to come to rest beside the flagship. After all, the *Emden* was the first ship of His Majesty's Navy in the Far East to go into battle with an enemy, even a merchant enemy, and very nearly the first German ship anywhere to do so.

Chapter 6

DECISION AT PAGAN

THE *Emden* had scarcely stopped on this warm, sunny day when the steam pinnace was over the side and Fregattenkapitän Karl von Müller was on his way to the *Scharnhorst* to report to his admiral on the activities of the *Emden* and the situation at Tsingtao. The other warships were already taking on coal, which meant to the men of the *Emden* that it would not be a long stay and that the squadron would soon be in action.

Von Müller made his report and returned. The *Emden* would coal the next day, he told his first officer. There would be a meeting of all commanders on the *Scharnhorst* in the morning, and there the strategy of the squadron would be decided and announced.

A barge from the *Gneisenau* came alongside the *Emden* that afternoon to inquire about mail. Thus it was learned that the *Elsbeth* had been sunk or captured, for she had been dispatched from Tsingtao so long before that only a disaster could have prevented her arrival before August 12. She had carried all the mail as well as coal for the squadron. The men of the fighting ships, then, were not to hear from the homeland again.

For the night, the officers were ordered to stand full war watches, to be ready for any attack; the men were not. The following day the crew was to have its first full taste of the hard labor of coaling. There were no Chinese coolies aboard the ship or on the rocky volcanic island, and the crew of the *Emden* would carry the coal. But in port the strictness of discipline was relaxed. Outside the harbor the *Titania* prowled nervously back and forth, day and night, watching for dots on the horizon, and she could be expected to guard the squadron against surprise attack. When the captain had returned from the *Scharnhorst* he had brought with him dispatches and orders concerning the ship. Among them was a promotion list, on which the ship's ensigns were listed. Several of them were promoted to Leutnant-zur-See, after three years of service, and these included Prince Franz Joseph. Naturally the promotions called for a celebration, and so there was much trading of watches while First Officer von Mücke looked indulgently the other way, and that night the champagne corks popped merrily in the officers' mess.

The work of the next day began at six o'clock in the morning. The ship's bell called the entire crew to duty, and war watches were maintained on a minimal basis for the men so most of them could help with the coaling. Tea and bread was the breakfast for the crew, and then the work began. It would have to be carried out in the morning and evening hours. Midday in the tropics was far too hot for confined work. Fenders were hung over the sides of the *Emden*, the boat davits were made clear all around the ship, and the coaling gangways were laid out. Shovels and empty sacks for coaling were broken out. The awnings on the poop deck were folded up and put away to save them from the soot.

Oberleutnant Lauterbach had been delighted on entering port to see his old command—the *Staatssekretär Kraetke* was one of the bevy of merchant ships at anchor there. Now he took a small boat over to the steamer and personally conned her back to the port side of the *Emden*. There was much shouting and laughter as he brought the big ship smoothly alongside. On the starboard side the *Gouverneur Jaschke* was brought up. Then the dirty work began. The men picked up their shovels and sacks and went into the holds of the merchant ships. The new Leutnant von Hohenzollern, Prince Franz Joseph, supervised the coaling from the *Staatssekretär Kraetke*, and another of the new lieutenants did the same on the other ship. Added to the heat and the dust was the unsuitability of these two mail and passenger ships for coaling. Their holds were deep and inaccessible, which meant long journeys for the men up and down gangways and steel ladders carrying hundred-pound sacks of coal on their backs.

But there were compensations. The band was turned out on the poop of the *Emden* to play rousing tunes and make the men forget the misery of their work. There were extra rations for meals, and a long break in the heat of the middle of the day.

While the men made the ship ready for war again, Captain von Müller was engaged in weighty deliberations of policy with the other commanders of the squadron. Around the scuttlebutt it was said that von Müller intended to propose that the *Emden* be detached from the squadron and be allowed to cruise alone in the Indian Ocean. The officers and men of the *Emden* backed this proposal heartily. Almost to a man they were fervent patriots, and they saw England as their primary enemy. If they could help "*Gott strafe Engländ*" they were eager to begin. Von Mücke's chalk talks to the sailors had begun to take effect.

Aboard the *Staatssekretär Kraetke*, the jolly Lauterbach was making a few solid preparations. In their exuberance in tearing out the niceties of the *Emden* wardroom the officers had left themselves a dismal flat, and even the businesslike von Mücke was sorry that they had gone quite so far. Lauterbach invited the officers who had no specific duties for the day to his old ship, and there they cracked open several cases from his private wine cellar and spent a pleasant day in his quarters.

Late in the afternoon, filled with the glow of good fellowship, he was struck by inspiration. He would refurnish the wardroom from the *Staatssekretär Kraetke*. Crewmen of the merchant ship were dispatched to infiltrate among the coalers and carry easy chairs, cases of wine, beer, and whiskey, and Lauterbach's extensive private library onto the *Emden*. Von Mücke started when he saw what was happening, but the other officers were so obviously delighted with this turn of events that he held his tongue and tactfully went to examine the yardarm while the unauthorized transfers were taking place.

While the furniture was being moved, Lauterbach discovered three deserters from the *Emden* hiding in his old ship. Had they been naval personnel it would have been a serious matter. They were not. They were the three Chinese washermen from the *Emden*. They had decided among themselves that they did not wish to risk their lives for a Kaiser they did not even know in faroff Berlin. They wanted to go home to China, Tsingtao if possible, but anywhere in the Middle Kingdom would do in a pinch.

Lauterbach had the three brought to his cabin, and he argued with them. They were obdurate. They wanted to go home. They would not stay under any circumstances. If forced against their wills to stay, they would not wash any more clothes.

This was a very serious matter to the officers, whose clothes they washed and ironed, and not a question to be dealt with either lightly or with Prussian discipline. Lauterbach was equal to the occasion. In fluent Pidgin he explained to the men that no ships were returning to China, nor were they to put in at any ports at all until the war was ended. This slight digression from absolute truth was a more accurate predication than Lauterbach expected, but even as a digression it could be forgiven, for these three were among the most vital members of the crew. It was essential that they be retained and be made cheerful again. The irrepressible Lauterbach succeeded by guile where the shouting Prussians who had tried before him had failed. The three went back, salaries increased, to be happy in their work in the hot bowels of the *Emden*.

By the morning of August 13 the men of the *Emden* had begun to believe that the *Markomannia* had either been captured or sunk, because she was two full days overdue. But that morning as they choked in the coal dust, the *Markomannia* steamed into harbor, bearing her five thousand tons of coal, more valuable to the *Emden* than gold or food. No one in the squadron knew what had happened to her, and no one aboard the *Emden* was to find out at that moment, for there was no time now for gossip.

While Captain von Müller was aboard the *Scharnhorst* attending the fateful squadron commanders' meeting, the boats of the *Emden* were sent out by von Mücke to do a bit of trading and scrounging. The important matters were beer and tobacco. The *Emden* had left Tsingtao without adequate supplies of either, since the Tsingtao garrison could spare so little. So in the heat of the day, when not a breeze was stirring and the smoke from the cooking fires in the ships pushed tendrils straight upward into the sky like gray vines crawling toward the heavens, the men of the *Emden* lay off the coaling to rest and gladly manned the oars of the trading vessels. They got their beer, or some of it, and their tobacco, although not enough to keep the crew for long. From the *Scharnhorst* they got yeast to bake bread, from the steamer *York* they got hospital supplies and medicines, from the *Prinz Eitel Friedrich* they got beer and fruit, from the steamer *Holsatia* they got cigarettes and even soda-water pills so the officers could enjoy their whiskey.

Then for the men it was back to work. From the *Scharnhorst* Captain von Müller sent the word that the *Emden's* coaling must be finished and she must be ready to steam out of the harbor with the squadron by nightfall. In midafternoon it became apparent to First Officer von Mücke that this deadline could not be met without assistance. When he communicated this to his captain, forty men from the *Scharnhorst* were sent to the *Emden* to help with the work.

For the officers, there were some changes. Kapitänleutnant Metzenthin was detached from the *Emden* and assigned to the *Gneisenau*, where there was a job for one of his senior rank. Two lieutenants came aboard, Roderick Schmidt and S.S. Gyssling. This brought the total personnel aboard the *Emden* to 399.

For the squadron the meeting aboard the *Scharnhorst* was descisive and fateful. Von Müller and the other captains were piped aboard in the morning and went to the admiral's suite, where he was seated in the middle of one side of a long conference table, his staff clustered around him. The squadron commanders sat across from the admiral. All were dressed in their formal summer white uniforms with gold braid and dark trim. The admiral looked peculiarly small and frail and sleepless.

Admiral von Spee gave his opinion of the situation first, punching his finger at the world map on the table in front of him as he spoke.

Although the war had begun, no one yet knew what Japan would do, he said. No one knew, but he was sure and he knew others felt the same, that Japan's attitude toward Kiaochow and the other German colonies in the Pacific was most threatening. But no matter what Japan did, the important thing for the cruiser squadron at this time was to remain disengaged. Uncertainty about the squadron's whereabouts and aims would occupy a great deal of the enemy's attention.

Also, there was the problem of coaling in an area where there was no coal. The *Scharnhorst* required ninety-three tons of coal a day if she was to cruise at ten knots. If she was to speed at twenty knots, which would be reasonable in action, her coal consumption quadrupled. The problem of her sister ship, the *Gneisenau*, was exactly the same. For these reasons the admiral had decided to take the squadron to the west coast of the Americas, where it would be possible to assure a supply of coal.

The admiral looked at his ship commanders, having finished his remarks, and asked if they had other opinions.

Fregattenkapitän Karl von Müller waited until the senior captains had their say. Then he spoke up.

He was opposed to the move east, he said. The plan would take several months to cross the Pacific. During that time the fleet would be ineffective against the enemy, except for the energy that might be spent in the search for its whereabouts. If the fleet was located then it could be written off until it moved out again from the west coast of America. Nor was there enough trade on the route east to make the plan worth while.

Von Müller spoke of the future of German sea power and the "fleet in being," a theory which held that the fleet, its whereabouts and strength known, served to immobilize enemy warships without actually engaging in battle. He believed the squadron ought to remain in Asia, but if the problems of coal supply were too difficult, he had an audacious proposal: Why not send one of the light cruisers into the Indian Ocean?

The admiral turned to Captain Schutz of the *Scharnhorst*. What did he think?

Captain Schutz agreed that the squadron ought to move east to assure its coal supply. But before it went, could it not stage one massive raid on an enemy port? This would throw enemy shipping into a panic.

That was quite correct, the admiral said. He agreed with Schutz that this was a fine idea. He thought it was better than splitting the squadron up into cruiser units, which would surely be picked off by the enemy one by one. But he also was certain that in the forty-eight hours that it would take to stage such a massive raid, Tokyo would declare war on Germany and then send out her entire fleet to close the route to the east—and the escape from frustration and destruction through lack of fuel.

The admiral had obviously considered every line of approach. Schutz had no more to say. Captain Maerker of the *Gneisenau*, Captain Schonberg of the *Nürnberg*, and Captain Thiereken of the auxiliary cruiser *Prinz Eitel Friedrich* all agreed that under the circumstances the move east in squadron formation was best.

Captain von Müller alone stuck stubbornly to his position that they should not abandon the Indian Ocean. If the British learned that there were no German warships at sea, then most of the British naval strength could be diverted to Europe.

Captain Fieltiz, the admiral's chief of staff, lent his approval to von Müller's plan. Let the squadron leave one cruiser to act independently in the Indian Ocean.

Admiral von Spee said that he had considered the idea of taking the entire squadron into the Indian Ocean to raid British shipping, but where would they secure coal? There was no friendly port available, and a neutral port would either be bound to intern them or to refuse them more than a brief refuge. Whether or not they could secure enough coal at Dutch ports was extremely questionable.

The meeting broke up with the admiral's promise to take von Müller's request under consideration.

Von Müller returned to the *Emden*. The squadron was to be ready to set to sea by five-thirty that afternoon, and it was nearly that when the conference broke up, and the decisions were made. Von Müller returned to his ship at just about the same time that a load of coconuts came in from a shore party. They were broken open by the thirsty coalers. A few moments later a boat came alongside bearing a message for the captain from the admiral. His request was granted. He would break away from the squadron at an appointed signal and the *Emden* would become an independent naval unit.

At five-thirty all ships weighed anchor and formed into two lines. The warships formed to port, the *Scharnhorst* leading the cruisers, the *Emden* tailing them. On the starboard was the line of merchant ships and auxiliary cruisers, headed by the *Prinz Eitel Friedrich*. During the night the starboard line disintegrated, and when dawn broke the warships broke formation disgustedly and went back to round up the stragglers. By eight o'clock it was done, and the squadron was steering a course almost due east. Then came the signal: "*Emden* detached. Good luck."

The *Emden* turned out of line, and from the line of merchantmen the *Markomannia* turned out too, for she was to be the *Emden's* companion and coaler on this lonely journey into the huge reaches of the Indian Ocean, where the German seaman would have no friends and a thousand enemies would lie in wait for them.

The course was south-southwest. The speed was twelve knots. Even the lowly seamen aboard the *Emden* had the idea that the *Emden* was going off to do battle alone.

~~~~~~

Chapter 7

THE FIRST COALING

FOR A DAY and a half the *Emden* steamed along the eastern side of the Marianas until it ran out of that group of islands. The next landfall was Yap, a German possession where there was a wireless station. Captain von Müller ordered his radiomen to make contact with Yap, and they called repeatedly for many hours, but there was no answer. Course was then set for Angaur Island in the Palaus. This island was leased by a German company that was exploiting the phosphates found there, and von Müller hoped to be able to add another German ship to his train and assure his coal supply for just that much longer.

The *Emden* steamed steadily at the economical cruising speed of twelve knots, the *Markomannia* following through the clear seas in her wake. The *Markomannia* could make sixteen knots when necessary and for that reason was much prized by the men of the *Emden*.

The voyage to Angaur lasted six days. Captain von Müller ordered First Officer von Mücke to spend the daylight hours in training exercises. The *Markomannia* was enlisted as a target tug, and Kapitänleutnant Gaede set his gun crews, magazine crews, and mast lookouts to work. Von Mücke supervised the erection of screens of woven hemp around the gun positions to protect the gun crews from flying fragments. Screens were put up in the wireless room, too. The engineering department spent its time changing boiler tubes and repairing the worn ones. The men of the torpedo branch were busy taking torpedoes apart, checking the warheads and operating mechanisms, and reassembling the weapons. Of all the crew the only unhappy men were the deckhands, for they must face the misery of coaling even now that the coaling was finished. The *Emden* carried 950 tons of coal in her bunkers, but now she was also stacked high with sacks of coal. Everywhere one could see the gray-white stacks that stood high in piles; there was also coal dust to seep into the cracks and crannies. The stacks of sacks rose so high that only a narrow passage, like a trench, remained of the old free decks. Men coming on deck invariably tracked coal dust inside the ship, and the deck hands spent much of their days with mops and brooms, dealing with the menacing dust and cursing coal.

So much relaxation of war watches and attention to training was possible because the *Emden* was well off the beaten track of steamers. She expected action in the next few days.

On August 19, at about eleven o'clock in the morning, the *Emden* sighted land, the first island of the Palau group. Sharp-eyed lookouts were posted then, because Captain von Müller had made arrangements by wireless with a German collier, the *Choising*, to meet them in the Palaus, but this casual arrangement did not bring the steamer. She never appeared.

Not long afterward the *Emden* reached Angaur. The island had two anchorages, one on the north and one on the west, and in each of these lay several heavy anchorage buoys, not more than 1,500 feet from the shore. The coral island dropped steeply into the sea and the bottom of the harbors was deep.

Captain von Müller took the *Emden* completely around the island once, to be sure that no strangers or enemies lurked in the vicinity, then he led the *Markomannia* into the north anchorage.

The *Markomannia* was tied up to one of the buoys and the *Emden* moved alongside and made fast for coaling. Nearly a week of steady steaming had cost the *Emden* a quarter of her coal supply, and Captain von Müller never wanted to miss an opportunity to replenish the precious fuel.

As the two ships were putting out fenders and beginning to throw gangways across the gap between them a small boat was rowed out from shore to the *Emden*. A handful of Europeans of the phosphate company came aboard, delighted to see a German warship and learn news of home. Their information about the war was very sketchy, although they had a wireless. Just three days before, they said, an English steamer had left their harbor filled with phosphates. Captain von Müller expressed his disappointment. Only three days earlier and he would have had another prize.

Among the civilians were a number of naval reserve seamen and officers. They volunteered to join the *Emden* then and there, eager to wreak havoc among Germany's enemies, but the captain said there was no room for them. She carried 34 officers and 360 men at this point, nearly twice as many officers as usual and a greatly augumented crew.

The war watches were reduced while the ship was in harbor, which meant a relief for the officers. The men had been taking light watches because they had other duties. The officers had stood the full war watches.

The manager and doctor from the island remained aboard for some time, hoping to secure some provisions from the *Emden*. They got little, for she had little to spare.

Later that day some of the supply problems of the ship were, or seemed to be, solved when the *Princess Alice* appeared off the harbor. She was the 10,000-ton merchant ship which had brought the squadron relief to Tsingtao that year. Now this North German Lloyd steamer came as close to shore as her deep draft would allow. She could not anchor, so she sat outside the bay maneuvering with her screws.

This meeting, too, had been planned by Captain von Müller by wireless. Arrangements were made for the captain, Prince Franz Joseph, and Lieutenant von Guerard, the adjutant, to visit the *Princess Alice*. There was some delay—young von Guerard was the busiest man on the ship; he was also wireless officer and as such he had gone ashore at the request of the civilians to inspect their wireless station. With him to shore in the steam pinnace had gone Dr. Ludwig Schwabe, assistant surgeon. Dr. Schwabe was a reserve officer who had been serving as surgeon aboard the steamer *Frisia* until war threatened, and he volunteered to take his reserve training that summer aboard one of the ships of the East Asia Squadron. He was in Tsingtao when the *Emden* returned with the captive *Rjasan,* and he was ordered by Admiral von Spee to join the *Emden* for the cruise to the South Seas, whereupon he was to be assigned to one of the other cruisers in the squadron. But when the *Emden* was given permission to detach herself from the squadron and operate as a free agent, Captain von Müller had decided that he needed the extra surgeon aboard ship, and Dr. Schwabe had remained with the *Emden*. He was a jolly young man, twenty-nine years old. He was the son of a Leipzig doctor and had gone to school at the gymnasium and the famous university in that city, then known all over the world for its medical school. He had interned at the Deaconness Hospital in Stettin, and then to secure more training had shipped out as a physician aboard several merchant vessels. When war threatened, his steamer was in Japan, and it was the load of rice she carried that brought her to Tsingtao under admiralty orders.

On arrival in Angaur, Dr. Schwabe went ashore to beg, borrow, or steal some clothes. All his equipment and his personal belongings had been left aboard the *Frisia*. It was sent to join the squadron with a load of coal, but it never arrived. Instead, the *Frisia* and all Dr. Schwabe's possessions fell into the hands of the English and landed at Hong Kong. So since leaving Tsingtao with one change of clothes, Dr. Schwabe had been wearing the castoffs of the officers of the *Emden*.

The pinnace was sent scurrying back to the island to pick up von Guerard before he kept the captain waiting an unseemly time, and Dr. Schwabe was left ashore to compare sizes with the civilians and to barter for what he could. Von Guerard was needed for the trip to the *Princess Alice* because as adjutant he was responsible for the records of the reserves, and he knew better than anyone else on the ship just what specialists the *Emden* still could use to round out her crew. In spite of having turned down the offers of the civilians at Angaur to serve with the ship, the *Emden* still had use for extra men. Captain von Müller did not want to deplete this German oasis in the unfriendly Pacific, so he had refused the civilians.

Those civilians did not know that Captain von Müller would embark another dozen men from the *Princess Alice* and the *Markomannia* within a few hours, bringing the total force of the *Emden* up to 412 officers and men. The captain decided that if hunting was good so many men would be needed to take prizes into port.

Von Guerard went to the *Princess Alice* to handle personnel matters. The captain went to discuss strategy and tactics with the captain of the merchant vessel. He had decided to make the *Princess Alice* a part of his fleet. Prince Franz Joseph and the *Schiffzahlmeister*, or purser, went aboard to requisition supplies. The purser

spent several hours filling out papers which would allow them to take
on supplies, grumbling about the red tape. The prince simply walked
into the officers' mess and asked for what he wanted—beer, cigarettes
and cigars for the *Emden's* officers' mess. Von Guerard took care of
the details of enlisting Kapitänleutnant Klöpper and eleven seamen
of the reserve, and inspected the *Princess Alice's* wireless to see that
all was in order.

The officers of the *Emden* learned here what had occurred at
Yap to keep the wireless station silent as they had passed. An English
squadron had appeared at Yap on August 7. The flagship had informed the men of the wireless station to take cover because in three
hours the wireless mast would be destroyed by shelling. It was
destroyed as promised, and the squadron steamed away.

The men of the *Emden* also heard more welcome news. The
Princess Alice had struck her blow for Germany. She had been carrying four million dollars in gold for the Indian government. When the
captain learned that the war had begun he changed course and instead of Hong Kong headed for the Philippines, where he delivered
the gold to the German consul. He also followed the consul's orders
and took on provisions and supplies. He was to join the East Asia
Cruiser Squadron.

But to counterbalance this good news, again, came the word
from the *Princess Alice* that Japan had sent an ultimatum to Tsingtao
to evacuate its military forces. Captain von Müller knew then that
war with Japan, too, was inevitable.

As the sun was sinking the *Emden* finished coaling and the
order was given to move on. She led the way out of the harbor, the
Markomannia fell into line behind her, and the *Princess Alice* further
yet behind. But from the beginning the *Princess Alice* misbehaved.
She missed a change in course and lost her way, or so it seemed.
Aboard the *Emden* officers and men believed the *Princess Alice* was
less than eager to join them in their search for battle. It was *possible*
that there was confusion; in order to keep from using the wireless
the captain established an awkward set of signals; by lantern from
the *Emden* to the *Markomannia*, which passed them on to the big
passenger ship. In any event the *Princess Alice* soon became separated
from the others. Two days later von Müller ordered the use of the
wireless to bring her to a rendezvous to ship the supplies, but then
there were excuses. The captain of the *Princess Alice* said he was

short of coal, although he had loaded coal at Manila. He then said his boilers were bad. Von Müller grew exasperated. He could not stand in the middle of the Pacific and argue all summer, much as he needed the provisions of the *Princess Alice*. He ordered the ship to return to the Philippines and steamed on without her.

The course of the *Emden* now lay toward a point in the Moluccas. She would steam by Mindanao and right through the Dutch East Indies, in other words, then make a right turn and head into the Indian Ocean.

In wireless code, the *Emden* was trying to get in touch with Tsingtao on the night of August 20 when suddenly the old German light cruiser *Geier* answered the call. She was not far away (she had remained hidden in a cove at Yap while the British bombarded the wireless station), and the two ships met on August 21. The *Geier* was accompanied by her collier, the *Bochum*. Korvettenkapitän Grasshof and his adjutant came aboard the *Emden* for discussions, and then Captain von Müller had another heartbreaking decision to make: What was to be done with the *Geier*?

She was old, she could not make more than twelve knots under full steam, and her armament was too light to engage in action with modern enemy ships. Von Müller needed firepower for his mission, but reluctantly he ordered the *Geier* to Honolulu where she would be interned. Then the ships parted company and the *Emden* steamed on.

The crew was now itching for action, because it wanted to glorify the red, white, and black flag for one thing, and because food was growing short for another. On the failure of the *Princess Alice* to meet and deliver her supplies, the *Emden's* officers and men were quickly reduced to a basic diet of corned beef and rice. The cooks were ingenious in disguising it; they made curries and treated it with chili powder, they fried it and baked it and boiled it; but still it was corned beef and rice. Nothing could be done to improve their diet until they could stop and take some of the small stores of live animals from the *Markomannia* or could find a German ship or capture an enemy.

On August 22, the *Emden* crossed the equator. If it had been peacetime there would have been ceremonies of initiation of "pollywogs" to become old salts, but this was war and there was no time for foolery. The ceremonies were passed over. The next day Captain von Müller was subjected to the worst frustration imaginable: A Japanese passenger ship appeared and although the captain knew that Germany would soon be at war with Japan he had no knowledge whether or not war had really come, and so he would not shoot at what he knew to be an enemy. (Japan began her blockade of Tsingtao on August 27.)

Now, at least, there was something for the men of the *Emden* to see. They were in strange waters and the sights were new to them. They steered between Celebes and Halmahera islands, but avoided both, trying to keep attention away from the cruiser.

Past the equator they headed through the Moluccan straits and for Timor. Here the *Emden* hoped for another rendezvous. In the heavy wireless traffic of the evenings and nights, Adjutant von Guerard kept his radio operators alert, and they had been in touch with the German steamer *Tannenfels* after the *Princess Alice* failed them. The *Tannenfels* had coal and food aboard and promised to meet the *Emden* at Timor to replenish her supplies. Up came the Nusa-berei straits, which lie between the northeast shore of Timor and the island of Letti. The *Emden* steamed ahead day and night, blacked out at night, keeping the smoke trail down to avoid detection. On August 24 she reached the point of rendezvous. She was a full day ahead of schedule, which meant welcome relief for the men for a few hours before the detested coaling must begin.

Now the coal on deck had been burned and the bunkers were only half filled, so no matter what would happen the *Emden* must coal again. If she were to be separated from the *Markomannia* for a week, even at reduced speed she would realize the nightmare of her commander: She would become useless and helpless by running out of fuel.

On the gray foggy morning of August 25 the *Emden* and the *Markomannia* steamed into the deserted little harbor where they were to meet the *Tannenfels*. They waited half the day but the ship did not appear. Afraid to wait longer, yet desperate for coal, the *Emden* took 470 tons from the *Markomannia*, thus cutting deep into her own reserves. The men were tired and dispirited. War, rather than bringing excitement and glory, was bringing them only heat, bad food, and the never ending filth of coaling. That day Prince Franz Joseph and three of the other lieutenants put down their tunics, picked up sacks of coal and helped with the physical labor. The prince offered the men of his port watch cigars if they carried more coal than the men of the starboard watch. So, buoyed by the spirits of their officers, the men made it through quickly, with even a rise to their sagging morale.

Those who were not engaged in coaling went on a foraging expedition on the island. Six cattle, two pigs, and several sheep were still left aboard the *Markomannia* and they were badly in need of fodder. Two of the *Emden's* cutters were released for haying, and a dozen men were given machetes to cut grass for the animals. A machinegun crew was assigned to protect them from the headhunters who had once lived on the island; whether or not they remained there on that August 25 was not known.

Had the captain called for volunteers for this expedition he would have received four hundred applications; every man aboard envied those who were allowed to go out and stretch their legs on land and breathe air untainted with coal. Danger was welcome. First Officer von Mücke led the expedition, eager to explore the island and he was accompanied by Gaede, von Guerard, and Leutnant Fikentscher, one of the deck officers.

The expedition began with a mishap. The boats were over the side and the officers and crew climbed down into them by ladder. Vice-Steerman Meyer appeared at the ladder just as his boat left the side of the ship. He was left behind. Or so it seemed. Meyer was not going to allow his tardiness to prevent his escape from the foul air of the ship, and so he leaped into the water after his boat and swam behind her as the crew back on the ship broke into laughter. Von Mücke saw what had occurred, and stopped the boats, and they waited for their dripping comrade to arrive.

The steam pinnace was too deep of draft to go into the shallow water, so her crew must stand offshore, guarding the others in the cutter as they rowed in and beached the boat. They cut one load of hay and went back for another. Then, before the eyes of their unhappy shipmates in the coal dust of the *Emden*, they stripped and took baths in the cool water of the sea before embarking in leisure to return to the ship.

There were no other incidents ashore. The boats returned filled above the gunwales with fodder before the coaling was completed. The *Emden* and the *Markomannia* left Timor then, headed for the Strait of Lombok and the Indian Ocean. The crew was nervous and primed for battle; the captain was hoping desperately that they would find their merchant steamer before long. Still another merchantman had been ordered to meet them at the island of Tanah Jampeia, which lay on their course, between Flores and the southern coast of Celebes.

On the morning of August 27, the *Emden* approached the islands, having steamed for two days down the coast of Timor, along its rocky shore, where the mountains rose from the water to a height of eight thousand feet. At Tanah Jampeia, they steered around the island to enter the bay from the south. Inside, they hoped, they would find a German merchantman waiting.

Instead they found a warship, larger than their own, approaching at full speed with her flags flying. From the distance they could not tell her nationality or her intention. The crew was ready, anxious, eager for action. No time was lost.

"Clear the ship for battle!" rang the cry and the alarm bells clanged and the fifes sounded angrily through the ship.

The men, at action stations, could not see what was happening, but a mile and a half now separated the *Emden* from the larger ship. At 2,500 yards firing could begin easily enough. Captain von Müller held his fire, straining at his glass. Finally when the tension had become nearly unbearable on the bridge he made out her ensign: Dutch. The battle flags were run down from the *Emden's* foremast and the crew was told to relax. Von Müller had rung up full speed; he now rang the engine down to half, and the two ships closed slowly. The loaders took their asbestos battle gloves off—no danger now that the cartridge cases would burn their hands. The gunners relaxed. The men in the crow's-nests had time to watch the spray scudding up from beneath the Dutchman's bow. The officers on the bridge could note the massive clouds of smoke she made, indicating to them, in their superiority, poor fuel management, or poor fuel.

Still, the quiet that precedes battle held on the decks of the *Emden*. Captain von Müller and Gunnery Officer Gaede stood still, tense even yet, as they would remain until they had passed the warship or the two had stopped for talk.

The ships approached one another slowly, warily. The men on the *Emden* saw that the other ship was the Dutch battleship *Tromp*. But had Holland entered the war against Germany? No one aboard the *Emden* was quite sure. The batteries were told to hold their fire, but the guns continued to be trained on the enemy ship and would be until her intentions were known.

The *Tromp* showed her intentions. Her guns were pointed straight over her bows in a peaceful gesture. So the amenities began.

The bugler was summoned to the deck of the *Emden* and blew attention, which brought the deck crew out to the rails, standing stiffly to honor the other ship. There was no recourse for the *Emden* in courtesy but to enter the bay and anchor, and she did so, the *Tromp* turning in courtesy and following her in.

At anchor, the *Tromp* sent a launch to the *Emden*, showing courtesy, but not so much that her captain bowed before the inferior vessel and came aboard. Then, of course it was necessary for von Müller to return the visit and meet the captain of the other warship, so the steam pinnace was lowered and he went aboard the *Tromp*.

Aboard the Dutch ship, Captain von Müller received bad news. His collier had arrived off the island, but had been driven away by the *Tromp*.

No warring ships could be permited to coal in Dutch waters if strict neutrality was to be maintained. Further, The Hague had ordered that warships of the warring nations would be allowed to enter in Dutch waters only once each three months and could then remain only for twenty-four hours. This meant, of course, that there was no chance of the *Emden* playing hit-and-run in the Indian Ocean, then using the Dutch East Indies as a base. One course of action which Captain von Müller had considered was outlawed for him then and there.

The courtesies ended, Captain von Müller returned to the *Emden* with the sad news for his officers. There was no time to consider the problem further, however, because the Dutchman must be fooled. Within an hour the *Emden* and the *Markomannia* steamed out of the harbor and headed northeast, back almost the way they had come, indicating that they were setting out into the Pacific. The *Tromp* accompanied them to the three-mile limit, then dipped her ensign in salute and turned back to her station. The *Emden* steamed on until the *Tromp's* masthead disappeared over the horizon. Captain von Müller laid the new course, first southeast to draw even farther away from the Dutch battleship, and then due west to make up for lost time. Two days' steaming and the ship would be at the entrance to her dangerous hunting ground, the Indian Ocean. The point of departure was ahead; they would first pass beautiful Bali, and then they would be in the straits, and on the other side were shark-infested waters. In the case of the *Emden,* the sharks were British warships.

~~~~~~

Chapter 8

THE BREAKTHROUGH

IN THE SUMMER of 1914 the Indian Ocean was a British lake. It was surrounded by British possessions or lands where Britain held protectorate, suzerainty, or enough influence to have its way. India and Burma lay on the north. On the west lay the Arabian peninsula and Africa. South and West was Australia. The only reasonable sea entrance not controlled by the British was that taken by the *Emden,* through the Dutch East Indies, but once inside this huge ocean, surrrounded by enemies, how was the *Emden* to survive?

Captain von Müller had no false hopes about surviving forever. He intended to live as a cannibal, off the captives of the *Emden.* The captives would supply her with coal and with food and clothing. As long as she could evade the hundred warships that the British could bring to bear against her she could survive. Von Müller knew that when he took the *Emden* through the Strait of Lombok he was steaming into a trap; huge as it might be, the Indian Ocean was still a cage to him and his points of exit were few and easily guarded. Von

Müller, however, gave no thought to points of exit. His problem was to effect an entry without being discovered and chased.

The first item in his plan was to find that right entry, and the one he chose, between Lombok island and Bali, took him through waters that saw little shipping. Von Müller also timed their arrival so they could pass through the strait at night. Leutnant von Guerard had been listening to the Dutch traffic on the wireless and from the liveliness of the communication, even though it was in secret code, von Müller was certain that the Dutch were increasing their watchfulness. He did not wish to be seen, for he expected that the Dutch would announce his presence in the area to the world after the *Tromp* incident, and if he were placed south of there it would be apparent that he had slipped into the Indian Ocean.

The *Emden* and the *Markomannia* steamed slowly among the lesser islands all day, taking care that no masthead came in sight above the horizon. As they whiled away the day, First Officer von Mücke worrying about the problem of secrecy, came forth with an inspiration. The *Emden* was easily recognizable as a German light cruiser by her size, shape, number and placement of guns, and her three funnels. British light cruisers carried four funnels, and there were no light criusers of other nations in this area. So wherever she might go, the three stacks of the *Emden* would be her trademark, and every spy in the Indian Ocean could spot her the moment she appeared. Why not, then, make her look like a British cruiser? All it took was the creation of another funnel. Von Mücke took his idea to the captain, and the captain approved.

It was afternoon. There was not much time to do the job, but von Mücke improvised expertly. He mustered a detachment of men and sent them below to bring up a supply of deck runners, strips of canvas about six feet wide which were used to protect the linoleum deck during coaling.

On deck a large wooden post was fastened to the planking in front of the forward funnel, and the deck runners were rigged around it to look like another funnel. From the side it was most impressive. From head on the framework left something to be desired, since it was skinny and badly proportioned, but passing through the straits they expected viewers to look at them from the side and not head on. The captain said it would do.

In the evening the round red sun came down to the sea and

plunged below the horizon, as it does in the tropics, bringing darkness very quickly. The *Emden* had been loitering near the entrance
to the strait until the last rays of red gold faded from the sky, and
even later. It was ten o'clock that night before she began her passage
through the narrow waters. She met one steamer and several sailing
ships in the passage, but none of them came near or showed any
particular interest in her. Still, before the passage was completed at
midnight the crew in the wireless room heard Radio Batavia announce that a four-funneled "torpedo boat" had been seen in the
area.

On the morning of August 29, First Officer von Mücke suggested that he could build a really effective funnel which would be
collapsible and could be used whenever the *Emden* wished to conceal
her identity. Captain von Müller gave permission, so the first officer
set to work. He brought up lathing and more sailcloth. He knew that
the British cruiser *Yarmouth* carried three round funnels and one
oval one, and he decided that the *Emden* would emulate this style.
In half a day he had constructed a most presentable funnel. The
Markomannia was instructed to circle the *Emden* and examine the
funnel, and she did so, directing a slight change here and there until
all was perfect, or as near perfect as a canvas funnel could become.

The funnel was rigged with wire-rope stays that were fastened
to the foremast, and these were marked so that the same position
could be attained each time the canvas rig was to be hoisted.

For the next few days the *Emden* and the *Markomannia*
steamed along the southern and western coasts of Java and Sumatra,
moving at about twelve knots, staying always around sixty to seventy
miles outside in order to avoid the curious. Captain von Müller expected a quiet time, and he had it.

The crew went to light war watches, which meant only two-
hour duty stretches with four hours off between them. There were
boilers to be cleaned and equipment to be repaired to be sure the
ship was ready for battle. There were no general exercises; only Gunnery Officer Gaede continued training for his crews. The others were
put to work painting the rust spots that suddenly began to stain the
outlines of the *Emden* and scrubbing down the coal-grayed decks.

In spite of the grime and heat there was a lightheartedness
about the ship that affected every man aboard. On August 30, which
was the dimpled Prince Franz Joseph's birthday, the ship's band

awakened him with a serenade. (He was ship's band officer as well as officers' mess officer these days.) Nothing could be done to save the blue-white linoleum of the cabins and the afterdeck from the ravages of coal, and the wooden decks elsewhere soon took on a dark gray. The handrails around the ship, once silver-bronze, became rusty and bent as the days went on, and the silvery sides were streaked with rust and dirt. The *Emden* could no longer be called a beautiful ship, but she was a very happy and stout one at this moment.

The first of September came, and with it the first results of the failure of the *Princess Alice* to deliver the supplies she had promised the *Emden*. Fresh food grew very short and was rationed to the men, who had to do the physical labor, while the officers began to live on canned meats. It was discovered in the officers' mess that they had a huge supply of paté de foie gras, which was welcomed in the beginning, but soon palled as a staple. The worst shortages, however, were in beer and cigarettes. There was plenty of wine aboard the ship, and for the rest of the voyage each man who sighted an enemy ship would receive a bottle of champagne as a reward. But there was not plenty of beer, and the cigarette supply was nearly exhausted. Worst of all was the shortage of soap. The supplier in Tsingtao had not delivered enough soap. So men first washed themselves with the soap, then saved the water to wash their clothes, and finally saved that water to wash the ship itself.

August 30, the Prince's birthday, was a Sunday, so worship was in order, and then cocktails in the officers' mess while on deck the men had a little of the remaining beer and First Officer von Mücke conducted his situation report to keep the men's morale and patriotism from flagging.

The following evening, as the *Emden* moved quietly off the coast of Sumatra, again heavy traffic on the wireless was noted, and the fact that it was in secret code indicated again that it was military traffic. It was actually the English heavy cruiser *Hampshire*, and although the men of the *Emden* did not know it, she was searching these very waters for German warships at that moment.

On the afternoon of September 3 the *Emden* approached the island of Simalur which lies off the coast of Sumatra. Captain von Müller intended to move into the harbor of Langini and coal there the following day. He did not wish to run at night, so the *Emden* spent the night cruising slowly back and forth well outside. Had she arrived twenty-four hours earlier she would have lain helpless in the bay, engaged in coaling, as the *Hampshire* came into the harbor to search. Even that night the English warship lay off the southern coast of Simalur at anchor.

On the following morning, the *Emden* and her collier moved into the narrow neck of Langini bay. It was an admirable spot for coaling. Inside the bay stood a small island, and behind that island a ship could anchor and no one outside could see any sign of life, and behind this was a chain of smaller islands with a deep channel running around them. The *Emden* came from the east and moved in from the north to Langini bay without ever knowing how close she had passed to an enemy large enough to destroy her.

At nine o'clock in the morning the tiresome task of coaling began again. The *Emden* could take on a thousand tons, including the extra loads for deck and the rear of the forecastle, but there was time only to load a few tons before the heat became oppressive and the captain ordered the coaling stopped. After lunch and a rest it was begun again, but it went dreadfully slowly. The lack of soap was torture here; some of the men were forced to wash their hands and faces in sand; the lucky ones guarded their tiny fragments of soap jealously.

The *Emden* lay so close inshore that the men who were off duty could examine the world of the jungle at first hand. In the inner bank stood a rain forest, filled with green trees, vines, and ferns that stood as tall as trees. To one side stood a grove of palms, and beyond, in back, the tall trees that shielded the ground and allowed little but brushy growth beneath them.

Not far from the spot where the *Emden* lay was a fishing village. At first the men of the *Emden* saw nothing, for the natives had hidden when the two ships steamed into their private paradise, but as the two ships lay quiet and no attempt was made to come to shore the islanders took courage and began to move out of their places of hiding.

In the afternoon, as the coaling began again, a few lucky men and officers sat on deck, amusing themselves by watching the birds and the natives on shore. Obermaschinist Berglin, a specialist who had no part in the coaling, sat on the poop deck with a fishing rod in hand and soon had a number of handsome large fish in a pile at his feet. Dr. Schwabe, the enthusiastic young surgeon, decided that he would try his hand at fishing and borrowed a pole and line. He fished mightily for an hour, without much luck, and then was forced to go below for a few moments, leaving his line in the water. While he was gone, Leutnant von Levetzow was seen to loiter near the doctor's fishing place, and when the doctor returned, suddenly he had a huge fish on the line. He reeled in and puffed mightily to make his catch, and when the hook and its burden broke water he saw it: an old boot, one of von Levetzow's finest.

As the doctor reeled in, von Levetzow had gathered the other officers around to see the fun, and when the prize was revealed in all its elegance, the crowd began to roar with laughter. The doctor endeared himself to everyone aboard that day, for once his moment of chagrin had passed he laughed more heartily than anyone else.

Toward evening the natives on shore became convinced that the men of the *Emden* and the *Markomannia* meant them no harm, so curiosity took over and they came out to the ships in tiny dugout canoes. Those who had sailed in the Polynesian islands were contemptuous of the canoes of these Malanesians—they were poor things, dug out of logs, and they lay so low in the water and were so poorly balanced that one crew member sat with a coconut shell in hand with the single responsibility of bailing lest the canoe be swamped in the clear, flat, windless bay.

The natives were dark-brown people, stringy with muscle, and they wore nothing more than small cloth or bark loincloths. They brought coconuts and oysters. Dr. Schwabe let the men have the coconuts, but he forbade them to eat the oysters of these hot seas. They also brought fish, pineapples, and bananas. The men could have the fruit, but the fish too was forbidden, since the doctor took one look at the filthy hands of the natives on board and began muttering about communicable diseases.

For this food the natives would not take money, but they were delighted to have old bottles, boxes and cigarette tins and went off happily, several of them holding bottles underwater until they were filled and then pouring them out with shouts of laughter.

The work of coaling was so very slow that it was continued until eleven o'clock that night, and still the bunkers of the *Emden* were not filled. They had drawn so heavily on the *Markomannia* in the last few weeks that her remaining supply of coal was deep in the airless hold, and with every will the men could not move at half speed in the intense heat and humidity.

They would have continued to work all night if necessary, but the captain took pity on them and called a halt until morning. So all the hammocks were brought above decks, and surrounded by hordes of mosquitoes the exhausted men tried to sleep.

That night Prince Franz Joseph and his roommate, Leutnant S. Schall, went to sleep in the wardroom. Their cabin was on the lower deck and it was far too hot for the tropics and far too inaccessible in case of an alarm, so the pair had permission to change their quarters. The prince slept in a hammock and Schall slept on a mattress beneath him.

At about three o'clock in the morning the prince was awakened by an unearthly noise. It was repeated and he realized that it was the ship's cat, somewhere beneath him, miaowing as if devils were in pursuit of her. He cursed the cat and his luck, and lay down to sleep again. The noise was repeated and repeated again. He sat up and tried to find a match in his trousers pocket. He fumbled, then discovered one and lighted it, grumbling because he had to go to the trouble while the confounded Schall lay there, much closer to the cat, without moving a muscle.

Match in hand, the prince looked down and began to laugh. Beneath him the half-naked lieutenant lay on his back, snoring, and between his legs lay the ship's cat and four kittens who had just come into the world.

After some stirring and mattress-turning the ship settled down again for the night, until six o'clock, when the bells rang and the fifes blew and the men arose for a drink of cold tea and to begin coaling once again.

Having been in harbor for nearly twenty-four hours, the captain was certain that the *Emden* had escaped detection. This meant that he had evaded the Dutch ruling which provided that a warship could call at one of her ports only once in three months. In case of need, then, he could seek refuge in a Dutch East Indian harbor.

It was a pleasant daydream, but at eight o'clock it turned out to be no more than that, because at that hour a lookout in the crow's-nest reported a white pilot boat approaching, flying the Dutch flag.

A few minutes later the little boat reached the harbor and anchored alongside the *Emden*, and the government officer came aboard.

When had the *Emden* arrived? he asked.

About nine o'clock on the previous day, the captain said.

The Dutchman laughed. Not exactly, he said. They had seen her turn into the harbor before seven that morning. The *Emden* would have to leave immediately, he said. She had already overstayed her twenty-four hour leave.

Von Müller said they could not leave, and indeed it was impossible, for the coaling was still in progress. So the Dutchman went down to the engine room and asked Chief Engineer Ellenbroek how long it would take him to get up steam. The engineer had steam ready for an emergency departure, but thought for a moment and said it would take him at least two hours to make ready.

So the smiling Dutch officer went back to the wardroom and sat, chatting, with the officers and men over whiskey and soda until eleven o'clock, while the sweating men of the *Emden* finished the coaling. The Dutch patrol vessel followed them for an hour as Captain von Müller travelled southeast, in the exact opposite of the direction he intended to go. Then the *Emden* turned, through a heavy cloud layer, and made a graceful sweep around to reverse her course. The destination was the steamer lane that ran between Khota Raja at the north end of Sumatra, almost due west to Ceylon, and around that island to Colombo.

Chapter 9

ACTION: SEPTEMBER 7-21

On the morning of September 7 the *Emden* reached the east-west steamer route to Colombo and began steaming west. The lookouts were alert and ready to sing out at the first sign of an object on the horizon. Now the *Emden* was seeking action rather than avoiding it. She was ready to do battle with any ship of lesser magnitude than a heavy cruiser and would avoid that or a squadron only because they could sink her while staying out of range of her guns.

Already she and the cruiser squadron were accomplishing their purpose. Admiral Jerram was searching the seas for the German East Asia Squadron, so far without success. His intelligence officers would puzzle in the days to come over the whereabouts of the squadron and over the reports that the *Yarmouth* was being seen in two different areas at the same time.

Half a dozen times that day the eager lookouts sighted smoke and the *Emden* turned and quickened her pace, only to have the smoke turn into a low-lying cloud.

There was nothing to be seen on September 7 but sun and sea and sky.

Captain von Müller sat in his chart room and conferred with Navigator Gropius. The intersection of the east-west steamer route that led to Singapore and the Colombo-Rangoon route lay a day's sailing north of them, so he ordered Gropius to set a new course and the next day they were there.

September 8: nothing. All day long the *Emden* moved toward the intersection of the steamer routes, without success. In disgust the captain talked in the afternoon of finding the Colombo-Calcutta line and following it north. That night they headed northwest.

At eleven o'clock that night the foremast lookout reported a light four points off the starboard bow, and the welcome cry to clear the ship for battle rang from the bridge.

With his night glasses, Captain von Müller strained toward the light. It was the after running light of a ship, but what kind of a ship he could not tell. He ordered full speed and the *Emden* leaped ahead, the *Markomannia* laboring after her at fourteen knots but falling rapidly behind as the *Emden* hit twenty knots. Looking up, von Müller was displeased to see a shower of sparks and a black cloud of smoke coming from the stacks. In their eagerness the stokers were piling on too much coal too fast and making smoke instead of speed. The captain wanted to surprise his quarry, not announce his presence to the world. He made a note to discuss the matter with the engineering officer at the first opportunity. If this was a warship he had already given a warning that might decide the course of the battle.

But it was not a warship, as he could make out shortly through the night glasses. It was a single-funneled merchantman, traveling away from him. He told Gaede to put a shot or two over her bows, and the gunnery officer moved his crews into action. Two shots rang out, two projectiles moved across the merchantman, and then the Morse lamps were flickering.

The message was in English: "Stop your engines. Don't use the wireless."

The merchant ship obeyed.

The doughty Lauterbach had already won his position as prize officer, partly because of his excellent command of English, and he rounded up his prize crew. It included a wireless operator, a Morse signalman, helmsmen, engineers, and seamen—all the men it would take to run a ship if necessary. They were armed to the teeth. Lauterbach carried a pistol at his hip and in his belt a dirk. The others carried guns and pistols.

A cutter was put over the side and they stepped into it and were rowed to the merchantmen. Now the *Emden* came close alongside, and the captain and the first officer stood on the bridge nervously waiting for Lauterbach's report.

Lauterbach puffed up the rope ladder that was flung over the greasy side of the merchantman and jumped onto the rusty steel deck. He spoke to the captain in English.

"What ship is this?"

There was no answer.

He spoke in French. This time the little captain fingered his filthy hat and replied.

"Ah," he said. "A British cruiser."

"No," Lauterbach replied. "A German cruiser."

The captain blanched and pleaded that his was a Greek merchantman. "He was a neutral," he said.

Lauterbach demanded to see his papers and his bills of lading. The captain tried to lie his way out. He said he was bound from Calcutta to Karachi, carrying coal. The papers were being sent by train.

Lauterbach knew he was lying and said so. The captain produced his ship's papers, and Lauterbach instructed the signalman to flash a message to the *Emden.*

"The Greek *Pontoporos,*" blinked the light.

Captain von Müller and the crew were stirred with disappointment. Their first prize in the Bay of Bengal, and she turned out to be a neutral. But then Lauterbach's second message came. The captain had finally produced his bills of lading and charter.

"Carrying 6,500 tons of coal for the English government. On her way from Calcutta to Bombay."

This put a different light on matters. The neutral ship was carrying an unneutral cargo. It could be called contraband and confiscated. Since it was coal there was no question about the interpretation the *Emden* would put on it. She needed coal more than her men needed food. The *Markomannia's* bunkers were too nearly empty for comfort.

Von Müller signaled back that the Greek could consider herself captured because she had contraband aboard. Lauterbach complied.

A few minutes later Lauterbach brought the captain of the *Pontoporos* over to the *Emden* to discuss his situation. It was a ticklish matter for the *Emden,* for while the cargo was English the ship was really neutral. It was resolved because the Greek captain agreed readily to change his charter and accept German money instead of British. He would be glad to work for the Germans, he said. It made no difference to him.

Now Lauterbach was sent back to the *Pontoporos* as prize

officer to take command of the ship. The armed guards were replaced by seamen who would supervise the operation of the Greek ship. Lauterbach on this trip also brought with him an English-language newspaper printed in Calcutta a few days before which carried a shipping-news column. He was able to point out on the chart the approximate positions of several merchantmen which had left port a few days earlier.

The newspaper gave the names of the ships and the destinations and times of departure. Lauterbach knew most of the ships and was completely familiar with the merchant shipping lanes of the area. Now they set out with direction as well as inspiration.

It was a slow and ungainly caravan, for the Greek could only steam at nine knots and the *Emden* was forced to cut well below her slow cruising speed to let the merchantman keep up. The *Markomannia* kept to port of the *Emden* and the *Pontoporos* to the starboard, where she could be kept under surveillance. They continued to head for the Colombo-Calcutta steamer lane, since Lauterbach's newspaper showed most of the ships from Calcutta taking that route.

All day long on September 9 they moved toward the steamer lane. They expected to reach it on about September 11, and they had little hope of finding more prizes before then. But at nine o'clock on the morning of September 10 a lookout won his bottle of champagne when he spotted smoke on the horizon, and the *Emden* detached herself from her entourage to investigate. This was a proper prize, the S.S. *Indus*, a British merchantman.

As the *Emden* ran down the Englishman, First Officer von Mücke complained laughingly to the captain. He said von Müller had done grave disservice to the cause of Germany by capturing that dirty Greek. What the captain needed to do now was take a prize bearing a load of soap. Von Müller promised that he would do his best.

The captain of the *Indus* supposed that the warship bearing down on him was a British cruiser. What else could it possibly be? So with the confidence of a yachtman asail on a private lake he ran up his Union Jack while the *Emden* was still far off and did the Germans the favor of identifying himself immediately.

Captain von Müller was still concerned with the niceties of sea warfare. There were distinctions and differences to be observed. She was an Englishman, this prize, but the condition of her charter was all-important. If she was carrying private goods it was one thing; if she was chartered by the British admiralty, it was another. If she was owned by the British government she was a warship. In the first case the ship might be liable as a prize but the cargo not, in the second the cargo might be a prize but the ship should be sent to port and sold off. In the third case the cargo could be confiscated and the ship sunk without question. War was considered to be a matter between governments, not between representatives of governments and individuals of the enemy power.

When the *Emden* came within easy range, the *Indus* placidly keeping to her course, the German ensign was hoisted suddenly and a warning shot went whizzing across the merchantman's bow.

The sea was calm, calm enough so that as the *Emden* came close alongside the British merchantman, Captain von Müller on the bridge could plainly hear the Englishman's response to the hail and warning not to try to use the wireless.

"Damned German," said the English captain in a voice that carried clearly between the two bridges.

Since Lauterbach was aboard the *Pontoporos*, Leutnant von Levetzow was sent to the *Indus* in charge of the boarding crew.

Vice-Steerman Meyer, who had taken the dunking when he flew off the deck of the *Emden* after the haying boats, was the senior noncommissioned officer, and he armed himself to the teeth for the encounter with the hated enemy.

As the boarding crew descended into the cutter, they could not see the deck of the English ship, and the captain was otherwise occupied. But in the bowels of the *Emden* the engineering crew, looking through the lower portholes, could see papers burning as they fell to the sea. The Englishman was burning his code books and secret orders. It was to be expected.

This prize was a prize. She was a 3,400-ton passenger-freighter, en route from Calcutta to Bombay, chartered by the English government from the Indian government. She was an enemy no matter how one looked at her. Further, she was a military ship, for the conditions of her charter held that she would be used to transport men and horses from Bombay to the European war front. Her decks were latticed with white-painted stalls for the horses. Best of all, because she was to embark troops for transport, the *Indus* was well-equipped with food and other supplies. Here was First Officer von Mücke's soap ship, just as the captain had promised.

Captain von Müller now faced a new problem. Should he take the *Indus* into his train and search for a hidden harbor where he could transfer supplies? Or should he take what he could here in the middle of the ocean and then sink the enemy? He decided on the latter course because he was in the middle of a British lake, the chances of detection if anchored even in a deserted harbor were very great, and there was no possibility of sending the *Indus* as a prize to a friendly port. Within the Indian Ocean there was no friendly port.

Now an entirely new set of arrangements must be made. First, Lauterbach, the merchant captain, must be relieved of his job on the *Pontoporos*. He was the expert in the loading and movement of supplies. The navy men—warriors—found themselves now forced to depend on skills that were never taught in the maritime academy or on the training ships. To relieve Lauterbach, a new officer must be found for the *Pontoporos*, because the Greek captain was totally unreliable and Lauterbach half expected him to try to flee at any moment. The mate of the *Markomannia*, a loyal German, was sent to the Greek steamer, and Vice-Steerman Meyer was detached from the boarding party to be head of the German armed guard on the ship. One of the cutters was sent to the *Pontoporos* to make these changes, and then both cutters were dispatched, one carrying Lauterbach, to begin what the sailors on the *Emden* called *sägen*—sawing. This process of unloading and loading on the high seas was to be repeated many times.

Lauterbach started up the rope ladder of the *Indus*, lost his footing, and, pistol at hip and dagger in belt, fell into the Bay of Bengal. He was fished out in a moment, spluttering and laughing, and was up the ladder this time with the skill of a trapeze artist, slightly shamefaced after his fall but ready to share the joke with all the others.

There was very little time for joking with Lauterbach about his mishap. His advice was needed about the unloading, and he fell to work immediately supervising the transfer of supplies.

There was enough soap to last the men of the *Emden* for six months. There was fresh meat and flour and all the other supplies they needed so badly at that moment.

Before the supplies were shipped, the English crew was taken, every man, from the *Indus* to the *Markomannia*. Kapitänleutnant Klöpper was sent to the *Markomannia*, too, with a military guard to be sure that the prisoners did not seize the *Emden's* collier and make off with her.

Then the cutters were ready to load and unload supplies. Captain von Müller maneuvered the *Emden* into a position in the middle of his three steamers. All the ships pivoted around the *Indus*, which lay stopped in the water. Although the seas were quiet, a breeze had sprung up, and the *Emden* had considerable difficulty in maneuvering so that she always presented a lee side for the boat traffic.

At noon First Officer von Mücke went aboard the *Indus* to check on the loading and see that the men had not missed anything of importance to the *Emden*. He commandeered all the sextants and other instruments of navigation.

All day long the boats scurried back and forth. By four o'clock in the afternoon the *Emden* had refurbished her lockers, and although there was plenty more left aboard the *Indus*, Captain von Müller felt they had lingered in this stretch of Indian Ocean quite long enough and gave the order to the loading crews to abandon the ship. They came, bearing the last of the provisions they wanted or needed, including a sampling of nearly everything, from live hens to pencils.

A sinking party then boarded the *Indus*. One of the engineer officers took a petty officer and three stokers to the English ship in one of the cutters and they set to work below. They took the doors off the bulkheads between the boiler rooms and the engine room and then opened the sea cocks so the water could pass freely through the lower compartments. Then they returned to the *Emden*.

To speed the process of sinking, Gunnery Officer Gaede was told that he might use the English ship for a bit of target practice. He sent four shells into the ship. Still she did not seem to be inclined to sink rapidly. Captain von Müller did not want more ammunition wasted, so he told Gaede to stop, and then the vigil began. It took her an uncommonly long time to go down, even with her sea cocks open and shellholes at the water line. She was an hour in listing heavily and then shipping water so that the bows sank. Finally she sank, gurgling. The air in her exploded and scattered debris, and the masts sprang out of the water and fell back onto the surface. Several boats were wrenched loose from their davits and lay floating.

Captain von Müller was annoyed, particularly by the boats.

They bore the name of the *Indus* and were as good as a calling card left upon the surface of the sea. But there was no time to destroy them, and so they were left, the *Emden* steaming ahead, the *Markomannia* following her, and the ponderous *Pontoporos* ordered to meet them later at a rendezvous.

Now von Müller must make another important decision. How much risk was there in remaining in the steamer routes now that he had sunk his first prize, and how much should he risk? He decided to remain in the steamer route until he had definite word that the British knew he was there and sent out warships to search for him. That would be time enough to begin playing tag with the enemy. The boats of the *Indus* were lying nearly unsinkable on the surface of the ocean, haunting him, but there was no time for recrimination. They had learned, and they would conduct themselves more professionally when they took their next prize.

The search for that next prize now began.

All night long on September 10, First Officer von Mücke stood as overlord of the new supplies, doling them out to the various divisions aboard the *Emden*. Some of the plunder, which he decided was unnecessary, he ordered thrown over the side. The *Emden* was a raider, not a pirate, and there was no thought of accumulating gold watches and private possessions from the captives they destroyed.

Beginning on the morning of September 11 the prizes began to come more rapidly. The *Lovat* was next, another English ship equipped to carry troops, also on her way to Bombay to pick up the Indian detachments destined for the war in France. Lauterbach was boarding officer. It was a little embarrassing, he told his fellow officers in the wardroom that evening, because the captain of the *Lovat* was an old friend of his from the days on the China coast. But war was war, and the captain was shipped, along with his crew, over to the *Markomannia* to await the discovery of a suitable *Lumpensammler*, or junkman, on which both crews could be placed.

There was no looting of the *Lovat*. She had plenty of supplies aboard, but Captain von Müller had no time to search among them to fill the *Emden's* minor needs, and the *Indus* had filled her major requirements for the moment. A few shells and the opening of sea cocks, and the waiting began. Again, the *Lovat* did not sink properly, and eventually the *Emden* steamed away from the listing freighter, leaving nature to take its course.

From the *Lovat* Lauterbach had brought newspapers to the *Emden*, Captain von Müller was interested in them alone. He wished to see if his entry into the Indian Ocean had yet been discovered by the press. It had not.

There was good news. It came from the *Markomannia*. The captain of that ship had entertained the two English captains with drinks in his cabin and in the course of conversation had learned that three more merchantmen were under charter and were following directly behind the *Indus* and the *Lovat*, all bound for Bombay, all destined to carry troops to Europe.

Captain von Müller could not have asked for a more effective intelligence report. All he need do was sit on the Calcutta-Colombo steamer route for a few more hours.

Transport number one showed up at ten o'clock that night, right on schedule. She was the *Kabinga*, 4,600 tons. But when Lauterbach boarded the *Kabinga* he discovered that the Englishmen either did not know what they were talking about in the *Markomannia* or they had been pulling the captain's leg. The *Kabinga* was laden with a cargo of jute and was bound for New York under charter to an American firm.

Here were complications. Captain von Müller could sink the *Kabinga*, because she was an English ship. But then Germany would have been bound to pay the American firm for the cargo. Von Müller did not wish to cost his government money, and he could use the *Kabinga* as a junkman, besides.

Lauterbach arranged affairs on the *Kabinga*, and the crews of the *Indus* and the *Lovat* were moved aboard that ship. She then joined the train. The *Emden* led now, followed by the *Markomannia*, then came the *Kabinga*, and last the poky *Pontoporos*. The convoy, when it kept together, was reduced to travel at nine knots.

Early in the morning of September 12 the *Emden* dashed off from her charges, awakening the men to action stations as she ran. Lieutenant Franz Joseph von Hohenzollern, the prince, rubbed the sleep from his eyes as he stumbled from his hammock in the wardroom and into his trousers, then groped his way down the passage and the companionway to the torpedo flat two decks below. There he could see nothing and could hear only what the bridge chose to deliver as information through the speaking tube. For fifteen minutes he and his men stood, waiting, then the word came that it was another merchantman and there would be no action from the torpedo division. He came on deck to watch the show.

Again it was an English ship, but again it was not one of the promised transports. It was the *Killin*, a collier, bearing 6,000 tons of Indian coal from Calcutta to Bombay.

The *Emden* had more Indian coal than she wanted. Captain von Müller decided to sink the *Killin* without delay. The ship's company was informed, and the cutters began their work in the rising seas, carrying the men and the few possessions they were allowed to take with them from the collier to the *Kabinga*, which came lumbering up with the other ships of the train. Von Levetzow had boarded the *Killin* in Lauterbach's absence. Now both officers returned to the *Emden* and the sinking party did its work on the *Killin*, with more speed and more accuracy than before. The shells that were fired into her were better placed, and she went down before the satisfied eyes of the men of the *Emden* in a very few minutes. She went down as had the others, only her funnel broke off at the very end and popped to the surface to bob around like a cork for a moment or two and then sink slowly.

It was midmorning before the transfer of crews was completed, then came a cheerful lunch of fresh foods, eaten with much gusto and many mock toasts to King George V of England and the British Isles. In the afternoon, the officers who were not on duty began a bridge game in the wardroom, sitting on Lauterbach's prized easy chairs. The off-duty crew wrote letters or slept or read some of Lauterbach's books. His library had been distributed and went from hand to hand among the officers and the crew.

Prince Franz Joseph and his companions were at the bridge table, having just completed a rubber, when the word was flashed that another steamer was in sight. There was no call to action stations, for it was obviously not a fighting ship. Lauterbach led his ten-man boarding crew to the ship and soon the message came back. She was the *Diplomat*, 7,600 tons, carrying a thousand tons of tea from Calcutta to London.

There was nothing here for the *Emden* and so the *Diplomat*, too, was to be sunk without delay. Captain von Müller was less than pleased with the performance of his engineers and stokers in the past. This time he decided to use a different technique. The officers and crew of the *Diplomat* were moved to the *Kabinga*, while Oberleutnant Witthoeft, the first torpedo officer, went aboard the *Diplomat* with a crew from his division. They carried explosives. The captain had ordered Witthoeft to make sure that the *Diplomat* sank quickly and cleanly.

Witthoeft and his detachment opened the sea cocks and laid their charges. They left the ship, and ten minutes later, after a series of small explosions, she went straight to the bottom.

All the officers of the *Emden* were eager to lead boarding parties. Prince Franz Joseph was promised that he and von Levetzow could take the next ship, but when she came she turned out to be an ally, or so it was officially. The ship was the Italian steamer *Loredano*.

Italy had joined Germany and the Austro-Hungarian Empire in the Triple Alliance before the beginning of the war. Through his two boarding officers, Captain von Müller asked this ally for a little help, since Italy was not yet in the war. He requested the captain to take the crews of the four British ships into Calcutta. It meant taking on some two hundred people in all, including the wife of the captain of the *Kabinga*.

The Italian refused. Prince Franz Joseph conducted the negotiations in French, because he spoke no Italian and the Italian spoke no English. But the prince was not above a ruse.

What would the captain do if the *Emden* put all these crews in boats and turned them adrift?

The captain would pick them up, of course.

So it was arranged, but by this time Captain von Müller was annoyed and decided to keep the *Kabinga* as his dump ship. The captain of the *Loredano* was reminded of his neutrality, and he promised that he would do nothing to give away the position or the condition of the *Emden*. Then he steamed away toward Calcutta and the *Emden* moved off south, as long as the Italian ship was in sight. Captain von Müller changed course and headed northward, but off the steamship route from Calcutta to Colombo and onto that from Madras to Calcutta. When Prince Franz Joseph returned to the *Emden* he reported that the Italian captain had been stiff-necked and unfriendly throughout their interview. Captain von Müller decided not to take any chances on the Italian's good will.

As if they had not had enough trouble, Lauterbach related his experiences of the day. He had gone aboard the *Diplomat* to be greeted by a bearded captain who wore a topee and insisted that he be allowed to take his nineteen cases of curios aboard the *Kabinga*.

He also had a suitcase, a bag of golf clubs, and a tennis racket in his hands. He was furious when he was relieved of all but the suitcase. He turned on the crew and insisted that they take his nineteen cases of curios, but his crew members preferred, they said, to save their own belongings. Lauterbach shook his head dolefully as he told the story and drank down some good English beer.

In the evening they met another Italian, and this time instead of identifying themselves and going aboard, von Müller simply hailed the ship and when she identified herself steamed away without a word, following a false course to keep the enemy off the trail.

By the time the *Emden* doubled back she had lost her companions, and she spent half the night searching for the other ships. In darkness and heavy weather she nearly ran down the *Kabinga*, saving them from collision only by reversing her screws at the last moment. But having missed an accident she had found her lost ships and brought them quickly into line on the Madras-Calcutta run.

The next morning the *Emden* spotted a superstructure on the horizon and began steaming toward it. It was not a merchantman, von Müller discovered to his chagrin, but the pagoda of the great temple of the city of Puri.

This was most unwelcome news. From the English ships captured, Captain von Müller and Navigator Gropius had amassed a fine collection of British charts of the Indian Ocean. All of them agreed that the waters around Puri were extremely shallow and dotted with mudbanks. The *Emden* was very seriously in danger of becoming a warship stuck in the mud. Captain von Müller reversed their course, then headed northeast toward Calcutta, to find the safety of deep water.

This was September 14. On this day Captain von Müller decided to lighten his load, abandoning the *Kabinga*. He realized that once he had done so he would reveal to the world the secret of the *Emden*'s presence in the Indian Ocean and that the fourth funnel would be of little value in the future. But there was not much alternative. The supplies aboard the *Kabinga* were running low, and he was not in position to operate a sea-going prison camp. The extra ships slowed his passage and created dangers, as was illustrated to him by the near collision of the night before. The English would have to be sent off, no matter what new dangers this might cause for the *Emden*. The prize crew came away and the military guard returned to the *Emden* and the *Kabinga* was given her position. Then there was a brief delay. Another British merchantman was taken, the *Trabbock*, a 4,000-ton collier which was in ballast, coming to Calcutta for coal, just as arrangements were being made to free the *Kabinga*. The crew of the new vessel joined the crowd on the dump ship and sailed away for Calcutta as Leutnant von Levetzow went to place the demolition charges in the collier.

The *Trabbock*'s end was not quite like that of the other merchantmen. When the blasts went off in her hold they ignited the coal dust and she exploded and burned brightly in the gathering night before she sank. The *Emden* moved away, for her silhouette would stand against the flames.

Half an hour later the lookouts reported a light on the starboard beam and the *Emden* turned. She hailed, but instead of stopping, the other ship increased her speed and turned to run. She ran, but the *Emden* ran faster and soon was in position to begin firing.

Shots were fired across the bow of the other ship; still she did not stop until one was placed very close by and she was told that the next shots would land on the ship itself. Then she hove to.

The captain hailed the ship, and from her bridge came the word that she was the *Clan Matheson*, on voyage from Southampton to Calcutta.

"English?" asked the *Emden*.

"British," came the firm reply. The captain was a Scot.

Captain von Müller had a good chuckle on his bridge over that remark. Lieutenant Lauterbach had a far less pleasant time of it. When he went aboard the *Clan Matheson* he discovered she was carrying a load of Rolls-Royce automobiles, locomotives, typewriters, and other precision equipment of the kind to warm the heart of a man who loved the good life. She also had on board a racehorse destined for the stables of the Calcutta Racing Club and reportedly the favorite in the coming Calcutta Sweepstakes. There were other thoroughbreds aboard as well.

There was nothing to be done, however, except the usual, so Lauterbach reluctantly told the captain to shoot the horses, while the sinking crew did its work.

The men of the *Emden* were acquiring real skill now in their destructive work. It took them only forty-five minutes to stop the *Clan Matheson*, remove her crew, transship them to the *Markomannia*, and set the charges and sink the ship. She went down and the *Emden* turned east.

Captain von Müller now sought a deserted island with a good sound harbor. It was time to coal. The *Emden* had not taken time for coaling, the captures came so quickly. It was nine days since they had left the East Indies, and the cruiser's bunkers were running low. Von Müller always grew restless and testy when this was the case; now he sought deserted seas.

His decision to move off the steamer route came in good time. That night the *Emden* intercepted a message sent in clear by the Calcutta lightship for the information of all steamers. It gave the position of 86° 24' east, 18° 1' north, and reported that according to the Italian steamer *Loredano* the *Emden* had sunk the *Diplomat*, the *Kabinga*, and the *Pontoporos*. This message annoyed von Müller and infuriated his officers. The Italian captain had broken his word of honor!

It would have made no difference, however, as von Müller knew, for the *Kabinga* was soon in port and gave out the true information. She had the proof, the ships' companies. And within a few hours it was known to the British admiralty that the *Emden* and none other was in the Bay of Bengal and that she was doing great damage to shipping.

The admiralty had no desire to frighten the wits out of British and Indian ships, so the news of the *Emden* was carefully kept an official matter for the moment. The naval station at Colombo was alerted and units of the British fleet began the search in earnest for the German raider.

On September 15, the *Emden* and her two steamers cruised slowly in a deserted region almost due south of Calcutta but well off the lines of travel. She would coal and then she would move discreetly away from the scene of these triumphs to another region.

The next day Captain von Müller decided to try coaling at sea. There was no suitable secret harbor in the area, and the sea was as calm as a lake at evening.

The *Pontoporos* was brought to the starboard side of the *Emden* and fenders and improvised fenders of washboards and hemp matting were placed between the two ships to reduce the friction damage. The *Emden* moved ahead slowly on her starboard engines and the *Pontoporos* stopped hers. Then the coaling began.

It was hot, but the men had grown used to that and to slow coaling because of it. There was no surprise in the heat. There was surprise when the two afterholds of the *Pontoporos* were opened and the officers looked down at the coal. The Chinese coal they had been burning came in large pieces and burned strongly. The Indian coal in this Greek ship was dusty and slack, and the engineer officers knew the moment they saw it that it would burn badly and smoke frightfully.

The coal was heavily compacted in the hold, and it could be gotten loose only by boring a hole so that men could reach it from two sides. But as soon as the hole was bored the coal slid down and closed the hole, and the process was unending. The dust of this coal was twice as heavy as that they were used to, and the entire process slowed so dreadfully that some Indian coolies who had been aboard the *Clan Matheson* were pressed into action to help.

After thirteen hours of coaling the men and the civilians had succeeded in transferring only 450 tons of coal to the *Emden*. The cruiser's bunkers and deck loads were not filled, but this was all the exhausted men could do in one day, and the ships could not remain tied together any longer. The lines were cast off and the fenders were withdrawn. The *Pontoporos*, then, was sent to a rendezvous at Simalur island. The first officer of the *Markomannia* and Vice-Steerman Meyer remained in charge of fourteen men of the armed guard to be sure that the Greek ship did not slip away. Bad as they had discovered the coal to be in coaling, it was the only known supply, and they could not allow it to escape. The *Emden* steamed away, the *Markomannia* in her wake, and the Greek ship vanished behind the horizon.

A few hours later, when the *Emden* began to burn the Greek's coal, Captain von Müller was too far away from the *Pontoporos* to recall his crew and sink the vessel. That might have been done had she remained, for the coal was even worse than it had looked. There was no more steaming without black smoke. The stokers must work twice as hard to keep the furnaces going, and the boiler tubes, which had been cleaned only once every ten days or two weeks, now must be cleaned thoroughly once a week.

On September 17 the *Emden* cruised in the upper Bay of Bengal. She crossed the Madras-Rangoon steamer route and the Calcutta-Singapore route, but without seeing any vessels of any kind. That night the course was changed and the ship headed for the Bay of Rangoon.

All day long on September 18 the lookouts strained their eyes but saw nothing until four o'clock that afternoon, when a smudge of smoke on the southern horizon was sighted. The captain saw no reason to waste coal chasing her, since she was heading north toward Rangoon, so the *Emden* changed course to intercept and came up with the merchantman at nightfall. Lauterbach and his boarding party moved to the other ship and shortly made their report.

It was a disappointment. The ship was the *Dovre*, a Norwegian and a neutral. She was of no use to the *Emden* at all, unless she would take the crew of the *Clan Matheson*. For a price, the captain said, he would do so. Von Müller gave him a hundred Mexican dollars and the captain was satisfied, since he would have had to take them without pay if von Müller had insisted.

The crew of the *Clan Matheson* were very pleased with their prompt release and good treatment. As they were being transferred to the Norwegian, von Müller went aboard the ship himself and talked with the captain. He learned that the Norwegian had been scoured the night before by a warship's searchlight, although the warship neither stopped nor identified herself. He also learned that the ship had come from Penang, and that in harbor lay the French cruisers *Montcalm* and *Dupleix*. This last news made von Müller's eyes sparkle.

It was nearly dark when the *Emden* steamed away, southward, and the *Dovre* moved north to Rangoon. As the ships parted the erstwhile captives of the Germans gave three cheers for the enemy who had treated them so handsomely.

During his stay aboard the Norwegian, Lauterbach had picked up some recent newspapers from Penang. They told of the exploits of the *Emden*, or some of them, and they predicted that the German ship would be captured or sunk within a very few days. The officers laughed, but not too loudly. They knew, certainly, that they could not stay forever in the Indian Ocean aboard the *Emden* unless they went to the bottom with her. But they were also determined to remain afloat as long as possible and to wreak as much damage to British shipping as they could. So far they had captured or sunk nine ships. They wanted many more.

On September 19 the *Emden* took more coal from the *Markomannia* while at sea, since Captain von Müller learned that the British were searching for him in strength. From time to time the wireless calls of a ship that signed herself QMD were heard, and one night a shore station inadvertently told the *Emden* that this was the British heavy cruiser *Hampshire*. She was in these waters, and from time to time she came very close to the *Emden's* course.

That night of September 19 the wireless transmission noises from QMD were so loud that von Guerard estimated the *Hampshire* was somewhere within ten miles of the *Emden*, but luckily the weather was dirty and the blacked-out *Emden* could not be seen.

In reading the newspapers Captain von Müller realized that the British were most concerned about the effect the presence of his ship would have on shipping in the region. He could also be sure that the British would not broadcast the facts of his victories, for the same reason. He decided that he wanted to frighten the people of the region just as much and as quickly as he could, and he came to the conclusion that the quickest way to make the *Emden's* presence known to the most people was to stage a strike on a shore installation. For this publicity gesture he chose the important Indian city of Madras.

Chapter 10

MADRAS

THE JOURNEY TO MADRAS occupied four full days of steaming. It meant traveling straight across the Bay of Bengal from Rangoon. In the middle of the voyage the *Emden* stood directly below Calcutta, and on September 22 she was as far from that city as she had been when she lurked in the waters just off the capital of Burma.

From the reports on the wireless the officers gathered that they had been sunk. So said some of the news dispatches, as newspapermen speculated and wondered where the *Emden* might have gone. She was heading for a city of half a million people and would come in sight of land and open her guns on land installations, but this idea was quite outside the thought patterns of the British. For a hundred years no European vessels had dared stir a finger to challenge British superiority in India.

This was exactly the point of Captain von Müller's decision. Madras was chosen for several reasons—first, because it was far from Rangoon; second, because its port installations were readily accessible from the sea and the *Emden* need not worry about trying to thread a mine field; and third, because one of the members of the crew had once worked in Madras and could give them a good description of the port facilities and particularly of the oil storage tanks of the Burma Oil Company, which would be the prime target of the *Emden*'s guns. The tanks were located in the south end of the harbor, inside the mole. The harbor was overlooked by Fort St. George, which mounted a battery of 5.9-inch guns. They were old guns, dating back to the 1880s, but if a shell from one of them struck the *Emden*, even on her armor plating, the damage could be considerable.

As the *Emden* cruised across the bay, out of the steamer lanes and unseen, the crew relaxed and the officers occupied themselves in playing bridge and reading their collection of English newspapers when off duty. Duty itself was relatively light. There was no training on September 19, and on September 20, a Sunday, the usual rituals were followed and the men rested during the day.

On September 21 the atmosphere changed aboard the ship. Captain von Müller staged a war exercise, with the *Markomannia* going off to play the part of the enemy. When she was sighted again, the call for action stations rang through the ship. This practice, like all the rest, bored the crew, but the captain and Gunnery Officer Gaede said it was necessary. The *Emden* had earned a reputation already, but she had not engaged in battle with another armed ship, and her gun crews' experience with shot and shell had been confined to shooting across the bows of peaceful steamers and using them for target practice. Now that she was to be so audacious as to steam right into an enemy port, the *Emden* must be prepared to take some punishment as well as give it.

The captain slowed his ship on the afternoon of September 22. He did not wish to arrive in Madras too soon, for it was to be a night attack. The afternoon was spent bringing in the hammocks and the awnings from the decks and stowing them safely below, out of the reach of fire. The ammunition in the turrets was doubled. The log was secreted in a place off the bridge, safe from shells.

After lunch the officers were called to a meeting by First Officer von Mücke. He outlined the duties and responsibilities of every officer at his action station and established the chain of command for the future should he and the captain be killed in this attack. The men then took fresh-water baths. If there were to be wounds, the captain wanted the men as prepared as possible to resist infection.

Toward evening the *Markomannia* was detached, and a rendezvous was made. She would be nothing but a hindrance to the *Emden* in such an action and was best sent safely away. They would meet again the next morning if the *Emden* was successful.

At dark the fourth funnel was set. The *Emden* had made sparing use of it in the Bay of Bengal, and no one was quite sure whether the enemy had discovered its use or not. In any event, with the fourth funnel attached the *Emden* did look like a British cruiser and there was a good chance that she could move almost onto the city without detection.

The arrogance of the British was unbounded, the Germans discovered at eight o'clock when the Madras light came in sight. The light was burning brightly, a beacon to any enemy in the vicinity. Of course, there was only one enemy in all the Indian Ocean, and that was the *Emden,* but the crew of the German cruiser found the carelessness of the British both contemptible and in keeping.

Madras expected anything but an attack—so much was apparent as the *Emden* steamed toward the city. The city spread along the beach for sixteen miles, inland for about eight miles. Throughout, Madras was as brightly lighted as in peacetime; the glow of the lights illuminated the shore clearly and could be seen very far out at sea. The harbor lights burned brightly, showing the installations and particularly the *Emden*'s target, the red-striped white tanks of the Burma Oil Company.

Around nine o'clock, as the ship steamed forward, the captain ordered the men to battle stations and the war watch was resumed.

The *Emden* increased her speed and came in at seventeen knots. She still had reserves in case she needed them.

At nine-forty-five the ship reached a point about 2,500 yards off the beach and stopped. The ship's searchlights began to play, until one of them found the white oil tanks. The order was given to fire and the first salvo cracked out in the night over the starboard side. The first shells overshot the oil tanks and hit the battery on the other side in Fort St. George. But soon the gunners found their aim and flame began to spurt from the tanks. Other shots were fired into a steamer, and still others were sent into the city. In all, 125 rounds were fired. The oil tanks burned brightly, casting light across the city, to match the flashes of the guns on the *Emden*. The British manned their artillery, or part of it, but not a single shot fell closer to the *Emden* than a hundred yards, and most of the men on the ship did not even know that the British guns were firing at them.

Most of the harbor guns, however, were unmanned, perhaps because a large dinner was in progress at the Madras club that night, celebrating the news of yesterday: the announced sinking of Germany's one ship in Indian waters, the *Emden*. The celebrators were in the dining room when a servant padded in to call their attention to the fires burning brightly in the harbor and in the town.

The wind was blowing offshore that night, and this lucky fact probably saved half the town from burning. But as the *Emden* fired her last shot and turned north, the fires were burning brightly enough to suit the captain. He had expended all the ammunition he cared to on this target, and he felt that he had accomplished his purpose, brought surprise to the enemy and destruction to one of his major cities. For one lonely light cruiser this was no little accomplishment.

All night long the fires flamed in Madras. The crew of the *Emden* could see them as the ship reversed her course and turned south again, and when they were ninety miles out at sea the sky was still aglow.

The *Emden* steamed now past Pondicherry, the French colony south of Madras, hoping to find some ships at anchor there or in the harbor at Cuddalore, but there were none lying in the roads outside. The cruiser moved on to make its rendezvous with the *Markomannia*, then steamed ahead, eastward, apparently, to confuse any watchers ashore. Out of sight of land the ships turned south. The

new destination was to be the water off the Ceylonese port of Colombo.

The *Emden* was now truly playing with fire. Admiral Jerram
had learned of her presence in the Indian Ocean on September 16
after the *Loredano's* captain had come into port at Calcutta. He had
dispatched the *Hampshire* and a Japanese cruiser in Indian waters
to search for the *Emden*. The Japanese was to coal at Colombo and
the ships were to rendezvous off Madras, on the night of September 19. At some point the *Emden* might well have run into one or
both of them. As luck would have it, the *Hampshire*, which had
been so close to her for several days, received a false report of the
Emden's position far to the east near Akjab, and chased that down
as the German boat was steaming toward Madras. The rendezvous
out of the question, the Japanese cruiser moved elsewhere and Admiral Jerram's intuitive gesture went for nothing.

Captain von Müller faced two problems now: He knew that
the enemy would be searching hotly for him, and he must find more
coal—and this time good coal. On the trip south to Ceylon he considered coaling again from the *Markomannia*, but the seas were
running high and there was no time to search for a landfall and a
hidden harbor. He decided on the risk of running low on coal.

The plan was to steam around Ceylon, at a distance offshore
of sixty to seventy miles so as to remain hidden from the land. On
September 24 the *Emden* was moving south off the east coast of the
island when von Guerard's wireless room intercepted a heavy flow
of military traffic. Not long afterward other communications clearly
indicated that a Japanese warship had passed them, about sixty miles
off their port beam, sometime during the day. The hunt was drawing
closer.

Sitting in the wardroom, the officers of the *Emden* talked of
two matters. They wanted newspapers, to see what had happened
in Madras, and they wanted good coal. At the moment they were
using the Indian coal from the *Pontoporos*, and it smoked so much
that they were constantly afraid of detection even at a distance of
sixty miles from shore. The officers joked with Chief Engineer Ellenbroek about it; they said that every night when he said his prayers
he asked God to send him a British ship from Europe, loaded with
Cardiff's finest coal. Prince Franz Joseph even promised the chief

engineer that in a few days they would find him such a ship and capture it.

On September 25 the *Emden* passed around the southern tip of Ceylon and moved inshore to a point twenty miles from the beach. The engine-room crew switched back to the good Shantung coal. It gave no smoke.

After lunch that day the ship approached the Colombo-Penang-Singapore steamer route, and very shortly afterward they sighted a smoke cloud ahead. Without increasing speed the *Emden* drew up on this ship, then hoisted her battle ensign.

The enemy was the *King Lud*, a 3,600-ton merchantman traveling in ballast from Suez to Calcutta. Except for some flour and potatoes, there was nothing of value on the ship—no coal to speak of and no newspapers of recent date. She was sunk without delay after the captain and crew were moved to the *Markomannia*. Supplies from the *King Lud* were also taken aboard the collier, because she had housed so many foreign seamen that her food and other provisions were running low. Prize Officer Lauterbach advised the captain and the other officers to ransack their stores for whiskey and soda. The *Markomannia*, Lauterbach told them, was completely out of them. There had been too many English visitors lately.

As darkness fell that night, the *Emden* lay thirty miles off Colombo, and the captain saw something that indicated to him the results of his Madras raid. Four searchlights stabbed out to sea from the naval base, guarding the entrance to the harbor. All night long they ranged back and forth. Colombo was not going to be surprised as Madras had been.

At nine o'clock that night the searchlights were six degrees off the starboard side when the lookouts sighted a light four degrees to port. The *Emden* gave chase, but when hailed in English as a precaution, the ship reported itself as the Norwegian tanker *Oceanis*, and the *Emden* dropped back without identifying herself. In these enemy waters, off the coast of the enemy's naval base, the captain did not wish to attract any attention, no matter how hungry he and his crew were for news of the effect of their exploit at Madras.

The *Emden* then turned toward the island of Minicoy, whose light was a guidon for ships coming east from Aden. At ten o'clock they saw a ship moving out of Colombo harbor, silhouetted time and again against the searchlights inside. For a time they steamed on a parallel course, then when the merchantman was well outside land they turned and hailed her. She was the English steamer *Tymeric*, carrying a cargo of sugar to England.

Prize Officer Lauterbach and his ten men went over the side and boarded the English ship. This time Prince Franz Joseph was selected as the second officer. They intended to take the *Tymeric* with them for perhaps a hundred miles to get her safely away from the Colombo area before sinking. Lauterbach so informed Captain Tulloch of the *Tymeric*.

The captain refused to conn his ship. The chief engineer refused to man it. The captain told Lauterbach he would order his men to refuse to obey any order from "damned Germans."

In a way the captain's anger was understandable, even to Lauterbach. The British master had sat in the port captain's office in Colombo two hours before and had been assured that the *Emden* was a thousand miles away and that there was nothing to menace his ship between Colombo and Aden.

The worst part of it was that there had been no reason to pull in to Colombo except that the captain wanted to discover the whereabouts of the *Emden*. Had he sailed on by he would have been out of range. By stopping for reassurance he found himself under the guns of the *Emden*, while not yet outside the range of the searchlights of Colombo.

Lauterbach was a master of discretion, and heretofore he had never encountered resistance when he boarded a ship and informed its captain that he was a victim of the war. "Fortunes of war" was a term that fell often and sympathetically from his lips.

But the master of the *Tymeric* would not be comforted or drawn into jolly companionship. He swore again, and again refused to cooperate. He swore at the Germans, but he swore even more loudly against the port officials of Colombo and the British navy.

Lauterbach became disenchanted with this Englishman and watched him closely. Captain von Müller ordered him to move the ship out and not sink it, and he hastened to comply. Then he caught a few words spoken by the captain and the chief engineer from the corners of their mouths. They were hatching a plan to tamper with the engines so the *Tymeric* would not be able to keep up with the *Emden*. If they could stall until daybreak either the *Emden* would have to move away from the area and let them go or the *Emden* might be caught by a British warship.

When Lauterbach flashed this information to the *Emden* and requested permission to sink the *Tymeric* immediately, von Müller did not hesitate. He trusted the judgment of his prize officer. So the British captain and crew were ordered to abandon ship. The demolition crew from the *Emden* moved immediately in the cutter to the merchantman, and the crew began filing off, complaining because they could not take their belongings with them. There was no time.

For his plot, the captain was arrested and taken with the chief engineer to the *Emden,* where Lauterbach could explain what the two Englishmen had tried to do.

As the English captain boarded the *Emden* and was escorted to her bridge, he was smoking a cigarette and did not bother to remove it from his mouth. First Officer von Mücke, furious, snatched the cigarette and upbraided the Englishman for his conduct on a man of war. The captain and the chief engineer of the merchantman were then taken to the port side of the quarterdeck and left under guard while their ship was sunk and the *Emden* again got under way. Later they were moved to an improvised brig to contemplate the dangers of defiance. (Still later, when they were taken to join their crew, they nearly caused a riot. Some of the British seamen rose up in arms at the captain for defying the *Emden* and forcing them to lose the valuables they had bought during shore leave in Japan. It took the armed guard to put down the trouble.)

The *Tymeric* caused trouble all the way around, then, but she brought welcome news. In searching the ship Lauterbach discovered the newspapers he wanted, even that day's editions from Colombo, and the officers of the *Emden* were able to learn what damage they had caused and what fear they had brought in their raid on Madras.

The official government press report was terse and still informative:

The German cruiser *Emden* appeared before Madras last night (Sept. 22) at nine o'clock and shelled the city. As a result of the first two salvos the gasoline storage tanks of the Burma Oil Company were set afire. Then the cruiser fired several more salvos, damaging a number of houses. The telegraph office was hit. A shore battery responded after the third salvo; the *Emden* ceased its fire then and retired. Two policemen on duty near the oil tanks were wounded. The steamer *Chupra* of the British India Company was in the battle zone, and eight of her crew were wounded. The principal result of this incident has been to stop the return of confidence of shipping men, of which the signs are already visible.

There were other little stories. One told of the manager of the Burma Oil Company, who was asleep in his bedroom when a shell struck nearby and arose to look out the window and see his oil tanks ablaze. Another told of the terror struck by the *Emden* into the hearts of the natives and the maritime industry around Madras. For days afterward the Indian population continued to desert the city, certain that the *Emden* would return and fearful that a German expeditionary force might follow.

And for two solid weeks not a single ship entered or left Rangoon harbor, so great was the fear that the *Emden* would return to that area.

Captain von Müller's guess that a strike at a land installation would be valuable in destroying British morale was justified, and the officers of the *Emden* could even be generous to their unfriendly enemies. Captain Tulloch and his chief engineer were given playing cards to while away their time aboard the *Emden*, where they were still kept separated from the others, and several of the ship's officers found it possible to speak kindly to them in the euphoria of victory.

Chapter 11

THE PARTING

Two DAYS LATER the prayers of Engineer Ellenbroek were answered. The *Emden* captured her Cardiff coal, 6,600 tons of it.

It came in the nick of time. Captain von Müller wanted to remain in the excellent hunting grounds around Colombo, but to do so he must have good hard coal that would burn without leaving a telltale smudge on the horizon. The *Markomannia*'s supply was very nearly exhausted. The *Emden* had last taken coal from her on September 19, before the attack on Madras, and by this time, six days later, Captain von Müller was again feeling the gnawing hunger for coal.

The newspapers captured aboard the *Tymeric* had a great deal more to say about the *Emden* than simply to describe her Madras adventure, and in the wardroom at midnight on September 25 the officers off duty were reading aloud to one another so that none should fail to be proud of their heroic exploits. That is how they were termed even in the enemy newspapers, and Captain von Müller was compared several times to a knight of the days of chivalry for his gentle treatment of the crews from the vessels he captured.

Even the advertising columns noted the exploits of the *Emden*: An advertisement for one brand of soap boasted "the soap is so good that even the *Emden* took it from the *Indus* and used it." That ad gave Prince Franz Joseph and his friends a considerable amount of amusement. They could not understand the English mentality that would make this effective advertising, but they appreciated the notice. They also appreciated the English love of fair play which caused the newspapers to praise an enemy ship that was wreaking havoc at that moment in Indian waters.

At one o'clock on the morning of September 26 the alarms sounded and the papers were put down and the officers rushed to battle stations. It was a merchantman again, not yet their coal ship, but the 4,000-ton ship *Gryfevale,* bound from Aden to Colombo in ballast. The crews of the *Tymeric* and the *King Lud* were considerably overloading the *Markomannia,* and Captain von Müller decided it was time to create another junkman which would house the prisoners captured in the next few days.

Two other ships were passed that day. One was a Dutch freighter, which was careful to observe her neutrality, so careful that later in the day the *Emden* heard a wireless conversation between the Dutchman and an English ship, and when the Englishman asked if he had seen the *Emden,* the Dutchman replied, "For reasons of neutrality, answer refused."

The second ship announced herself in messages in clear to Colombo as the Danish motor ship *Fionia.* The *Emden* passed her in the night and saw a clearly lighted passenger ship. This was the approved manner in which all passenger ships traveled, be they English or German or neutral, and in Captain von Müller's war, based on the old chivalry of the sea, he would not think of attacking a passenger ship. Lieutenant Lauterbach said he was willing to wager that this ship was one of the famous British India liners, but it made no difference to the captain. He would not have attacked her under any conditions, for he did not want the responsibility of dealing with passengers who would include women and children.

At three o'clock on the morning of September 27 the marvelous coal ship appeared out of a cloud of dense smoke. She was the *Buresk,* carrying coal for Admiral Jerram's ships from England to Hong Kong. She, too, was added to the *Emden's* retinue, and the next few hours saw frenzied boat activity among the ships of the little squadron. The transfers of crews to the *Gryfevale* were being made. All were transferred except a handful of Englishmen aboard the *Buresk,* who said they would remain with their ship even as prisoners of war rather than be shipped back to port as passengers.

So on September 27 as dawn deepened into morning the ships steamed across the calm sea under a clear sky. Nothing could have seemed more peaceful than the *Emden* leading her flock, the *Buresk* on her port side, the *Gryfevale* on the starboard, and the *Markomannia* behind the *Gryfevale.*

It was Sunday and Captain von Müller led the Protestant services on the middle deck. The band played a hymn, the captain read from the Bible and gave a short sermon, a few prayers were said, and another hymn was played and sung. In the forecastle Prince Franz Joseph led the services for the Catholics of the crew. The job rightly belonged to Lieutenant von Guerard, but he was busy in the wireless room and could not be spared that day.

After church the officers and men relaxed. The officers assembled in the wardroom for their traditional cocktail. The indefatigable Lauterbach had obtained new stores of liquor and beer from the *Gryfevale*. One of the Chinese stewards aboard that ship had been his pantry boy on the China run, and he had opened the liquor locker for his old captain.

Lauterbach was not even aboard at the time; he was supervising activity aboard the *Gryfevale*, where the crews of three ships were bunched together. All was quiet on the sea and in the ships. In a few moments luncheon would begin on all of them.

Then hell broke loose on the *Gryfevale*.

When the kindly Lauterbach had told the officers and men of the *King Lud* to take some liquor with them after their capture they had been only too willing to do so. They had carried this liquor aboard the *Gryfevale*, and some of the seamen had broken into it that calm Sunday morning. One of the drunken seamen decided to settle an old score with the Chinese steward.

The steward was carrying a tureen of hot soup to the luncheon table when he was grasped by the pigtail and swung around and given a clout. He responded by pouring the scalding soup over his enemy's head, thus putting him out of action. But the drunken one's chum took it upon himself to enter the fight now. He snatched the tureen from the Chinese steward, broke it over his head, and then a knife flashed. Others, friends and enemies of both, began to move into the fray, and a general insurrection was stopped only by the interference of the armed guard from the *Emden*, who pulled out their pistols and ordered the fighting stopped before someone got shot.

Lauterbach stood in the galley entrance, pistol in hand, and ordered three drunken Englishmen put into irons. They were taken off deck and thrown into a lazarette for temporary safekeeping. All those involved in the fighting were herded into the forecastle and guards were posted there to prevent further outbreaks. Then Lauterbach handed a pistol to the captain of the *Gryfevale* and asked him to help keep order. The captain apologized for the behavior aboard his ship and promised to do so.

This was not quite all. Lauterbach signaled the *Emden* that he was having trouble aboard the ship because of drunkenness. Captain von Müller was outraged, and for the first time he was annoyed by his ebullient prize officer. Frostily, he ordered the confiscation of what liquor was left aboard the *Gryfevale*. He did it personally. The *Emden* pulled up alongside the merchantman and the captain delivered his anger and his instructions through the megaphone in clear, unmistakable tones.

Thus the insurrection was quelled and the quiet of a Sunday afternoon returned.

Aboard the *Emden* that day the officers were just sitting down to their lunch—soup, corned beef with rice, and stewed fruit—when the ship veered so sharply and increased speed so rapidly that the table moved on its gimbals and the water slopped in the glasses. The soup spilled over onto the table cloths, but no one was there to mind, because the entire wardroom spilled out onto the quarterdeck to see what was happening.

It was another smoke cloud. For a few moments the captain hesitated before calling the ship to battle stations, then a single funnel showed, and the tension relaxed. Another merchantman.

This ship was the steamer *Ribera*, the *Emden*'s fourteenth capture since the beginning of the war and her thirteenth in less than three weeks. The *Ribera* was in ballast and had nothing to offer the *Emden* except fresh provisions to supplant the corned beef for a while, a complete British signal book, and the captain's information that the Germans would not find many more ships in the Indian Ocean. He had just learned by wireless, he said, of a port embargo of ships in the Bay of Bengal. No more were to sail from any port until the *Emden* was destroyed. Further, the captain reported, even if the government had removed its embargo the captures of the past fortnight and the bombardment of Madras had sent insurance rates in that area skyrocketing until it was prohibitive for a ship to sail.

The crew of the *Ribera* joined the unruly ones on the *Gryfevale*, and now Lauterbach had the men of four ships to worry about.

The *Emden* was again cruising in the direction of Minicoy Island. Hunting was very good indeed, but it could not continue much longer. It was now eight days since the last coaling; the supply of smokeless coal was nearly gone, and Captain von Müller knew that the captures and sinkings of five ships in the past week would bring a flock of enemy warships to the area.

It was hard to disengage. At nightfall the *Emden* came across the 4,000-ton steamer *Foyle*, removed the crew and sank her. The charges had not been placed when another ship came into sight and the *Emden* rushed away again. This ship, however, turned out to be a Dutch mail packet and yielded no more than a few cigarettes for the officers who had boarded her. They came back the envy of officers and crew alike, as by this time the *Emden*'s cigarette stores had been exhausted.

The crew of the *Foyle* was added to the *Gryfevale*, making it impossible to stack another man in that ship. She was dispatched then to Cochin, with instructions to sail on a certain course lest she be torpedoed by other German warships in the area. This warning was Captain von Müller's bluff, given to throw the British pursuers off his scent. He had the feeling that this area was becoming much too dangerous for him and was taking every possible precaution to avoid engagement with the British fleet. The *Gryfevale* steamed off on her prescribed course, and the men of the *Emden* were pleased and flattered to hear their enemies give three cheers for them as they sailed away.

Captain von Müller ordered Navigator Gropius to set a course for the Maldive Islands then. This little chain was off the beaten path, and the chance of the *Emden* encountering either an enemy or a prize was very slim.

The men needed a rest, and the ship needed coal and a chance to stop somewhere so that the bottom could be scraped. She could not manage her top speed now, even burning Shantung coal, for the resistance of the barnacles was too great. Captain von Müller had quite given up the hope that the *Emden* could be kept or restored to her prewar trim condition, but matters that affected her speed and seaworthiness were something else again.

No one spoke of it, but now, on September 28, not a man in the crew expected to see Germany again. Each night the atmosphere screeched with wireless messages, many in code but so many in clear that von Guerard could report an estimate that at least sixteen enemy ships were now in pursuit of the *Emden*.

Some were British, some were French and some were Japanese. Every one of these capital ships was more powerful than the *Emden*; each one outgunned her and could sink her in an even battle. The *Emden* relied for her life on stealth and speed—not even speed, except speed in flitting about her self-imposed prison in the Indian Ocean, for all these ships were not only heavier but faster than she.

Captain von Müller had made the probable fate of the *Emden* clear to his officers and men at the outset of their voyage, and he did not speak of it again. When they passed the equator, First Officer von Mücke told others in the wardroom that he was then quite content to go to his death, for this had been one of the wishes of his life.

The officers and men of the *Emden* were not discouraged; quite to the contrary they were uplifted by a patriotic zeal that made them proud of their position as raiders. They were among Germany's first heroes, and they knew it. They would sacrifice themselves, and by showing their willingness they were exhibiting the highest love of the fatherland.

All this feeling of impending martyrdom sat close beneath the surface. It served to buoy the men's spirits when they stood without sleep for twenty-four and forty-eight hours at a stretch. But somewhere there must be a breaking point, and on the capture of the *Foyle* it was nearly reached.

On September 28 as the *Emden* steamed toward the Maldives the men rested. Except for clearing the ship to coal, most did nothing, and even the war watch was distinctly relaxed. Some simply collapsed in their hammocks. Others sat on deck and played with the ship's cats, Pontoporos, Lovat-Indus, Kabinga, King Lud, and Diplomat, the runt.

The runt was also sometimes called the little idiot by the officers, who took great pains to keep him from his chosen desire, which seemed to be to march overboard. The runt got lost. In the relaxation of the ship the kittens were sitting up on the poop, rolling and playing in the sun, when someone noticed that there were only four of them. The officers on "kitten-watch" assured their threatening fellows that the kitten could not have fallen overboard. A search of the ship was ordered and carried out, but no kitten appeared. The officers sat down to afternoon coffee, berating the careless ones, and even the afternoon band concert did not go as well as it should have. Then, on the evening watch, the kitten was found. He had fallen down from the poop, twenty feet into the rear magazine, and was discovered peacefully asleep in an ammunition box, sore in one hind leg but otherwise safe and sound. The ship could relax once again.

On the morning of September 29 the men were rested enough to begin the necessary coaling, and before eight o'clock, as the *Emden*, the *Markomannia* and the *Buresk* steamed toward the Maldives, a coaling crew was sent aboard the German collier to make her ready. At eleven o'clock the Maldives came in sight, and the *Emden* led the way through a tortuous series of passages until Captain von Müller was positive that they were out of sight of ships on the high sea. No one would find them there unless they came looking especially, and in this case there was absolutely nothing to be done.

Coaling began at eleven and continued for twelve hours. The result was shipment of 570 tons, not very much considering the time, but very much indeed considering the weariness of the men and the heat of the tropics. The men were hampered too because they had drawn so much from the *Markomannia* that they had to go deep into her holds to fill their sacks.

The work was stopped before midnight and the men slept. The captain, who had moved one of the easy chairs from the wardroom onto the bridge, slept fitfully in his chair and worried over the problems of his command. He decided that night to release the *Markomannia* to find the *Pontoporos* at the rendezvous, coal from her, stop in at a Dutch port and buy what provisions she could, and then return to a given rendezvous with the *Emden*. The coal of the *Buresk* should last until her return, for the *Buresk* carried a thousand tons more of good coal than the *Markomannia* had held when they left Tsingtao in August.

On the morning of September 30, First Officer von Mücke gave the orders. The men were to write home if they wished. The *Markomannia* would carry the mail. Coaling was suspended.

The *Buresk* moved slowly alongside the *Markomannia,* made

fast, and took off her surplus of oil and water. The officers of the *Emden* spent the morning writing their own letters and censoring the mail of their men. Like the others, Captain von Müller wrote home to his mother in Germany. He wondered if the letter would ever reach her and said so in the letter. That was why he could not discuss operations: The letter might fall into enemy hands. Nor could he give her the place or date of his letter. "I see with calmness what fate will bring to my ship and to me," he said. "Sadly I give thanks to you, dear mother, that on your birthday you must go through so much difficulty along with my dear sister Elfriede and brother Richard and his family."

He referred to the war in Europe, but only briefly, because, he said, he was totally without news of the war. He sent his love to all the family. And that was all.

What could he say? What could the others say? Some of the men sent home unbridled statements of patriotism. Others said little or nothing. All expressed the greatest admiration for their commanding officer and concern for his welfare. Von Mücke was especially impressed by the regard of this crew for the captain. If they were singing at their work and someone passed the word that the captain was asleep, they stopped. If he wanted them to coal all night, they would do it without grumbling. He was quiet and austere and he smiled seldom and raised his voice even less often, but about him there was some quality that brought the men to their finest, made them ready to lay down their lives. All this and personal references, some of them bald enough to make the officers blush, were in the letters home.

After lunch the writing and the censorship were completed and the *Emden* moved again alongside the *Markomannia* to finish the job of coaling. By half past seven the cruiser was again loaded with a thousand tons of coal.

Zahlmeisterapplikant Bordeaux, one of the ship's clerks, went aboard the *Markomannia* to carry the mail and post it from a port in the East Indies. He also took fifty English pounds, to buy provisions. The *Markomannia* could not buy so much as to make her purchases obvious, of course, but some needs could be filled.

At eight-thirty that evening the *Markomannia* steamed away, followed by the cheers of the men of the *Emden* for her safe journey. The plan was laid: They would meet again at the beginning of November at a designated rendezvous. Many brave words were spoken that night, but aboard the *Emden* few really believed they would ever meet their friends of the *Markomannia* again.

~~~~~~

Chapter *12*

ACTION: OCTOBER 1-20

CAPTAIN VON MÜLLER was a precise and careful man. As long as the *Markomannia* remained in sight he steamed back and forth outside the Maldives. There was no question of distrusting his comrades aboard the faithful collier; he was taking elementary precautions. If the *Markomannia* was captured it was best that no one aboard her know in which direction the *Emden* had been heading when last she was seen.

When the *Markomannia* passed beyond the horizon, Navigator Gropius gave the helmsman a new course, and the *Emden* began steaming straight south toward the Chagos Archipelago, a group of islands so nearly deserted that it was unthinkable they would meet trouble there. The *Emden* now needed time and quiet more than anything. After three months at sea she was not recognizable as the pride of the East Asia Squadron. Only a few swatches of her silver-gray paint could still be seen on her sides; the rest was reduced to rust and coal dust. The railings around the ship were bent and broken from the weight of coal and the accidents of coaling. The linoleum on the decks was tattered and broken; much of it needed replacement. There was no thought of replacement, so it must be ripped off and the decks treated.

Below, the engines and boilers needed major overhaul, which could be accomplished only when they were shut down to cool.

The *Emden* needed a good week in drydock, but since this was impossible in the midst of enemy waters, Captain von Müller sought a deserted coast where she could be run in and canted so her barnacles could be scraped, and where there would be no ships to chase them or be chased and the engineers could do their work.

The cruiser moved slowly south, the engine-room crew doing as much repair work as possible while at sea. On October 3 the ship reached the Chagos Archipelago, and she began moving slowly among the islands, anchoring here and there. The tubes in the boilers were changed. Only four of her boilers were in use at any time; the others were under work. The engines were stopped alternately and the machinery was repaired and cleaned. The condensers were overhauled and the salt scraped.

On deck the hammering and scraping went on day and night. The rails were straightened and rebuilt. The rust was scraped away. New lines were fitted to the boats and the moving parts of the davits were oiled and repaired.

From the ship's stores the men drew new clothing and underclothing to replace that which could not be repaired. The Chinese washermen doubled as tailors and repaired the officers' clothes. The seamen sewed and cut their own.

The ship's small arms were brought out and oiled and inspected. There was infantry practice and infantry drill for the men to keep them in condition while the ship was out of action. Kapitänleutnant Gaede put the *Buresk* to work towing targets and staged gunnery practice, and this time the stokers and engine crews were given turns on the guns so they could serve in emergency.

Now that there was a bit of leisure, Kapitänleutnant von Mücke had the crew break out some spare pipe and rigged showers on deck. Each man, thereafter, could have as many seawater showers each day as he wished, and some of them took showers three times a day.

It had been the custom of the ship's band to give an evening

Karl von Müller, the Captain of the *Emden*

The *Emden*, one of the proudest ships in the German Navy

Here, in the harbor of Nanking, on the Yangtze, the ships of
the Great Powers lie at anchor. At far right, the *Emden*

The harbor at Tsingtao

Captain von Müller attends a social event with other naval officers
in Tsingtao before the outbreak of the war

The *Emden* under a full head of steam

Burning oil tanks in Madras, after a shelling by the *Emden*

This photograph was taken from the deck of the *Sydney*, just after she had beaten the *Emden*, which lies aground in the distance

The raiding party in council

The bridge and deck of the *Emden* after her final fight

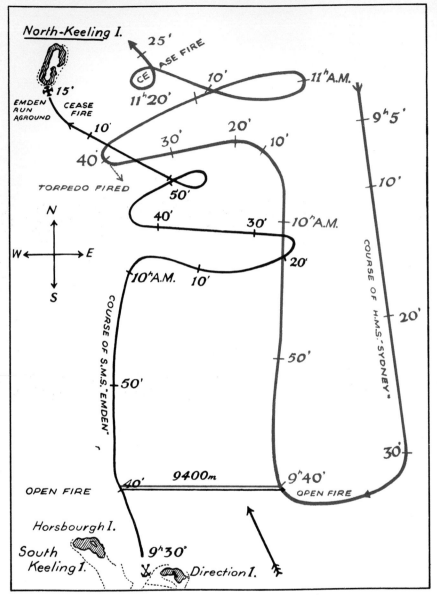

This is a plan of the *Emden's* last fight

concert. During the past few weeks the custom had suffered, but now the band turned out every night. It played every kind of music. The men sang and sometimes, when the band played waltzes and two-steps and polkas, they danced. The concerts ended nightly with the singing of *Die Wacht am Rhine* by the ship's company.

First Officer von Mücke took this freedom to distribute some of the delicacies that had been collected aboard the captive steamers. Hams and sausages and beer and chocolate were given to the men, and morale rose noticeably. Von Mücke also took time out to read the captured newspapers to the men, making it a point to inculcate in them a goodly suspicion of the words of the enemy. (His most effective gesture here was to read to the men the Reuter report of August that said it was officially confirmed that the *Emden* was sunk in battle with the Russian cruiser *Askold*.)

On October 9 all was done that could be done without cant-ing the ship so that the bottom could be exposed and the bottom and sides could be painted. At seven o'clock that morning Captain von Müller ran the ship into the harbor at Diego Garcia, the south-ernmost of the islands. He chose this little bay because it was sur-rounded by high ground and could not be seen from the waters outside.

The *Emden* and the *Buresk* were making ready to coal, but no sooner had the anchor been dropped than the men on the bridge saw an English flag run up on the island, and very shortly there-after a boat drew alongside the *Emden*, rowed by natives. Out of it stepped a grizzled old Frenchman, his red face beaming. He brought with him gifts of fresh eggs and vegetables, which were hoisted on deck, and he came up the Jacob's ladder hand over hand. It was an English island, but he was the assistant manager of the oil company that was exploiting the island's resources. He spoke only French, but soon the officers of the *Emden* learned that he was from Madagascar, that he was one of two Europeans on the island, and that he knew absolutely nothing about the war, not even that war had been declared.

This old man was taken to the wardroom (where the cap-tured English newspapers were hurriedly cleared away) and given copious drinks of whiskey and soda with ice. He explained then that the only contact between the island and the outside world came from

Mauritius. Once every three months a sailing ship arrived from there bearing mail and provisions. The ship had not come for the past three months.

The Madagasque was delighted to see German sailors. He could not remember having seen other German warships since 1899, when the *Bismarck* and the *Marie* had run into the harbor for a brief stay.

He wanted to know all that the men of the *Emden* could tell him about the outside world, so the officers not on duty began to spin fairy tales about a friendly peaceful world that had ended two months earlier.

Not long afterward, the manager of the oil company appeared alongside the ship and came aboard. He was an Englishman, and he was far less ebullient than his French companion. He wanted to know, straightway, what a German ship was doing in that part of the world, particularly a ship in such bedraggled condition. He looked suspiciously at the oil-stained deck which had once been blue-white and examined the deep scratches and fraying with a jaundiced eye. He saw the thick matting hung about the guns as a protection against shell fragments, and he noticed all around the ship the shadowmarks where something had once stood that was now gone. He looked into the wardroom and said something about the strangeness of having an officer's mess with a gun in the middle of the room. He said he had looked over the deck and he commented on the lack of paint and the repairs that were under way. Captain von Müller had a tale for him. The repairs were necessary because the ship had just come through a terrible storm, which had nearly caused her to capsize. The islanders nodded. They could understand storms like that. The ship was in these waters because she was taking part in "world maneuvers" which involved the united fleets of Germany, England, and France. Both men nodded happily. They were pleased to hear of the international camaraderie.

The suspicions of the pair were completely allayed when the manager asked for some assistance in the repair of their motorboat and Captain von Müller immediately assigned several men to the job. They went ashore delighted and made preparations to repay the courtesy.

First Officer von Mücke was not involved in any of these conversations. He was attending to the business of the ship while the captain did the honors. Arrangements were completed, the fenders were hung, and the coaling from the *Buresk* began. At the same time some of the watertight compartments in the *Emden* were opened and filled on the opposite side of the ship and the *Emden* was thus canted, to starboard and then to port. As she was canted crews swarmed over the sides and scraped the barnacles, then scrubbed the sides and bottom as far as they could reach, and repainted her, below the waterline with rust protector and above with their gray hull paint.

This task and the coaling took all the rest of the day until midnight, and then was renewed again in the morning.

After his motorboat was repaired, the grateful manager sent a formal letter inviting the captain to breakfast. Captain von Müller declined gracefully, saying his presence was needed aboard the ship. The real reason was that his inventiveness was nearly exhausted. Having informed the islanders of the death of Pope Pius X he really had no information at all to give them that did not deal with the war, and it would never do to talk to them about that sad affair.

Not to be outdone in hospitality, the islanders deluged the *Emden* with gifts the next morning. They came aboard bearing chickens and pigs, fish, and fruit. The natives offered to go out and catch lobsters for them if they would wait until afternoon.

Again Captain von Müller demurred. It was October 10, and they had spent ten days out of action. It was time to return to the shipping lanes. At eleven that morning the two ships moved out of the tiny harbor and began to cruise northwest on their decoy run. Out of sight of land they changed to a northeast course, cutting in and out of the Aden-Australia shipping lane. The captain of the *Ribera* had volunteered the information that hunting for troopships ought to be good in this territory. What they would do with the troops if they captured a shipload of them was never determined, because they saw no signs of shipping.

Their search was interrupted that very night. Leutnant von Guerard came to the bridge all smiles, bearing a wireless message he had intercepted from an English ship and a reply from the Colombo station. The ship had inquired about the safety of the Aden-Colombo steamship lane and the whereabouts of the *Emden*. The station had replied that the *Emden* had left the area more than a week ago and that the lane was completely safe.

Captain von Müller was delighted. He ordered the return, forthwith, to the hunting ground around Minicoy light.

Two days later the British heavy cruiser *Hampshire* appeared at Diego Garcia in company with its auxiliary cruiser, the *Empress of Russia*. The *Empress of Russia* steamed inside the little bay, while the big cruiser stayed outside in case the *Emden* was lurking somewhere in the vicinity.

The *Emden*'s stout friends of a few hours before, the Frenchman and the Englishman, were told what serpents they had clasped to their bosoms. They gave the course of the *Emden* when she left, as they knew it, and the British warships set out in hot pursuit, apparently two days behind.

The *Hampshire* then cruised up the eastern side of the Maldives while the *Emden* moved up the western side. Again the *Hampshire* at one point was within a few hours of her quarry without knowing it.

The *Emden* stopped briefly in the Maldives to take on the maximum load of coal from the *Buresk*, and then the *Emden* was ready once again to become the terror of the Indian Ocean.

On October 15 they captured the *Clan Grant*. She carried a mishmash of goods, including live cattle, and—wonder of wonders—prodigious supplies of beer and cigarettes. First Officer von Mücke went aboard the *Clan Grant* after Lauterbach had delivered his preliminary report. The methodical first officer took with him his list; the various divisions all reported on their needs. They wanted screw taps, soldering irons, brooms, a sheet of rubber, iron bars, firebricks, and machine oil. He scoured the merchant ship for them. While aboard, some of his crew decided they wanted to bring back some oil paintings and other curios. No loot, said the first officer firmly; nothing would be taken except those items the *Emden* really needed.

The cattle were shipped aboard the *Emden* and her transport, and 250,000 cigarettes were brought aboard the *Emden*.

The ship now had a definite barnyard smell about it. Besides the cows, for whom the carpenters built stalls on the middle deck, there were the grunting pigs and the cackling chickens, each adding its bit to the effluvia. When the ship was in motion all was well, but when she was stopped on the windless sea it was another matter.

Taking part of his cargo, First Officer von Mücke returned to the *Emden*, leaving Lauterbach and one of the young lieutenants from the *Emden*, Leutnant Fikentscher, in charge of the prize crew. The *Clan Grant* would be kept with them for a short time, until she was emptied of the valuables.

It was Lauterbach's sorry duty to report to the captain of the *Clan Grant* that his ship would be stripped and then sunk, sorry because the captain was an old China hand and Lauterbach had seen his scrubby beard and broad beam in many a port before. They were, in fact, old friends of years' standing.

Lauterbach waited until the correct von Mücke had left the ship before he broached the subject. He and Lieutenant Fikentscher went into the captain's cabin. The captain invited them to a stengah, Far Eastern talk for a strong whiskey and soda. They had one, and Lauterbach gave his melancholy news. They must have another to help the captain assuage his sorrow.

The captain was a model host, Asiatic style, and each drink was stronger than the last, on the theory that the only good hospitality was plenty of it. Lauterbach was an old hand at this game, and since he did not want to get drunk, he drank a little of each drink and shot the rest out the porthole when his companions were not looking. Leutnant Fikentscher was not so experienced and he drank each drink to the dregs, three of them.

Lauterbach sent Fikentscher below to sleep and said he would take the first watch. Fikentscher was to relieve him at five o'clock, but when five o'clock came, there was no Fikentscher. He went below and rousted him out of bed, a bedraggled sick youngster with eyes like mackerel dabs. From that day forward, Leutnant Fikentscher claimed that the captain of the *Clan Grant* had drugged him.

That following day, October 16, the *Emden* sent seventeen men aboard the merchantman to clean her out of supplies that could be used. The *Emden* replaced her crockery and table linen, and the engineering department got its firebricks in quantity. The cigarettes and beer came out by the caseload.

The unloading was proceeding, even though there was a heavy swell that day, when a smoke smudge came up on the horizon. Captain von Müller trained his glasses on it and recalled Lauterbach from the merchantman for more prize duty.

The *Emden* raced toward the smoke. As the silhouette became clear the captain was puzzled. It did not look like a merchantman. Perhaps it was a new model of destroyer. He ordered the crew to battle stations.

The tension grew until the *Emden* closed with the other ship, and suddenly seeing it broadside on, it was apparent from the bridge that they had wasted their adrenalin on an ocean-going dredger.

Lauterbach and Lieutenant Schall went aboard, not even bothering to take the prize crew, for what prize was this? The prize would be the information as to what she was doing out in the middle of the ocean.

In the gathering swell, Lauterbach leaped aboard the low deck of the dredger from the boat, slipped and fell on his portly backside. Mustering as much dignity as he could under the circumstances, he got up.

He did not need his dignity that day. The men of the dredger were delighted to see the *Emden*. They were delighted to see anyone and anything that would get them off that dredger—the rolling coffin, they called it. They had read and heard of the *Emden's* exploits and they knew that they would be well treated and sent back to port if they were captured.

This was their second try: they had started out with another dredger bound for Tasmania and it had capsized in the Indian Ocean. Now, on their second voyage, they were four months out and still far from their destination. It took three shells from Gunnery Officer Gaede's men to put this dredger on her back, too, and then she sat upside down in the water and would not sink until the gunners poured another half dozen shots into her.

The men from the dredger went to the *Buresk* and the *Emden* went back to ransacking the *Clan Grant* until Captain von Müller declared an end to it and the ship was sunk. The rest of the day remained quiet until just before midnight when the *Emden* came up on the 4,800-ton steamer *Ben Mohr*, loaded with machinery. The captain had the crew removed and sank her at once.

October 17 and 18 were quiet days, with no sightings except a Spanish mail packet, which the *Emden* turned to avoid. It was apparent that the port officials at Colombo suspected their presence in the area if they could not confirm it, and shipping was either being diverted or stopped.

On Sunday, October 19, the captain decided to try the Colombo-Bombay shipping route, and that afternoon they took the Blue Funnel liner *Troilus,* which was also carrying an extremely valuable cargo of metals and rubber destined for England and the war effort.

The captain of the *Troilus* was furious, and in his anger he revealed a valuable military secret. The Colombo-Aden traffic had not been stopped, but had been routed thirty miles north of the usual lane. The *Emden,* in moving, had just happened to catch the *Troilus* on her way.

Lauterbach comforted the captain as best he could. Then came a new complication: there was a lady aboard this passenger-freighter, a lady who knew Lauterbach from the days on the China coast. She had been a passenger aboard his *Staatssekretär Kraetke.* He was courtesy itself, and she was vastly amused at her capture by an old friend done up in a pirate suit.

With the capture of the *Troilus,* the *Emden* embarked on a period of swift action and great complications. The news that the steamer lanes had been changed caused Captain von Müller to take the *Troilus* into the train for the moment. He did not wish to waste daylight hours in transferring passengers and crew and in sinking her. Besides the *Buresk* was now very full, and something must be done to get the men off her. He would not send the *Troilus,* with its valuable cargo of war material, back to port as a dump ship, and he had no time to dump the cargo, even if his men had been able to do so.

The simple solution was to capture another passenger freighter, preferably in ballast, and send the noncombatants to safety in her. So the scouring began.

That evening the *Emden* found just what she wanted: the English steamer *St. Egbert,* carrying a cargo to New York—British ship, neutral cargo. There was their new junkman.

Now the captures followed so quickly that there was no time for changing the guard. Lauterbach was left aboard the *Troilus* for the moment. Prince Franz Joseph and Leutnant Levetzow were selected to be the next boarders, because still another boarding crew was on the *St. Egbert.* Anyone could now see why Captain von Müller had taken so many extra men aboard the *Emden* in Tsingtao and in the South Seas. Fourteen men had already left the *Emden* aboard the *Pontoporos;* one was on the *Markomannia;* sixteen were aboard the *Buresk*; and now two steamers were in the train, each with a prize crew of a dozen officers and men aboard, and still another prize crew must be formed.

Shortly after midnight the *Emden* captured the third steamer of the day. She was the *Exford*, carrying coal. Captain von Müller could not pass up the coal, so this ship was added to the little fleet. It was a rough night and a troublesome one for the men of the *Emden*. The prince, aboard the *Exford*, found it difficult to keep up with the *Emden*. Leutnant Geerdes, aboard the *St. Egbert*, misunderstood instructions, turned north-northeast instead of northwest, and was out of sight for many anxious hours. He stopped the ship and hove to; then, when the seas slackened, he moved back to the course and tried to find the impromptu convoy. Luckily the captain had considered what might have happened, and he stopped the convoy early on the morning of October 19 so the *St. Egbert* could catch up. She did, but not until seven in the morning. He went out and found her, leaving Lauterbach on the *Troilus* in command of the flotilla.

This day, October 19, was as busy and confusing as any day in the *Emden's* voyage. It began with the transfer of the various ship's crews from the captured vessels to the *St. Egbert*. From the *Buresk*, German boat crews were needed to ship supplies for the use of that collier and to ship extra supplies aboard the *St. Egbert* for the civilians.

Lauterbach had a chance to chat with the lady passenger for a time that morning. She was the wife of an architect friend in Shanghai, and she confided that her voyage home to England had been stopped three other times.

She had been aboard a steamer that had turned back to Hong Kong when the news of the *Emden's* first exploits was learned. She had sat there for several weeks. Then she had gotten on another ship as far as Singapore, when it stopped in fear of the *Emden*, and she had waited there. The third time she had come to Colombo, and after delay was now captured by the *Emden*. What, she asked, would be done with her?

First Officer von Mücke appeared on the *Troilus* that morning and told her that she would join the other English aboard the *St. Egbert*, and go back, this time to India. While he was there making arrangements for the transfer, and the *Emden's* four boats were scurrying from one ship to the other, some seventy officers and men were outside their ship. Just then, with all boats over the side, the *Emden's* lookouts shouted that smoke appeared on the horizon.

One cutter was hoisted in to hold the boarding crew if there was to be one, and a junior lieutenant was sent aboard the S.S. *Chilkana* of the British India Company with a very small, inexperienced prize crew. She was new and was carrying a fine load of supplies. The captain took her in charge, too. Now he had a six-ship fleet.

Aboard the *Troilus,* First Officer von Mücke was transferring supplies to the *St. Egbert* for the noncombatants. He was also negotiating with the captain of the *Troilus,* who wanted to ship his harmonium with him because it had sentimental value. Von Mücke could not resist sentiment and he gave his permission, so the instrument, the size of a small grand piano, was hoisted over the side and into a boat.

Aboard the *Exford,* Prince Franz Joseph was negotiating with the stokers. They were Chinese and they were willing to continue aboard the ship, working for the Germans, if they were paid their usual wages. The prince was glad to have them, for the *Emden* needed its own stokers.

Then the captain returned in the *Emden* and ordered von Mücke to stop taking supplies from the *Troilus* and transfer his attention to the *Chilkana.* So three boatloads of hams, sausages, canned goods, tea, chocolate, condensed milk, and all the table linens, extra cooking supplies and cups and coffee pots were taken from the *Chilkana* for the new passengers on the *St. Egbert.* On board the *Chilkana* young Leutnant Zimmermann discovered a new wireless set, and First Officer von Mücke, now on that provisioner, ordered it dismantled and sent aboard the *Exford,* which would be another collier for the *Emden.*

Boats from the *Buresk,* the *St. Egbert,* the *Exford* and the *Emden* ranged around the two condemned supply ships, carrying off the loot. Finally the confusion sorted itself out, and the captain ordered all boats clear of the *Troilus.* Gunnery Officer Gaede put several shots into the ship at the water line, but all she did was list a little.

His attention and the captain's was then diverted by a frantic message from von Levetzow in the *Exford.* Her engines would not function astern, and she was moving into the side of the *Emden.* In a few moments she would strike.

The gunnery was stopped and the captain gave his full concentration to avoiding this lummox. The sinking of the *Troilus* had to wait. Navigator Gropius was dispatched to the *Exford* with an experienced crew to repair the old ship's steering and engines and keep her traveling in the right direction, and the prince and von Levetzow were relieved.

Back on the *Emden,* Gunnery Officer Gaede was whiling away the time until he could get back to the business of sinking the *Troilus* by gunfire. She sat in the water, hardly any lower at two o'clock than she had been at one. Gaede was amusing himself by shooting at sharks with an ordinary rifle. Suddenly his hat, a white tropical helmet, fell overboard, and one of the sharks seized it. Gaede shot the shark before it could take the hat down, and the shark disappeared in a whirlpool of froth and blood, its fellows following to devour the beast in its death throes.

Soon it was three o'clock in the afternoon and the *Troilus* was still afloat, to the embarrassment of all, a monument to British shipbuilders. Gaede began shooting again, this time with the big guns.

At four o'clock von Mücke announced that the unloading of the *Chilkana* and the provisioning of the ships had been completed. He then took personal charge of the blasting party that sent her to the bottom in a few minutes.

The *Troilus* was still afloat. Gaede continued to shoot. There were snickers now aboard the *Emden.*

The *St. Egbert* was dispatched to freedom and young Leutnant Geerdes came back to the *Emden* to repeat proudly the orders he had given the captain. This ship was to take his six hundred civilians away from India. If he put into an Indian port he would be torpedoed.

Captain von Müller listened to Geerdes and blanched. This was the exact opposite of the orders he had issued, to someone, sometime during that afternoon. He *wanted* the ship to put into an Indian port and thus create unrest among the Indians and bring a little more fear into the hearts of shipowners.

Would Gaede's guns never sink that *Troilus?*

At half past six they did sink her; she gurgled and went to

the bottom. The *Emden* hoisted in her boats, signaled to the *Buresk* and the *Exford* to follow her and set out to pursue the *St. Egbert* and correct the orders. It was after dark when the job had been done and the false course had been taken and corrected, and the *Emden* was again steaming where she wanted to go, southward now.

The captain lay back in his easy chair on the bridge and announced that no matter what came in sight, except a warship, he was not to be disturbed. They were not capturing any more ships until the morning. It had been a very trying day.

Chapter 13

ATTACK

THE SOUTHERN COURSE set that weary evening of October 19 soon gave way to new settings: south-southeast, and then southeast, and later it would be due east. The *Emden* was headed toward a goal. She would steam into Penang harbor on the eastern coast of the Malay Peninsula and attack the warships anchored there.

Captain von Müller had decided on this plan as the ship lay in harbor at Diego Garcia. He had been delayed only because the wireless had brought him the welcome news that the Colombo-Aden line was "safe" and undefended. Having taken advantage of that information he was now prepared to return to his plan.

Early on the morning of October 20 two ships were sighted,

one at two o'clock and the other at three, both traveling at high speed, both running with sidelights only. The *Emden* and her two colliers steamed ahead, blacked out, and were unobserved. Later the men of the *Emden* discovered that they had been criss-crossing the path of the *Hampshire* and her auxiliary, the *Empress of Russia*. In their search the two English warships turned through the Maldives after they had come part way up the side, and once again they passed very close to the Germans without sensing their presence in the area. The other ships crossed and moved north. The *Emden* moved south, slowly but steadily, making around ten knots, so that her slow freighters could keep up.

October 20 was a quiet day, given to First Officer von Mücke's division of the spoils and to minor ship repairs. The captain had laid the course to remain away from shipping, and no smoke or sail was seen. The next day was the same, except that the course came over more eastward as they rounded the tip of Ceylon again. In midmorning the ships stopped briefly while an engineering officer from the *Emden* went over to the *Exford* to examine her boilers and engines and von Mücke arranged exchanges of provisions with the two colliers so that the division was evened out. A rendezvous was arranged with the *Exford*. She was to steam to a given point west of Sumatra and remain there hidden in a tiny, out-of-the-way harbor until her provisions ran out or the *Emden* appeared. That evening she was detached and moved away, leaving the *Emden* and the *Buresk* to continue east.

On October 22 the men of the *Emden* held a birthday party. It was the birthday of the Kaiserin. At eight o'clock in the morning the colors were run up and saluted, as usual, but this morning, the masthead flags of a German warship were also run up. At ten o'clock the officers and men formed into divisions in their dress uniforms and Captain von Müller inspected them and gave a speech about Her Majestey's good works, as far as he could remember them. It was short on the virtues of the Kaiserin and long on the virtues of German womanhood, but even a captain could not remember everything. He ended the speech by calling for three cheers for the Kaiserin, and this provided a fittingly enthusiastic memorial. The band played the national anthem, and many of the crew gulped, stirred by patriotism. The Kaiserin's nephew, the prince, was particularly moved.

There was a feast, fresh meat and vegetables, and wine and beer, in honor of the day. In the wardroom First Officer von Mücke made a little speech for the officers. The captain had retired to his bridge and ate alone, as usual.

All was quiet on October 23, 24, and 25, quite intentionally. The captain wanted as much rest for himself and his men as he could obtain. Their next objective was the most difficult they had attempted. Singlehandedly they would dash into the harbor of the enemy, select a target, fire, and attempt to dash out again without being destroyed. No one knew what they would find in Penang harbor, except that von Müller was quite certain it was being used as a base for capital ships. He might find the *Montcalm* and the *Dupleix* there, both larger than the *Emden*. In fact, nearly any cruiser he might find would be larger, faster, and more heavily armed than his own ship.

On October 26 the *Emden* and the *Buresk* pulled into Nancowrie harbor in the Nicobar Islands, which lie northwest of the northern tip of Sumatra. It was time again to coal. For the first time since war had begun the decks were cleared of coal. Captain von Müller made sure that no extra fire hazard would be available as a target for enemy guns. As the coaling ended, the name and port of the *Buresk* were painted out, and she was sent to the rendezvous west of Sumatra to await the coming of the *Emden*. Kapitänleutnant Gropius, the *Emden's* navigator, was left aboard as captain of the ship. Von Müller wanted no slip-ups where his coal supply was concerned.

On the evening of October 26 the *Emden* set her course for Penang harbor and steamed slightly faster than she had been able to move with her colliers, at twelve knots. Early on the morning of October 27 that speed was increased to fifteen knots. The object was to come to the lip of the harbor just before dawn of the next morning and to dash in and make the attack at dawn.

On the morning of October 27 the captain called his officers together as he had before the Madras strike and the battle plan was revealed and emergency instructions were repeated. The duties and lines of succession differed, because Gropius was out of the ship.

All day long the leisurely preparations for battle continued, building the tension of the men, who had not been told their destination or object. At five o'clock, however, the entire crew was assembled on the afterdeck and the captain announced his plans. The crew bubbled with enthusiasm, for they were warriors, and many of them were growing sick of carrying out a task they said the auxiliary cruisers were invented to do.

At eight o'clock that night the *Emden's* speed was increased to seventeen knots and the fourth funnel was hoisted into place. The captain remained on his bridge examining charts of Penang harbor.

The harbor lay between the sandy coast of the Malay peninsula, on the east side, and the island of Pulo-Penang on the west. There were two openings, one to the south and one to the north, but the southern opening was too shallow for oceangoing vessels; thus as far as the *Emden* was concerned the harbor was inside a bottleneck formed by the channel, which was a thousand yards wide. The *Emden* must move around the north side of Pulo-Penang island and close in to avoid beaching on the sandy Malay coast. The port facilities were located on the island, in and around the town of Georgetown. The course for the *Emden* was simple and clear. She must run in very close to the island, at high speed, with her helm hard astarboard as she rounded the point, and then Captain von Müller must be prepared to take in the situation in the harbor at a glance and decide in a few seconds how to make his attack. All depended on what he found in the harbor. He expected to find it dotted with merchantmen, but he was not seeking merchantmen this time. He must spy out the capital warships immediately, head for one of them, loose his torpedoes and gunfire, sweep around, and charge out of the harbor. The greatest danger was that a torpedo boat might be lurking near the edge of the harbor or might be able to reach the bottleneck before he could make his sweep and emerge. Then the *Emden* would be a clear target for a torpedo. But that was unavoidable, the known risk he must run.

At midnight the ship went on full war watch. Two hours later the lights of Penang came into view. The captain ordered the ship slowed and she cruised at eleven knots back and forth, out of sight of the harbor in her darkness. They saw a steamer enter the harbor and stop near the brightly lighted buoy, apparently waiting for the pilot. Still they waited, moving nervously back and forth outside.

The moon went down. At four-thirty the officers were warned to be ready for action and the *Emden* turned toward the harbor mouth. She passed a small island near the opening of the bottleneck,

5

and saw a pilot boat a few yards abeam. The boat was heading for the stopped steamer and paid no attention to the four-funneled cruiser.

At four-fifty the commands rang through the ship.

"*Achtung. Achtung. Achtung.*"

The night had been extraordinarily clear; all the more fuzzy then were these few moments before the dawn. The searchlights were trained, but not yet lighted. The guns were loaded but not yet trained. The men waited, half breathing. In the torpedo flat, the prince checked the tubes. Both were loaded. The electric release gear was in place and connected to the bridge, where First Torpedo Officer Witthoeft stood with the captain.

Just before entering the harbor, Captain von Müller reduced speed and looked around him. Even in the grayness the lights stood out. On the port side were four particularly bright lights, evenly spaced, that at first seemed to belong to houses on the far shore. But as the earliest golden rays of dawn appeared, the lights separated and disclosed large funnels and the superstructure of a capital warship.

Torpedo Officer Witthoeft shouted to the prince through the speaking tube to be sure the starboard torpedo tube was clear. He checked again, and reported. While the ship waited, Captain von Müller stopped the engines.

In these brief moments the dawn was breaking full, and now the officers and some of the men recognized the ship before them. It was the Russian light cruiser *Yemtschuk*. Oberleutnant Lauterbach knew her well. He had been the guest of her commander in Vladivostok harbor.

Captain von Müller ordered the engines started and moved toward the quiet enemy. The battle flags were run up the masts, declaring to the world the identity of the German ship, and she turned hard aport to bring the port torpedo tube to bear on the beam of the Russian cruiser. At 500 yards, as the dawn broke from the bridge, the captain and the torpedo officer could see a steam pinnace pulling away from the Russian, toward the town of Georgetown. Captain von Müller stared at her for a moment, worrying lest she be a dreadful enemy herself. No. It was only the cookboat, bearing the petty officers and cooks who would go in early morning to the market to buy fresh supplies.

A few seconds and the *Emden* turned to port, and now her port torpedo tube was properly aimed. At 300 yards, still without a stir from the cruiser, Torpedo Officer Witthoeft pulled the release handle and the torpedo leaped from the tube, its propeller whirring. It was five-eighteen when Witthoeft shouted:

"*Torpedo los!*"

On deck the men strained in the gathering light and could see the telltale track of bubbles. At the searchlights the crewmen waited for the order, but it never came—their lights were no longer needed; the enemy was in plain view and not more than 250 yards away.

Now there was stirring aboard the *Yemtschuk*, movement on the bridge and on the decks. It was too late.

A second passed, and then another. There was a muffled explosion, below the water line, and the *Yemtschuk* seemed to leap out of the water, a large splash appearing against her hull just below the second funnel. Then she fell back and settled as far as the flagstaff on the poop.

From the conning tower Witthoeft's muffled voice could be heard over the tube system in the torpedo flat, where nothing could be seen. The torpedo had struck, but had not finished off the ship. Another run was to be made.

As the torpedo splash was seen from the deck of the *Emden* the men began to cheer, but their first cheer was drowned by the thunder from the *Emden's* guns, which opened on the Russian, aiming at her forecastle where the men were sleeping.

The bright blaze of the sunlight was joined now by blazes from the ship. She was afire, deep in the water, and the *Emden's* shells were gouging into her.

Captain von Müller speeded around in a turn to port, to fire the starboard tube. In these few moments of maneuver the *Yemtschuk's* crew, or some of them, managed to move to action stations and some shells began to whistle across the decks of the *Emden*. Not far away from the Russian cruiser lay the French destroyer *d'Iberville*, which had been the *Emden's* buoy neighbor in Shanghai during the difficulties of a few months before. She opened fire now on the *Emden* with her guns.

A few minutes' maneuvering and the ship was aimed and the hiss heard on the bridge said the torpedo was away. First Officer von Mücke began to count: "*Eins . . . zwei . . . drei . . . vier . . . fünf . . . sechs . . . sieb—*"

The torpedo exploded with a sharp crack, cutting him off in midword. This second shot struck below the surface at a point beneath the armored bridge and penetrated into the torpedo storage of the cruiser. There was a second explosion, and the center of the ship raised high, she broke into two pieces and splashed back into the water.

Immediately smoke broke out, thick yellow, white, black and gray smoke laced with the flickering tongues of flame. There was a sizzling and a hissing in the water and a cloud spread around and above the Russian cruiser.

Now the firing from the *d'Iberville* was very noticeable. The firing from the *Yemtschuk* stopped, and the only action that could be seen through the smoke was that of a handful of survivors swimming in the bay.

The *Emden* could not stop to pick up survivors. She was too closely hemmed in by the merchant ships in the harbor and was under fire by the French destroyer. She turned again, and as she turned the men of the *Emden* could see what remained of the *Yemtschuk*. She was completely sunk; only the tips of the masts projected from the water of the harbor.

The captain considered the possibility of moving to deal with the *d'Iberville*, which was screened from him by merchantmen. Then his attention was drawn to a ship approaching them at high speed from the mouth of the harbor, trailing a dense cloud of black smoke of the kind that he associated with the fast torpedo boats.

He turned hard aport and began running toward this new enemy at maximum speed. At six thousand yards Gunnery Officer Gaede opened fire on her with the *Emden*'s guns trained dead ahead. The boat turned and showed herself as a government pilot boat, quite harmless to the cruiser. She had received only one hit in the funnel, and that had not disabled her. The interruption had, however, caused the *Emden* to run so far out of the harbor that it was foolhardy now to turn back in and attack the *d'Iberville* or any of the twenty merchant ships lying at anchor.

The battle flags were hauled down as the *Emden* moved past the entrance buoy, and in a few moments the men were released from battle stations.

Not long afterward, First Officer von Mücke called the men aft and explained the progress of the battle to them. A few had seen the entire fight, but most of the men had seen at best a portion of it, and some, who served below decks, had not seen any of it, including the men in the torpedo division who had sent the deadly explosives into the Russian cruiser. The captain also came aft and reminded the jubilant men that the credit should go to the Kaiser for giving them the opportunity to serve him. They gave three cheers.

The ship settled down. The ammunition cases were cleared away and the guns were cleaned and reloaded. Breakfast was served.

At seven o'clock the ship was called again to action stations as smoke was sighted on the port horizon. At first the lookouts thought this vessel was an auxiliary cruiser, but she turned out to be an ordinary merchantman—not quite ordinary, because she flew the yellow flag that indicated a cargo of explosives. Lauterbach and the prize crew were sent to the ship, the *Glanturret,* to carry out the usual procedure. She would be sunk.

Lauterbach was talking to the captain when the signal lamps from the *Emden* began to blink furiously. He was to deliver a message: Captain von Müller wanted to express his apologies to the men of the *Yemtschuk* for not stopping to pick up survivors and to the British pilot boat for firing on an unarmed craft. He had thought the pilot boat was a torpedo boat, he said, and he knew there were plenty of boats in the harbor to pick up survivors, so he had not remained.

The message was hardly delivered when Lauterbach's signalman was again at his side, telling the boarding officer that their orders were changed. The *Glanturret* was to be set free and they were to return immediately to the *Emden.* From the starboard an enemy was approaching at high speed and there would be another fight. There was no time to waste on merchantmen.

Lauterbach clambered back into his cutter and they rowed to the *Emden* to be hoisted on board. He tumbled out and ran to the bridge, for in the absence of Gropius he was the *Emden's* navigator.

Less than five thousand yards from the enemy the *Emden* raised her battle flags, and the order came to begin firing. As they closed the *Emden's* gunners began to shoot. The ship turned to port and the starboard guns were brought into action.

The enemy came ahead, then loosed two torpedoes and turned, presenting her beam as a target. The torpedoes passed harmlessly astern, and the *Emden* began to fire effectively. From the silhouette Captain von Müller could tell they were dealing with a destroyer, and from the tricolor streaming from her mast he could tell she was French.

The tricolor did not stream long. After two salvos the *Emden's* gunners found the range and the third sent the flag dropping. One shell must have landed in the boiler room because white clouds of steam rose high above the ship.

The French manned their guns, particularly a machine gun forward of the conning tower, which sent bullets swarming above the *Emden*—like bees, some of the crew said.

At the end of the tenth salvo Captain von Müller ordered Gaede to cease fire. He was waiting to see if a white flag was run up from the badly holed ship.

No white flag showed.

Two more salvos were fired.

The eleventh struck home, and the firing aboard the French ship ceased. The twelfth also struck, and then the destroyer began to sink.

Captain von Müller ordered Lauterbach to move the *Emden* in closer. Lauterbach demurred. They were approaching very shallow water, he said, and if they went in much farther the *Emden* ran the danger of going aground.

Von Müller listened and agreed. They stood off and continued firing. At the end of the twentieth salvo the captain again ordered the firing stopped. The destroyer was down by the bows. Then her stern rose for a moment, and the entire ship disappeared.

The *Emden* moved in to about 200 yards, going very slowly and sounding as she went. Lauterbach was careful not to lose the channel. Two of the cutters were put over the side, and in one of them Dr. Schwabe carried bandages and medicines to treat the survivors they could see swimming in the water.

It took a few moments longer to launch the second cutter, because as was customary before a fight the boat had been filled with water to keep it from catching fire if struck. The other, Lauterbach's cutter, had come back aboard too late for that treatment.

As the cutters approached, the French swam—but away from the boats, not toward them. They were afraid, the men of the *Emden* later learned, that they would be shot if the Germans picked them up. They preferred to take their chances in the sea, and one French sailor did actually swim all the way to Penang, but many of the survivors chose drowning rather than capture.

The *Emden's* boats moved slowly through the water, picking

up the wounded, who could not swim away. Then some of the
sailors saw that they were not being murdered in the water and swam
toward the boats. In all, thirty-six seamen and one officer were rescued and brought back to the *Emden*. The wounded were left in
the boats while the unwounded climbed aboard the ship, and then
the boats were hoisted on the davits amidship and the wounded
were taken to the sick bay forward. Some of them were badly hurt,
including one whose entrails were falling out of his belly and two
whose legs were so badly injured that they had to be amputated by
the two German surgeons.

The unwounded Frenchmen were placed in the waist on the
starboard side and were given an awning for protection against the
sun. A few were questioned, and from them the captain learned that
he had sunk the French destroyer *Mousquet*. He also learned that
the destroyer had been on patrol duty at the north entrance to
Penang harbor on the night before, but that she had ignored the
Emden when she saw her approach because her captain saw the fourth
funnel and was certain she was an English cruiser. When the French
heard the noise of action in the harbor they had scurried in, passing
the *Emden* on her way out, but again they had believed her to be an
English ship and had paid no further attention. Even when the destroyer had seen the *Emden* later that morning they had thought she
was an Englishman until the *Emden* opened fire on them. The captain, who had erred so badly in turning his broadside to the enemy,
had distinguished himself at least by bravery. His legs had been shot
away in the fight, but he had had himself lashed to the bridge and
had gone down with his ship.

As the wounded were treated and the able-bodied were made
comfortable and given food and clothing from the *Emden's* stores,
Captain von Müller decided to move quickly away from the vicinity.
Two more French destroyers lay in the harbor, he learned, the
d'Iberville, with which he was familiar, and the *Fronde*, of which
he had been unaware because she was anchored some distance away
from the Russian cruiser.

Leutnant von Guerard appeared on the bridge with wireless
messages intercepted from the Penang station, reporting the sinking
of the *Yemtschuk* and the *Mousquet*. If any of Admiral Jerram's
cruisers were in these waters they would soon be nearing Penang.

The captain turned to Lauterbach and ordered him to move out. The *Emden* began to steam north at twenty-two knots, hoping to throw the enemy off the track before turning south and west to join her colliers at the Simalur rendezvous.

~~~~~~

Chapter 14

THE RING CLOSES

As THE *Emden* sped away from the scene of her triumph the messages from Penang continued to inform the allied fleets of her presence in the area. Captain von Müller was not long in discovering also that he was being followed by an enemy destroyer, which kept him in sight and most certainly kept Penang informed of his course and progress.

This destroyer was identified by one of the French survivors as the *Fronde*, a sister ship of the *Mousquet*. Adjutant von Guerard reported from the wireless room that her transmissions did not cease. They were in the clear, and they told the story of the "assassination" of the *Mousquet* and kept reporting on the course, speed and position of the *Emden*. The *Fronde* took care not to come close enough for the *Emden* to close with her. Von Müller's solution was to try to jam the enemy's transmissions and make them unintelligible with his more powerful wireless, and to shake this French bulldog from his tail. His great hope, of course, was that within a few hours she would reach the danger point on coal and be forced to return to Penang.

Lauterbach plotted the course west-northwest and the *Emden* steamed ahead. Around noon she plunged into a violent rain squall and in this cover changed course to north-northwest. When the *Emden* emerged from the squall fifteen minutes later on the new course the *Fronde* was nowhere to be seen. The sea was clear and blue and the sun had never seemed to shine more brightly.

As damage-control officer, First Officer von Mücke had found absolutely no work as a result of their recent engagements, although the *Emden* had been fired upon by three different ships. There was not a single wounded man aboard, nor had any part of the ship been hit by gunfire. Remarkably, she had come to grips with an enemy her own size and had come through unscathed while sinking the other. This was now confirmed as von Mücke inspected the ship and reported to the captain.

Von Mücke's time for the next few hours was taken up in making arrangements for the comfort of the French prisoners. The canvas awning was replaced by a temporary "doghouse" built in the waist of the ship of framework and canvas so the prisoners might have a greater feeling of security and protection from the monsoon storms. No one was quite sure how long they would be with the ship or what was to be done with them.

Two of the *Emden*'s seamen spoke fluent French, and they were relieved of their routine duties and assigned to interpret for the Frenchmen in the hospital and in the doghouse.

Captain von Müller decided that he would capture a ship and send the Frenchmen to safety in it. That would be his first mission. The *Emden* turned to the Penang-Rangoon shipping lane then and reduced speed to seventeen knots. She cruised along the ship lane until four o'clock in the afternoon, but found nothing. Then she turned west-southwest, but still found nothing.

Toward evening the port engines began running hot and Chief Engineer Ellenbroek asked for some time to stop them and repair them. Captain von Müller then sought the safety of the Nicobar Islands again. It would never do to have the *Emden* suffer any break-down her own men could not repair, for there was no port at all to which she could turn for assistance. Breakdown meant disaster.

She ran into St. George Channel between Great Nicobar and Little Nicobar islands, and the port engines were stopped while she cruised very slowly on the starboard power plants. The French prisoners were worried when the high wooded coasts came into view. They were afraid that they would be abandoned on these lonely islands to take their chances of survival and rescue, and it was necessary for the officers of the *Emden* to reassure them that this was not the captain's intent.

Despite the attentions of Dr. Luther and Dr. Schwabe, two of the most seriously wounded Frenchmen died during the night of October 28. The following morning at eight o'clock they were buried at sea with full military honors. The crew of the *Emden* fell in on the decks in dress uniform. The ship was stopped so every member of the crew could attend the ceremonies. The officers came forth in uniform with medals and a guard of honor prepared to salute the two dead heroes who had died for their country. The bodies, wrapped in sailcloth, were covered with the French tricolor and placed on the starboard deck on biers. Captain von Müller made a speech in French, paying tribute to the two men and reading from the Catholic prayer book. Three volleys were fired over the sea as the biers were tilted and the weighted bodies slipped over the side. The men and officers of the *Emden* saluted, standing beside the Frenchmen they had conquered.

That next day the doctors labored over the other wounded and the captain searched vainly for a merchantman. None was found. On the night of October 29 another Frenchman died.

Early on the morning of October 30 the *Emden* captured a 3,000-ton freighter, the *Newburn*, carrying a cargo of salt to Singapore. Lauterbach went aboard and talked with the captain, who agreed most readily to interrupt his voyage and take the Frenchmen into Khota Raja, a nearby port on neutral Dutch Sumatra that was reported to have a modern hospital. The French lieutenant, in particular, was in very poor condition and would die if he did not receive more complete care than the *Emden* was prepared to administer. His right foot had been amputated, but the wound was not closing properly. He needed drugs and freedom from the movement of the ship.

The French sailors were questioned about their intentions and were made to promise that they would not fight again against Germany in this war. They did promise, and the transfer of the healthy and the wounded began. Dr. Schwabe went aboard the *Newburn* and supervised arrangements on that end. Dr. Luther watched over the movement of the wounded from the *Emden's* sick bay. The French officer, as he left, asked the prince if he might have one of the *Emden* hatbands as a memento, and it was given. The captain of the *Newburn* was given his course and told that by steady steaming he could be in Khota Raja by nightfall.

Then the *Emden* steamed away. By nine o'clock, when the last French sailor, the one who had died the night before, was given military burial, she had gone through the motions of setting the false course for the benefit of the *Newburn*, then changing to her true course, and she was running to the rendezvous where she hoped to find the *Buresk*. Coal was again the need.

This day the captain sat down in his sea cabin and recapitulated the results of their cruise. They had been out for three months. They had sunk or captured twenty-three merchant ships, including a sea-going dredge and the *Newburn*, which had just been released. They had terrorized a city and attacked it singlehanded. They had sunk an enemy cruiser and an enemy destroyer. They had traveled thirty thousand miles, most of it in the heart of enemy territory, and they had used six thousand tons of coal. They had inflicted many millions of dollars worth of damage on the enemy, and most important of all, Captain von Müller knew that he was leading the enemy navies a merry chase. He would have been even more proud if he had known that at that moment he was occupying the attention of the naval chiefs of England, France, Japan, and Russia. The little *Emden*, the *Kleinkreuzer* as they called her, was the object of frantic search by no fewer than 78 of the ships of the combined allied navies.

On the accomplishment side, the record was very impressive. As to the future, the prognostications could not be so clear or so happy. From the French prisoners the captain had learned that the *Pontoporos* was captured. She had been seen, escorted by a warship, moving into Singapore harbor. He also learned of the presence of five Japanese heavy cruisers in Singapore—more enemies to be avoided. It was a month since the dispatch of the *Markomannia*, and there was no word from her. If she did not appear at the rendezvous, he must presume her lost to the enemy, too. Now his task was to find the *Buresk* and the *Exford*, and then what? The *Emden* was showing signs of her travels and her fights, lucky as she had been. The engines were wearing, and parts needed replacing, but he had no replacements. It was simply a matter of time until something gave or broke down. But here, in the heart of the enemy's holdings, he had no recourse but to keep going, dodging and shifting, sinking and fighting, until the end. That was the plan, that would be the plan.

The *Emden* met the *Buresk*, as planned, on the morning of October 31, and the two ships steamed slowly along the deserted western coast of Sumatra. Two days were given to cleanup and repair and rest. Promotions of various enlisted men were announced in a ceremony on the afterdeck, and later that day the officers were invited to the captain's cabin for a drink in celebration of their accomplishments.

November 2 was given over again to the dirty work of coaling. They had learned that they could not come inside the Dutch harbors to coal, and they had become quite expert at coaling on the high seas, so they undertook the process eight miles out, protected from the never-ending swell of the Indian Ocean to some extent by the land, but still well outside Dutch territorial waters.

Coaling at sea involved a different technique from coaling in port. The constant rubbing of the ships meant fenders wore out quickly, so the *Emden* improvised her own. Logs were used, covered with extra hammocks. First Officer von Mücke had appropriated a number of automobile tires from one of their captures, and these made excellent fenders. The worst problem of coaling at sea was damage from bumping caused by the motions of the ships. The *Emden* carried two guns in her swallow's-nests, small elevated structures fore and aft. The forward nest was always in peril from the boom and the heavy bags of coal, and several times it was damaged. On this occasion, as they took five hundred tons from the *Buresk*, the cable broke and a sack of coal fell on the leg of one of the torpedomen, breaking his thigh. He became the *Emden's* first casualty of the war.

At lunchtime while the coaling was halted temporarily a sailboat came alongside. First Officer von Mücke, thinking it was a fisherman, bawled out at the helmsman, asking if he had any extra fish to sell. Just then out of the little cabin stepped a man in green-gray uniform who signaled for a ladder. He was a Dutch official, and von Mücke was red-faced at having caused his ship such embarrassment.

But the Dutchman was amused, not angry, and he came into the wardroom for a drink. He had come aboard to be sure that the

Germans were outside the three-mile limit, which they were, although probably just barely. He told the men the only news he knew: that Portugal had just declared war on Germany. This was a matter of no interest to anyone except the prince, whose sister was Queen of Portugal.

The *Emden* parted from the *Buresk*, making a new rendezvous with her, and steamed into the Sunda Strait, which separates Java and Sumatra. After two days she had not encountered a single ship, so in disgust she turned away west toward the Cocos or Keeling Islands, where she was to meet the *Exford* and the *Buresk*.

On November 7 the *Emden* arrived at the rendezvous and the *Buresk* was there. The *Exford* was not. They searched all day and through the night for her.

The captain had cause for worry. On the night of November 7, Leutnant von Guerard had approached the bridge to report on an unusual amount of wireless traffic being intercepted in the radio room. Lauterbach was on the bridge, and he and the captain accompanied von Guerard to the wireless shack to listen and make what they could of the racket. The messages were in code, but as usual the names of towns and ships were sent in clear. The word "Newcastle" was caught. The captain thought it meant the small cruiser *Newcastle*. Lauterbach corrected him. He said he was sure it was the port of Newcastle in Australia. They could make very little of it otherwise.

Lauterbach went back to the bridge and the captain went back to his sea cabin to try to get a little rest. Not long afterward a huge seabird of the variety that the seamen called *Döskopp* landed on the bridge. Lauterbach, among his other enthusiasms, nursed a love for natural history. He sent the word below to the wardroom that there was a *Döskopp* on the bridge and that everyone should come up and see it.

Von Mücke, cruel man, threw back his head and roared.

"Tell Lauterbach we've known that for years," he said to the startled seaman.

His brother officers, after drinking a joyful toast to the big fat *Döskopp* on the bridge, trouped up to see both of them.

All was well the next morning, when the *Exford* was found, fifty miles from where she ought to have been. The captain of the *Exford*, Kapitänleutnant Gropius, had seen a British convoy coming by and had changed his course. So the meaning of the intensive radio activity became clear. There were British ships and British warships in the area.

Captain von Müller had a premonition that he was about to get into a fight. He wanted all his regular navy officers around him when it happened, so he began to exchange crews. The jolly Lauterbach, valuable as he was, was not regular navy but a merchant captain and he belonged aboard a merchantman, while Gropius, good a captain as he made, was a regular navy man who belonged back on the *Emden*. Much to Lauterbach's disappointment the captain ordered them to change positions, and Lauterbach took command of the *Exford*, buoyed up at the last by the Captain's handshake and promise that they would meet again at a point a thousand miles west of the Cocos Islands in two to six days, and then he could return to the *Emden*. Leutnant Gyssling and Leutnant Schmidt, who had been in the *Buresk*, were brought back to the *Emden*, too. Then the *Exford* was detached, and the *Emden* and the *Buresk* steamed toward Direction Island, where the British maintained a wireless station and a cable relay station.

At this point the cables crossed. One set went from Australia to India. The other set went from Australia to Zanzibar and Africa. Since they were in the region, Captain von Müller decided to destroy the wireless station and cut the cable. Some of his officers suggested that he first shell the wireless aerial and knock it out quickly so the station could not call for help. He considered the plan, but said this would endanger civilian lives, which he had no desire to do. No, he would not do that, but would send a landing party ashore in the morning to destroy both the wireless station and the cables. They would go in early and hope that they could stop transmission of any messages. By now, he was certain the nearest enemy ships must be 250 miles away, which meant they would have almost a full day's leeway no matter what messages the station might send.

Chapter 15

THE LANDING

ABOARD THE *Emden* on the night of November 8, Kapitän-leutnant von Mücke made careful preparations for the next day's landing on Direction Island. So important a communications link deserved proper protection, and had the German position been reversed they would have stationed perhaps a hundred armed men on the island to repel attacks. That would be adequate protection against any single warship or any surface raider. No ship could afford to dispatch a landing force of more than fifty or sixty men, and an attacker would be reduced to shelling the installation from offshore. Effective as this might be temporarily, the destruction could be repaired rather quickly, and the important cables would be retained intact.

Since he must expect a vigorous defense of the island, von Mücke chose young men, but experienced men. The two officers he took with him, Leutnant Gyssling and Leutnant Schmidt, were well trained in infantry tactics. He chose thirty seamen, fifteen technicians, and two wireless men. Nearly all of them were nine-year men—sailors who had chosen to strike for petty officer and had elected to serve nine years in the navy, then would continue to make the navy their career.

Von Mücke commandeered all four of the *Emden*'s portable machineguns for the expedition. He would have taken more if they had been aboard. He also selected twenty-nine rifles and twenty-four revolvers. The men took the guns apart, cleaned them thoroughly, oiled them, and broke out new boxes of ammunition. The men laid out their whites, with boots or puttees, and they were issued topees to shield their heads from the tropical sun.

That night the *Emden* lay fifty miles off the island. Early in

the morning the fourth funnel was raised again and the ship began
to steam toward its objective, hoping to take the wireless station
quite by surprise and prevent any outburst of messages. The *Buresk*
remained at the point where the *Emden* had lain. If all went well
during the day she was to be called up for coaling after the destruction of the wireless station.

The *Emden* had been underway since well before dawn. By
sunrise she lay outside the entrance to Port Refuge. At six o'clock
First Officer von Mücke reported to the captain. He was ready to go
ashore. He saluted, Captain von Müller returned the salute, and von
Mücke stepped smartly off the bridge.

The two cutters were already in the water, and the officers and
men of the landing party had already taken their places in the boats.
The steam launch was ready too, with steam up. She would tow them
through the reef and into the little harbor.

Von Mücke in his topee and white uniform joined the others
and snapped orders to the men on the steam pinnace to move. The
distance was about two miles, through which the steam pinnace must
pick her way, since the water was very shallow in spots and the coral
was very sharp. As they moved slowly and carefully the island itself
was plainly before them. There was little to see. It was flat and quite
undistinguished, covered with palm trees through which could be
seen the roofs of the European-style houses of the station attendants
and the tall mast of the wireless station. After the landing party had
entered the lagoon, von Mücke on the steam launch ordered the
helmsman to steer for the wireless aerial. That would be their first
objective.

At six-thirty they were on shore. They drew up beside a small
white sailing ship. One of the officers asked von Mücke if that, too,
was to be destroyed.

"Certainly," said von Mücke. He ordered the lieutenant to
have a man prepare it with explosives.

As the landing party pulled into shore, it was met by nine
members of the staff of the wireless station. Von Mücke, in his heavily accented English, asked them the location of the station, and
since there was no point in refusing to answer, the Englishmen told
him. He also asked for the location of the house of the director, and it
was pointed out to him. He thanked his respondent and noted that
the *Emden* had "plenty of trouble with your wireless and cables."

Once all the men were on shore, von Mücke split the party

into three sections. He took one section and assigned one to each of his lieutenants. One section moved to the wireless hut, where an operator was sending messages. A second went to the quarters of the station to round up the personnel. Von Mücke took the second party himself. The third was set to work destroying facilities.

Von Mücke called one of the Englishmen aside and told him to bring the superintendent of the station. In a few minutes this portly gentleman arrived, agreeable and smiling. He was D. A. G. de H. Farrant, head of the Eastern Extension Telegraph Company's station on the island. He gave his keys to von Mücke, pointed out the various houses in which apparatus was located, and said he had no intention of resisting. He then congratulated von Mücke.

For what, asked the suspicious first officer of the *Emden*.

For the Iron Cross, said Farrant. Their wireless had picked up a German news bulletin which announced that the Kaiser had honored all the men of the *Emden*.

Von Mücke hid his pleasure and proceeded to the business at hand. All firearms were to be yielded to the Germans, he said. All Europeans on the island were to assemble in the square in front of the telegraph building.

The Europeans were assembled there and placed under a guard. Two men stood near them, and two others brought one of the machineguns from the cutters. Soon, however, the sun rose high and the square became unpleasant, so the civilians asked if they could shelter in the boat shed, and von Mücke said they could.

One party was sent to destroy the wireless mast. Von Mücke led his men into the offices, where they took axes to the Morse equipment, large demijohns of ink, and pieces of cable. They took all the papers and bundled them up in international code flags and prepared to take them back to the *Emden*. They took all the correspondence from the superintendent's office, hoping to find something that would be of interest to them and would tell the whereabouts of British shipping or other targets for the *Emden*. They destroyed the offices with much breaking of glass and smashing of paneling, then moved to the outbuildings, wrecking the engine room, the four dynamos, and the switchboards and the cables. They would have smashed up the ice plant, too, but the Chinese mechanic refused to let them into his engine room, and they understood his Pidgin and believed him when he said "This no b'long electric light, this b'long makee ice."

The destroyers were very thorough. They even wrecked an inoffensive seismograph that had been placed on the island to record earthquakes and other disturbances.

The third party had begun early on the wireless mast, but it caused them trouble. They drilled holes in the base and inserted dynamite cartridges. The first explosion had no effect at all. The second made the mast sway and list, but did not bring it down. The third blast knocked it down, just after seven-thirty in the morning.

As the men were laying the cartridges, one of the Englishmen came up and asked that the mast be felled away from the tennis courts. It was done.

Then came the problem of finding the cables. All over the island there were signs that referred to the cables, but there was no map that showed their location. At one point close to shore, however, stood a cluster of signs that referred to the cables, and von Mücke calculated, quite rightly, that this was the point where they entered the water. They used the cutters and grappling hooks to bring them up from the water. Although the cables were quite visible in the clear water it took some time to get them on the cutters, and then much longer to cut them with crowbars, axes and cold chisels. Finally, they cut two of the three cables and dragged the ends out to sea, in opposite directions, so it would be difficult for the English to find them again and make repairs. They did not find the third cable.

One of the lieutenants investigated a galvanized-iron storehouse where cables and other material were stored and blew this up with dynamite, just as von Mücke and his party were finishing with the cables.

There was time for a very little bit of conversation with the English, which was carried out in French, English, Dutch and Pidgin and very bad German. The English told them about their awards and the *Emden* men told the English about the battle at Penang.

Then from the distance could be heard quick bursts from the *Emden*'s siren, recalling the landing party.

Kapitänleutnant von Mücke assembled his men sharply on the beach. They loaded their guns and the captured documents and newspapers and books aboard the three boats, and set out across the lagoon. Behind them the Englishmen yelled goodbye and snapped pictures with their cameras. The little white schooner, which was to be blown up, was left intact. There was no time to destroy it, as the captain was calling them back to the *Emden* immediately. It was a matter of no consequence. Von Mücke could see from the shore that the *Emden*'s anchor flag was flying at half mast, which meant she was weighing anchor at that moment. He looked at his watch. It was almost nine-thirty.

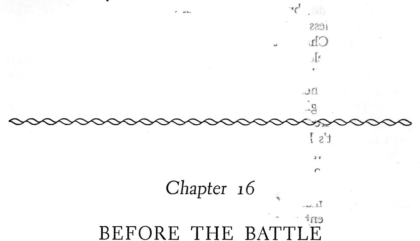

Chapter 16

BEFORE THE BATTLE

WHEN VON MÜCKE took the three boats ashore and they disappeared beyond the harbor entrance, the quiet in the *Emden* became almost unearthly. For the first time the ship must sit outside the harbor and wait, its men, and not the ship itself, occupied in the major task of the moment.

Captain von Müller paced the bridge and kept looking at his watch. He looked at the sky. It was a fair and calm day. He decided that he should waste no time, and sent word to von Guerard that the wireless men should call up the *Buresk* and ask her to come immediately to the island. They would coal before they went on.

No answer came from the *Buresk*. The order was repeated.

Then the island's wireless station broke in to ask what ship this was so nearby that was using wireless.

The *Emden* did not answer.

While this drama was being played in the wireless rooms of

the *Emden* and the station, and the steam pinnace was towing its two cutters toward shore, another series of events was launched on the island.

Very early a Chinese servant had noticed a strange ship lying in the entrance to the lagoon. It was not his place to awaken any one and tell him, but shortly after six o'clock that morning one of the night wirel men came off duty and began walking back to his quarters. The inese stopped him and told him what he had seen.

The wire ess operator climbed onto the roof of the wireless building, the tallest on the island, and looked out to the entrance to the harbor. T' re he saw a warship with four funnels. The station had been exchanying messages with H.M.S. *Minotaur* for several days, and he was sure this was the *Minotaur*, but he hurried off to the superintenden house to inform him of the arrival.

On the way to the superintendent's house he met the island's doctor, who also climbed the roof and through field glasses noted that the ship was not flying a flag and that her first funnel seemed to be a dummy made of canvas. He came off the roof in time to meet the superintend who had dressed hurriedly and was on his way to the office.

Inside, the men at the keys were involved in their strange encounter with the mystery ship. They reported. The superintendent ordered a message to be sent immediately:

"S.O.S. Strange ship in entrance."

This was sent several times with the station's coded signature. Then the message was jammed by transmissions from some nearby point, and the superintendent became certain that he was dealing with the *Emden*. The message was changed.

"S.O.S. *Emden* here."

This message was sent constantly, in spite of the radio interference from offshore, until von Mücke and his men burst into the wireless station and ordered the men away from the keys.

On the *Emden* the captain was annoyed to learn that the station had attempted to send out messages, but was not seriously worried. The plot of the evening before had convinced him that the nearest ships of any kind were now some 250 miles away and could not pose any danger.

He was assured of it when von Guerard came up to the bridge with a message from an unknown ship which was calling the wireless station. The message was coded, but the wireless operators could estimate from the strength of the transmission that the ship sending was 250 miles away.

The men of the *Emden* now prepared for coaling. The task took longer than usual; this was von Mücke's normal responsibility and he was ashore. Still it was done in good time.

At about seven-thirty in the morning several explosions were heard, coming from the island, and the tall radio mast slowly toppled and fell. All was obviously going as planned.

At nine o'clock Captain von Müller began looking at his watch again. Von Mücke was late; he was to have returned by nine o'clock. As the captain began to show concern about the time, a smoke cloud was reported on the horizon. He first accepted this as the mark of the *Buresk*, which was due around ten o'clock. Although the *Buresk* had not answered the *Emden*'s wireless call she had not specifically been told to respond.

The lookout reported a few moments later that he saw a single funnel and two masts. That was the *Buresk*. Lieutenant von Guerard climbed to the crow's-nest and verified this report.

Yet the smoke cloud was not that of the *Buresk*, or the *Buresk* was inadvertently shielding another ship. The smoke cloud became that of His Majesty's Australian Ship *Sydney*, a heavy armored cruiser. She displaced 5,400 tons, she had a speed of 25.7 knots, and she was armed with eight six-inch guns. This was much more powerful than the *Emden*'s 3,593 tons, 24 knots, and ten 4.1-inch guns.

After three months of solid good fortune, the fates of war had turned on the *Emden*. The convoy heard two nights earlier had not moved out of the area. At six-thirty that morning, when Captain von Müller was told that the ship calling the Direction Island wireless station was 250 miles away, actually this ship was the *Sydney*, fifty-five miles away, transmitting under reduced power.

Captain Silver, who was in command of the convoy, had released the *Sydney* to answer the station's S.O.S., and that transmission was the ship's reply to the station. All the while that Captain von Müller had been waiting impatiently for the landing party, the *Sydney* had been bearing down on the *Emden*.

At nine-fifteen, Captain von Müller became very impatient. He ordered the ship's sirens blown to warn von Mücke that he had exceeded his time limit and to call him in. As the sirens sounded, Captain von Müller saw the approaching ship change course and take on a different appearance. She sported the tall masts of a warship, and at that moment of turning she chose to show her white ensign bearing the Cross of St. George.

Within a few seconds Captain von Müller had ordered the anchor weighed, full steam in all boilers and the ship cleared for action. There was no time to wait for von Mücke and the landing party. If the *Emden* were caught at anchor she would have no chance.

Just before nine-thirty the frantic activity seen by Kapitän-leutnant von Mücke from the steam pinnace meant that the *Emden*, not more than half prepared, was moving out to battle for her life.

Chapter 17

THE END OF THE *EMDEN*

AT NINE-THIRTY, as the *Emden* steamed slowly forth to engage the enemy ship, the *Sydney* was moving due south. She was then about six miles east of Direction Island. Von Müller took his ship due north in the first move of this game. He was not eager to close with the *Sydney* until his steam was up, and that would not be for another half hour.

Captain Glossop of the *Sydney* gave von Müller no time to

maneuver. As the *Emden* moved out of the entrance to the harbor and ran up the black-and-white battle ensign, Captain Glossop turned the *Sydney* hard to starboard and came straight at her. As the *Emden* moved north, he adjusted his course. At nine-forty he had nearly halved the distance between them.

The *Emden* opened fire at 5,600 yards. The first three salvos of the *Emden*'s guns bracketed the *Sydney*. The fourth salvo struck, and bright-yellow flame began to flash from the center deck.

"Very good, Gaede," Captain von Müller said to his gunnery officer. It was better than good, although the German captain did not know it. One of those shells had struck the fire-control room, and the automatic aiming devices of the *Sydney* were out of action. Her guns must be operated manually from that point on.

That was good luck, but the last bit of it for the *Emden*. Moments later the superiority of the *Sydney* began to count. She was faster and she had steam up. She drew away from the *Emden*, past seven thousand yards, out of her range, but not out of the range of the *Sydney*'s guns. Then she began to cut the German cruiser to pieces.

Ten minutes after the fight began the gunners on the *Sydney* found the range. One of the first hits struck near the bridge, and splinters wounded Gunnery Officer Gaede slightly in the eye. Torpedo Officer Witthoeft was struck in the cheek, and a seaman was also slightly wounded. Captain von Müller was hit but did not even know it at the time.

That was the beginning of the carnage.

Next a shell struck squarely on the wireless room and destroyed it completely. All that remained were a few white-hot plates on the deck.

The *Sydney* drew steadily to a point just outside the *Emden*'s range, and kept that distance, pouring shellfire into the German. A shell struck behind the crow's-nest in the mainmast. Another struck one of the after guns, killing the crew and several of the ammunition carriers.

At ten o'clock there was noticeable slacking in the *Emden*'s fire. Why weren't the men shooting? Captain von Müller asked. The range was too great, Gaede replied. Von Müller swung the ship hard to starboard, then, trying to close with the *Sydney*, but Captain

Glossop immediately swung to port in a long curve, maintaining the distance.

The *Emden* now presented her port side to the enemy. One direct hit from the *Sydney* knocked out the *Emden's* aiming system. Leutnant Zimmermann, in charge of this division in the command turret, was unhurt and picked himself up. All his enlisted men were dead. He moved to the starboard No. 2 gun and began directing fire.

Torpedo Officer Witthoeft asked the captain to move in as close as possible, but it was not possible. The *Emden* had scarcely gotten to full steam, which was still an effective three or four knots slower than the *Sydney*, when a shot penetrated below decks and pierced some of the steam pipes. To the fires that sprouted now was added the heat and misery of steam.

A second hit just after ten o'clock killed every man in the port No. 1 gun crew, and a third hit struck directly into the ready ammunition supply of the port No. 4 gun, blasting crew and gun, including Leutnant von Levetzow, who was in charge of the after guns. In a moment the ship was ablaze aft.

At ten-twenty the *Emden* turned again, still trying to close the distance. The hail of fire continued. The steering system was knocked out, and so was the internal communication system. All that was left now were the men, a handful of guns, and their engines. Orders must be transmitted verbally and in person.

Navigator Gropius went aft to attempt to repair the steering gear. Another shell widened the flames in the stern and cut it off from the rest of the ship. The men retreated as the fire kept following them.

Below decks there was much less damage, since the armor plating gave some protection. Just after ten-twenty, however, a hit on the armored deck pierced through and cut below the waterline, sending a stream of seawater and gases from the explosion into the torpedo flat. Leutnant von Hohenzollern, the prince, ordered his men into their smoke bandages—gas masks were not yet in use.

The torpedo tubes were ready, and so were the torpedomen. They were busy now trying to close the hole that was letting seawater pour onto them. The prince sent a man to find carpenters, but the carpenters were busy elsewhere. He released compressed air from the tanks used to fill the torpedo tubes. This cleared the air, but the leaks could not be stopped. When he had used all the air in the tanks he signaled for more to the port auxiliary engine room. There was no answer. He discovered that the signal system had broken down and that a hit on the auxiliary engine room had knocked it out, too.

At ten-twenty-five the *Emden* managed, by the captain's skillful maneuver, steering with his engines, to close the distance between herself and the *Sydney*, but now most of her guns were silenced, and those that were firing were doing so intermittently. Von Müller asked Gaede why there was not more fire, and the gunnery officer replied that there was not enough ammunition on deck. This represented the carnage of the last half hour. Most of the ammunition handlers had been killed as they moved across the open decks, and those left found it difficult to move through the debris to serve the guns.

The speaking tube between the bridge and the torpedo room was still open. Through that, Witthoeft ordered his men below to prepare the starboard tube, and the prince did so. Above he could hear the constant clanging of metal and explosions as the *Sydney*'s guns punished the cruiser.

Ten-thirty came, then ten-thirty-five, and ten-forty, but there was no order to fire the torpedo. The *Sydney* had moved away and no longer presented her port side to the *Emden*. At ten-forty, in fact, she fired a torpedo at the *Emden*, but this missed.

The two fighting ships were paralleling one another and crisscrossing paths, as the captains fought for advantages. The *Emden*, most of her guns silent now, could hope to destroy the *Sydney* only with a lucky shot in a magazine or by torpedo, and it was to torpedo the *Sydney* that the *Emden* kept moving, trying always to get close enough but never coming half close enough.

At ten-forty-five the *Sydney*'s starboard guns faced the *Emden*'s port side and blasted furiously. There was a sudden shock, felt throughout the ship, and the foremast began to topple. Down it came, bearing a seaman and Adjutant von Guerard to their deaths.

Just before eleven o'clock another shot from the *Sydney* pierced below the armored deck and the water line. It made a sixteen-inch hole in the torpedo flat, and water began pouring in. The prince and his men abandoned the torpedo flat. First they tried to escape through the armored hatch, but the coaming had been bent by a shell and they could not get out. They moved to the torpedo storage hatch and made their way out, fastening the watertight doors behind them to control the leak in that compartment.

When the fire-control mechanism was knocked out and the internal communication system failed, Gunnery Officer Gaede began periodic rounds of all his guns. At one of the port guns he was struck by fragments of an exploding shell and mortally wounded. When the prince stepped up from his torpedo room, he found Gaede lying on the deck near the disabled gun, his uniform red and blood making a little pool around him. He was conscious and thanked the prince for words of condolence, then died.

Ten minutes later, the deck was a shambles. All three funnels were hit; two of them were demolished and the third lay at a crazy angle across the buckled deck. The foremast lay across the port side of the ship, its crow's-nest smashed and the tip underwater.

The surgeons and first-aid parties moved around the decks, searching in the debris for the wounded. There were not enough first-aid men, not enough bandages, not enough morphia to go around.

By eleven o'clock the electrical system in the ship was almost totally destroyed. The ship was being steered from the steering flat. Since the funnels were down the smoke from the boilers could not draw off properly, and the *Emden*'s speed was cut further.

At one of the few remaining guns a boatswain's mate was directing fire, and kept directing it until the end, although his right arm had been shot away and most of his men were wounded.

The end was near, now. A shell carried away the captain's bridge. Luckily he was on the main deck when it struck. The ship was barely navigable. Captain von Müller wished to make one last attempt to get within torpedo range, even though the torpedo room was down. With communications knocked out, orders were passed by a gunner down the engine-room skylight, and only thus was the *Emden* kept moving.

When he learned that the torpedo room was completely useless, and as his guns ceased to fire, and the ship continued to lose speed with her funnels shot away, Captain von Müller decided to run her aground on the coral reefs of North Keeling Island. He reasoned that thus the ship would not fall into the hands of the enemy and that only thus could he save the lives of many of his wounded crew and the men who were stationed belowdecks. If the ship were to sink, most of them would be lost.

Aboard the *Sydney* Captain Glossop realized that von Müller intended to run his ship aground, and he increased the rate of fire from the *Sydney*'s guns in an attempt to sink the German ship.

At eleven-fifteen the *Emden* ran aground on the south coast of the island. The engines were stopped, then started again, and she was firmly fixed on the reef. Then the fires were put out and the sea cocks were opened to let the water in. The captain hoped he had completely wrecked his ship so that she would be of no use to the enemy.

While all this was being done the *Emden* remained under enemy fire. At eleven-twenty the *Sydney* saw that the ship was aground and ceased firing at her. Instead of coming around to pick up survivors, however, she moved off in pursuit of the *Buresk*, which had fled north during the battle, having come up and seen what was in progress.

The captain and his few remaining officers then had an opportunity to begin counting noses and checking on the damage.

Captain von Müller toured the decks, trying to comfort the wounded and dying. As the shooting continued for the few moments after grounding, he gave the ship's company permission to jump overboard if they wished and try to reach the island, a hundred yards away from the reef on which they were fixed. He pulled together a party, led by the prince, to destroy the guns, instruments, and secret books aboard the ship. The locks were removed from the guns, the sights from the measuring instruments. Such treatment was given everything forward and amidships, but the crew could not move aft of the engine-room hatch. The metal there was still red-hot from the fires that had burned. They knew nothing of what had happened to Leutnant Gropius and his men, who had gone back to repair the steering.

The prince tried to go aft from the waist, by creeping between decks. In the laundry they found their Chinese washermen, who had been washing clothes even until the moment they were struck by a shell and crumpled on the deck, the wet garments beside them.

The search party discovered a few wounded men and brought them back to the main deck. They could go no farther aft. The metal was too hot.

The crew assembled above in the forecastle, which was the

least damaged part of the ship. Surgeon Luther was there; Surgeon Schwabe had chosen to try to swim to the island. The forecastle was crowded and smelled of sweat and iodine. The bandages soon ran out and the table linens were secured and torn into strips to serve.

At midday the captain discovered that he had a serious water problem. All the water tanks above the armored deck were destroyed, and the drinking-water compartments were located beneath the torpedo flat, which was filled with seawater. The compartments could not be reached, nor could the pumps be worked to draw the water. Even if the electrical system had been in operation the pumps were damaged by shellfire. The only drinking water available on the ship was that which had been left in the pipes, and this was drawn off. It was scarcely enough to wet the lips of the wounded.

The island represented salvation. Captain von Müller hoped to find enough coconuts there to serve the wounded at least.

As the sun stood high, the heat was oppressive. All the awnings and sailcloth were stored in compartments that were now underwater. The men were abandoned on the main deck to the sun.

They had no boats. The two cutters and the steam pinnace were in the hands of the landing party at Direction Island. The single remaining boat had been struck by a shell and burned.

A few men had managed to reach the safety of the island by swimming through the surf, and now an attempt was made to make contact with them. A line was floated to the beach by using empty ammunition boxes and matting. But the current sweeping around the island caught the line and carried it away from the surf. Once a line was put into the surf and the men held their breaths in anticipation. It caught on the jagged coral and broke in two. The life-saving gun was found and fired, but it did not carry. Two swimmers took lines around their bodies and tried to swim through the surf, but failed.

The wounded were troubled by the heat and the lack of water and the shortage of medicines. They faced another danger, even more gruesome. As soon as a man was left alone, he was attacked by vicious *Döskoppes*, those great seabirds, who hovered over the helpless and pecked at their eyes. A crew of guards was assembled to kill off these new enemies with cudgels and revolvers.

Captain von Müller counted his dead and wounded and missing, but the action was not yet ended.

All afternoon the survivors sat in the blistering sun. At four o'clock the *Sydney* reappeared, and when she came close enough to be identified the men of the *Emden* could see that she was towing two boats. They were the boats of the *Buresk*.

The *Sydney* had sped away from the helpless *Emden* to capture the *Buresk*, but when they caught the slower merchant ship, Captain Klöpper threw his papers overboard and also opened the seacocks and threw the valves overboard so the ship could not be salvaged.

The boarding party from the *Sydney* spent some time searching the ship and questioning the officers and crew after the capture, and then brought the crew and the boats back to the scene of the battle.

The *Sydney* stopped four thousand yards astern of the *Emden* and raised a signal. The *Emden*'s signal books had been burned or destroyed and no one aboard could read the message, so the captain ordered his signalmen to signal in Morse with flags "no signal book," and one signalman did so; the Englishmen either did not understand it or paid no attention to it. Not a gun on the *Emden* was firing and nearly no one was stirring, but suddenly the *Sydney* again opened fire on the wreck. It was a great tribute to the *Emden* that the *Sydney* would be so much afraid of this helpless enemy, but it was an expensive tribute in terms of lives. Men began to fall, killed and wounded by the shellfire.

Captain von Müller did not know what the enemy intended, so he shouted that his men had permission to jump overboard and swim for shore if they wished. Many did so. The prince seized a plank and jumped over the side, hoping to fight his way to the entrance to the lagoon and the safety of the island. But in a few moments he found half a dozen men had joined him on his plank and it was hopeless to try to navigate. They floated in the water, the gunfire starting new flames aboard the *Emden* above them. Half an hour later the gunfire had ceased and the prince and several of the others saw that they would never make it to the island, so they returned to the ship and were helped aboard by their unwounded comrades.

The captain had neglected, it seemed, to haul down the flag of his wreck, and the English did not know what to make of it, so they had taken no chances. When Captain von Müller hauled down his flag and ran up a white flag of surrender, the firing stopped.

The Australian cruiser still did not send doctors or men to help the wounded and helpless of the *Emden*. They dispatched one of the boats they were towing, which held Leutnant Fikentscher and some of the men of the *Buresk*. The cruiser sped south, this time to Direction Island, where Captain Glossop intended to capture the landing party of the *Emden*.

Now that he possessed a boat, Captain von Müller hoped to communicate with the men on North Keeling Island, but before an attempt could be made to do so, darkness fell, so the men of the *Emden* slept that night uneasily and without food or water. Leutnant Fikentscher took charge of the deck during that long night, burying the dead, tending the wounded, and putting out fires that sprang up.

At dawn the officers and able-bodied men were up again. They hoisted the *Emden*'s flag in an upside-down position, the international distress signal. They had half given up hope that the *Sydney* would return.

The captain again counted heads: Several of the wounded had died during the night, including one horribly burned man whose agonies had been stilled only by heavy inroads into the small supply of morphia.

The men of the *Emden* waited.

They could use the *Buresk*'s boat, but the passage through the surf to the island was treacherous, and if this boat smashed all might be lost. Captain von Müller chose to wait and hope that the *Sydney* would return.

At one o'clock in the afternoon the *Sydney* did reappear, her boats swinging in the davits as she came, showing the Germans that their enemies would take them off the hulk of their ship at last.

First two cutters came across to the dangerous *Emden* and one British officer bargained with the captain: The *Sydney* would only take off the ship's company if von Müller would take personal responsibility for the behavior of the crew.

The captain promised his enemies not to fight them aboard their own ship, and the slow process of shipping off the crew began.

The wounded were removed first, in heavy seas that pounded the *Emden* on her reef and made transportation painful and difficult. The able-bodied came next, and then the officers. The captain was the last man off the ship; he had spent the last hour before departure in unsuccessful attempts to build small fires near the magazines so the ship would blow sky-high and could not be reclaimed by his enemies. Small wonder that Captain Glossop of the *Sydney* had been to such pains to deal carefully with an enemy who normally would be considered helpless.

~~~~~~

Chapter 18

THE COST

NEAR THE END OF THE DAY the last man was taken from the *Emden*. He was Captain Karl von Müller, and he left his ship to step into the gig of Captain Glossop. Von Müller had requested, through one of the British officers, that no special honors or treatment be given him as captain, but there was nothing to be done if he wanted to leave the hulk of what had been his proud ship.

She sat stiffly on her reef, the surf banging against the sides, down at the stern, her mainmast still standing and some guns still projecting from their mounts, looking dangerous although they were totally ineffectual.

Aboard the *Sydney*, Captain von Müller was greeted by Captain Glossop with friendly words for his conduct during the battle, and the captain accommodated him in his own cabin. The officers were shown to the anteroom of the wardroom, where they would sleep. The men were put into the forecastle, and the wounded were taken into the waist on hammocks laid on deck, protected by awnings. This was the coolest and most healthful place on ship.

That evening Leutnant Schall of the *Emden* was sent ashore on North Keeling Island in a boat. He managed the difficult entry and took off the living and buried the dead on the island. Among the dead was Surgeon Schwabe, who had struck his head on the coral in coming through the surf and received a terrible crushing wound. He had floundered to the beach, but had died within a few hours.

Back on the *Sydney*, Captain von Müller and the others began to sort out the stories of suffering and heroism. Navigator Gropius, they learned, had been trapped aft by the flames that cut across the ship and had been forced steadily backward until the heat and smoke became unbearable. Then he and his men had leaped overboard, giving three cheers for the Kaiser. Three of the men had survived in the sea and reached the island. Gropius was not among them.

Von Müller also learned how uneven had been the fight all the way. The *Emden*'s fire struck the *Sydney* only sixteen times in all the engagement, and only four men were killed and seventeen wounded aboard the British ship. The shell that had carried away the range-finding equipment was responsible for most of the damage. Elsewhere he saw dents in the armor, which represented his shells that had exploded but had not done serious damage to the armored ship. There had been one moment of danger. A shell had entered an ammunition hoist and had thrown burning cordite into a magazine. But one of the *Sydney*'s seamen had unhesitatingly grasped the burning material in both arms and put it out.

The difference in degree of destruction was overwhelming. The *Sydney* was hardly struck. The *Emden* was almost totally wrecked. In comparison to the negligible damage and few casualties of the *Sydney*, the *Emden* had suffered heavily. The captain discovered that seven of his officers had been killed. So had thirty-seven subordinate officers and petty officers, ninety-two seamen, one civilian cook, one civilian barber, and three Chinese washermen.

The wounded numbered two officers, fifteen subordinate officers and petty officers, and forty-eight men. Only six officers, forty-four subordinate and petty officers, and sixty-seven men remained unhurt of the entire crew.

It was a sad ending to a brave ship. The British would float her off before the war was ended and salvage her and try to refit her, but she would never be the same.

~~~~~~

Chapter 19

PRISONERS

THE Emden WAS GONE, the Buresk was scuttled, and as Captain von Müller had feared, the Markomannia had run afoul of the enemy too and would cruise the seas no more. The Pontoporos lay in Singapore and the Germans from the Emden who had gone aboard her were in prison camp. All the men of the Emden, then, were accounted for save two groups: those in the landing party and those aboard the Exford, which had been sent a thousand miles west to await the Emden.

On that ship Lauterbach had a Chinese crew made up from the stoker gang of the Troilus. He also had two German petty officers from the Emden, one to command the deck and the other the engine room, and seventeen Emden seamen. He had the new wireless from the Chilkana, and thus although sailing westward as promised, he could pick up the wireless traffic of the area. On November 9 and the day after the air was filled with wireless flashes that referred to the Emden. But they were either in code or they were jumbled fragments which told him nothing. Yet when the Emden answered none of the Exford's coded calls, Lauterbach began to sense that something serious had occurred. He suspected that he would not see the *Emden* again.

The *Exford's* orders were unquestionable: proceed to the middle of the Indian Ocean and wait. So that is what Lauterbach did. He moved to the rendezvous point, a man-made point in a sea of salt water. This rendezvous was simply a set of coordinates on a chart. There was no land nearby, and no port from which they could replenish their dwindling supplies.

A week went by and then another. They circled the rendezvous point, waiting. Their food supply grew short. They had plenty of beer and cigarettes aboard, but the diet of corned beef and rice and potatoes soon gave way to a diet of potato pancakes and pickles. The Chinese complained, but it did them no good. They complained again, knowing it would do no good. Lauterbach was eating the same food they ate, and they knew it.

The *Exford* remained at her rendezvous point until the ninth day of December. Then and only then Lauterbach decided to take up the second half of Captain von Müller's orders: If the *Emden* did not appear or they ran short of supplies they were to head for a neutral port. The closest neutral port was Padang in Sumatra, seven hundred miles from where the *Exford* sat. Lauterbach had no charts, only his own prodigious knowledge of the eastern seas to guide him, but they made the run in three days using an atlas of the Indian Ocean as a chart. They arrived off Padang light and could see the houses of the city as the pilot boat put out for the ship when Lauterbach had the pilot flag hoisted.

Just then a ship crept out from between two small islands and approached the *Exford*. She hoisted the British war flag and asked the *Exford* to show her flag. Lauterbach ran up the German naval flag. The other ship, which he recognized as the *Empress of Japan*, a liner converted to an auxiliary cruiser, put a shot across his bow and ordered Lauterbach to heave to. A boat came over bearing the Lauterbach counterpart, a boarding officer and a prize crew. Lauterbach argued that he was in neutral waters. The Englishman said he did not care.

It was too late to sink the *Exford*, although Lauterbach had employed his crew earlier at boring holes in her and sealing them back again so she could be sunk, and given a little time he could have sent her gurgling to the bottom. He barely managed to throw all of his secret papers into the leaded bag and get it over the side. He did manage also to slip the compass from the bridge over the side, leaving his enemies only the compass at the hand steering wheel, which was four points off. He moved that to the bridge, hoping that the prize crew would use it for navigation and would pile the *Exford* onto the rocks. They did.

The officers of the *Empress of Japan* believed that Lauterbach was the commander of the landing party from the *Emden*, and it took some time to convince them that he was not. The captain, Commander Hamilton, treated Lauterbach royally while he was aboard the auxiliary, and with the greatest of respect, because he was an officer from the *Emden*. Eventually, however, Lauterbach was taken to a prison camp in Singapore, along with his men of the *Emden*. Some from the *Pontoporos* and the *Markomannia* were already there. The authorities offered Lauterbach transfer to one of the hotels in Singapore if he would give his parole, his promise not to try to escape. He refused, and he did escape later, to neutral Java and then to the United States, where he began a new set of adventures. He made his way back to Germany and was attached to the staff of Admiral Tirpitz for a time, reported to the admiralty on the exploits of the *Emden*, ran a flotilla of "mystery ships" which were actually raiders, sank several British ships of the same type, was trapped by six British destroyers and escaped in a small boat, commanded the German raider *Moewe*, and went safely through the German naval mutiny.

Captain von Müller and the survivors of the *Emden* were taken in the direction of Colombo aboard the *Sydney*. Several men died in the next two days of injuries sustained in the battle. On November 14 the wounded personnel were transferred to the auxiliary cruiser *Empress of Russia*, which had the room to become a temporary hospital ship.

The *Sydney* and the *Empress of Russia* arrived in Colombo on November 15. That same afternoon the officers and the able-bodied men were shipped aboard various transports, which had been liners. Captain von Müller, Surgeon Luther, Leutnant Fikentscher and the prince were taken on the *Orvieto*. Each had his own cabin on the upper deck, and their prison section was separated from the British officers' section by a wire grating and was manned by sentries. Twice a day they were allowed to walk on the promenade deck on the starboard side of the ship, and they ate in what was formerly the nursery. In walking and at meals they were accompanied by British officers. They were taken in convoy to Aden, to Suez, and finally, aboard the cruiser *Hampshire*, an old friend and an old enemy, to Malta, where they were imprisoned for the remainder of the war, Captain von Müller only being transferred suddenly to England in 1917. Others, including Prince Franz Joseph, remained at Malta until November 1919 and arrived home in Germany just in time for Christmas that year, five years after their capture aboard the *Emden*.

On the trip to Colombo, Captain von Müller and the others were cheered by one bit of information they received: The reason the *Sydney* had been so long in coming to the assistance of the *Emden* after her surrender was that the landing party of the *Emden* had escaped.

Chapter 20

THE MIRACULOUS ESCAPE

WHEN FIRST OFFICER Hellmuth von Mücke of the *Emden's* landing party saw the *Emden* begin steaming away from him, he was surprised and puzzled. It was true that he had overstayed his time ashore, but no one had expected the task of finding and cutting the submarine cables to take so much time, and since his captain was an understanding if a demanding man, the correct von Mücke antici- pated no trouble in explaining his tardiness.

At first, von Mücke believed the *Emden* was moving to meet the *Buresk* to bring her through the shoal water that surrounded the Cocos Islands. He expected to go outside and then catch up with his ship as she slowed to turn and guide the collier. Then he noticed that she kept increasing her speed until she hit something around sixteen knots, while his launch, laden with two tows, could make but four knots.

Suddenly, as they cleared the reef, he saw the *Emden* run up her battle flags, and saw, then heard, the flashes from her starboard guns as she began firing salvos at an enemy. He did not know what enemy, and he assumed it was a British freighter somewhere out of sight.

Then five spouts in the sea next to the *Emden* showed him that this was not a defenseless merchantman. The *Emden* was engaged in battle. He could not see her opponent from his position, because the island came between the two ships, but he did know that there was no chance of overtaking his ship and that he must wait until she returned. He turned the steam pinnace back to shore.

This time von Mücke knew exactly what he was about. There was no stopping to ask for directions. He sent men to raise the German flag on the staff, and he told the superintendent that the island was now under German martial law. The Englishmen were ordered into one place and their arms were again collected and confiscated. They were warned against trying to communicate with any other island or any ship.

The beach was cleared of civilians and the machineguns were removed to shore and placed so as to sweep the landing area. The sailors began to entrench. Von Mücke was determined to defend the island against a landing party if his ship should be defeated and it should come to that.

When the English superintendent, Mr. Farrant, saw what the Germans were doing, he asked on behalf of his men that the civilians be allowed to move to one of the other islands if it appeared that a fight was going to develop. He did not like the prospects of being targets without being able to fight back. Von Mücke assented to this course, and cordiality was maintained.

Von Mücke took two of his signalmen and climbed to the top of the wireless office, the highest building on the island. There he watched, as well as he could, the fight between the two cruisers. He saw the *Emden* under fire, and the *Sydney*'s shells falling around her, and commented, without knowing of the destruction of the *Sydney*'s rangefinder, on the poor shooting of the enemy. Then the gun aimers found the range, and before von Mücke's anguished eyes the *Emden* began to spout smoke and flame. He saw the forward funnel shot away, the shell that began the huge blaze aft that cost the life of Navigator Gropius.

He saw the quick turn to starboard and the fall of the foremast, and knew that it cost the life of some officer, but he did not know it was young von Guerard who died.

The ships moved northward, away from the island, and soon were out of sight, but von Mücke, a trained naval officer, need see no more than he had. He knew that the *Emden* had met a superior enemy armed with much heavier guns, that she was taking terrible punishment without being able to return very much, and that unless she could fire a torpedo that would stop or sink the enemy, her chances of survival were slim. He also could see that the other ship was faster than the *Emden*, and he knew how little was the chance that his captain would ever be able to fire that torpedo.

So von Mücke knew that he was now commander of a detachment of the Imperial German Navy and he alone must decide what use should be made of his troops. Even if the *Emden* escaped from the Englishman, and he now knew the other ship to be either the *Sydney* or the *Melbourne*, the German cruiser would be forced to run for some neutral port in hopes of making repairs and escaping again. She would never come back to Direction Island.

Whatever the outcome of the battle, von Mücke knew, he could expect a British warship to come to the island very shortly. If the enemy ship out there to the north was sunk, which seemed most unlikely, still there would be another cruiser along within a few hours at the most. Britain would not stand by and allow her wireless station to go unmourned or allow her cable system to remain out of commission forever. The very success of his shore mission had guaranteed his imminent discovery.

Von Mücke saw two courses, but they were not those a lesser man might have seen. First was to stay and fight, inflict as much damage on the enemy as possible, and then either die or surrender when the ammunition ran out. He did not consider surrendering without a fight. His second course was to take the little schooner that lay in the harbor and escape.

A lesser man would never have considered this plan. Von Mücke and his comrades were very much marooned. They were standing on an island, surrounded by enemies, possessing only the clothing they wore and the guns they had brought from the *Emden*. The island was a part of a British lake, surrounded by British territory and the lands of peoples allied to the British. To get home they must cross thousands of miles of unfriendly sea, where they could not expect to find a single friend and every ship's smoke would indicate another enemy. He must take a sailing ship, about which he knew nothing, not even if she possessed charts or a working compass, find stores, water and equipment, and escape so cleverly that the enemies who would search for him would not be able to find him with all their modern equipment.

Von Mücke said nothing to his men. He indicated the little schooner, the *Ayesha*, and expressed some interest in going aboard her. Her name, he discovered, was given to honor the favorite wife of Mohammed. Did she have ammunition or guns aboard? Ostensibly to discover this for himself he boarded the steam pinnace and went out to the schooner to see, really, if she was seaworthy.

The captain and one seaman were aboard. Von Mücke began asking casual questions and looking about, and he satisfied himself that she was seaworthy. Then he returned to shore and issued his orders. They would board the *Ayesha* and escape.

Captain Partridge of the *Ayesha* and Edmund Clunies-Ross and his brother Cosmo, sons of the owner of the Cocos Islands, were taken off the schooner and sent ashore to join the other English prisoners, who were now being held, guarded rather loosely, in the boat shed. No one was quite sure at this moment who was a prisoner of whom, but von Mücke made certain that the Germans kept their weapons about them.

Von Mücke then asked the superintendent just how good a stock of provisions he had. Superintendent Farrant said he had enough supplies to last the men of the island four months in an emergency. Von Mücke said he was sorry but he would have to take two months' supplies for himself and his men. He took down the address of the company at Singapore and assured Farrant that he would get word to the company within two months if possible that he had left the Englishmen on Direction Island destitute.

Then, setting his men to work provisioning the schooner, von Mücke allowed the English to disperse around the island. It was understood that if the British ship returned before they could leave that the Germans would fight, and the English civilians were warned to find hiding places for themselves if this was the case.

One of the German guards asked an erstwhile captive if he might write a letter to his mother, and he was taken to a room and given pen and paper. Those who were not moving supplies sat with the English and watched the smoke on the horizon and discussed the chances of the *Emden* in the fight.

Von Mücke loaded pots and pans, 150 gallons of water from the island's condenser tanks, half the supplies. He asked for old clothes and the Englishmen produced their wardrobes, generously giving much more than asked.

Captain Partridge offered some advice: The *Ayesha* was not as sturdy as she seemed. Von Mücke ought to look out for rot in her bottom, he said. Von Mücke listened politely but went on with his preparations. He had no alternative but to ignore the Englishman.

Late in the afternoon, as the *Sydney* was pulling up to the hulk of the *Emden*, the *Ayesha* was ready, and the Germans got into their cutters and the pinnace and made for the schooner, giving three cheers, "*Hoch, hoch, hoch,*" as they left. The English responded with hurrays, and then began snapping pictures of the departing enemy.

The Germans boarded the *Ayesha* and assembled aft. Von Mücke made a short speech; the German battle ensign was broken out on the aftermast and saluted with three cheers. The steam pinnace took a line from the bow of the schooner and towed her out of the lagoon. Darkness was falling as she moved outside the reef and her sails caught the light breeze. Had the *Sydney* been about her business, and she had pulled into Direction Island harbor that night, she might have captured the landing crew of the *Emden* even then, for laden with the pinnace and the cutters the *Ayesha* made much less than her eight knots. First Officer, now Captain, von Mücke climbed into the top of the foremast himself and conned his little ship through the reefs and shoals, for he had not a single chart and did not know the waters. He had the boatswain's whistle about his neck on a chain and tooted to the helmsman to steer port or starboard. It soon grew so dark that he could not see from the fore-mast, so he climbed down into the chains on the port side of the ship, and there, next to the water, gave his orders.

The *Sydney*, which drew up in victorious leisure beside the island, decided that the next morning would be quite enough time to send boats into shore and capture the landing crew of the *Emden*. And so the long quiet night passed, the last few men of the *Emden* inching their way out to sea and to freedom.

Chapter 21

THE *AYESHA*

Before dawn the *Ayesha* was out of sight of land, away from the many small islands of the Cocos group and safe in deep water where the long swell of the Indian Ocean helped the breeze fill her sails. Captain von Mücke called in his steam pinnace and told the crew to board the schooner. They had no further use for the big boat and she was a serious liability. The last man out of her started her engine and turned the rudder to port with a boat hook after he had stepped onto the deck of the schooner. The steam pinnace glided off into the night and vanished.

That night the men made do about the little ship, sleeping where they might. The next day Captain von Mücke set about, in his thorough navy way, to create order and discipline on his ship.

Some of the men had told Englishmen on Direction Island that von Mücke was a "regular Prussian." They were referring to his behavior, not to his Saxon parentage, obviously. But disciplinarian that he was, von Mücke proved before and was to prove again that he would never ask a man to do something he would not do himself, and he led his men, he did not drive them, into every adventure.

On the morning of November 10, the *Ayesha* was sailing nicely in a fresh breeze and von Mücke took his chance to look around him. His ship, his first command, was ninety feet long and twenty-five feet wide and had a burden of ninety-seven tons.

She was a copra ship, by and large, although at this time she was empty and in ballast, carrying iron pigs in the hold. She was painted white, with a figure of her Mohammedan namesake below the long bowsprit, and had three tall masts made from double spars lashed together. The foremast was square-rigged, but the mainmast and mizzenmast were rigged for fore-and-aft sails. This gave her the double advantage of navigability on the high seas and in the coastal waters where the wind is changeable.

She was intended for a five-man crew and was found for that purpose. Her two small boats, her cabins, her galley were all built for the small crew. This created the most difficult problem with which the men of the *Emden* had to deal on the *Ayesha*, since there were ten times as many of them as the ship could comfortably accommodate. The forecastle of the *Ayesha*, for example, could house only six men at the most.

The sleeping problem was solved by assigning most of the men berths in the hold. They had brought with them a few blankets and mattresses. But the men bedded down on the spare sails in the hold, with the iron ballast for mattresses. As time went on they solved the sleeping problem for themselves by making hammocks from ropes and sailcloth.

Below deck were two small cabins, which the Germans used to store the provisions they had taken from the island. Far aft was another cabin, which was called the chart room, where the petty officers were quartered. Captain von Mücke lived in the deckhouse in a small cabin, and his two lieutenants shared another the same size, and a third, still smaller cabin was fitted up as an officers' mess, smoking and wine room, also to be used by the officer on watch as his watchroom.

Immediate attention had to be paid to the problem of the galley, for it was totally unfit to serve fifty men. Several pigs of iron ballast were brought up from the hold and laid out to form a fireproof stove. Pieces of sheet iron and tin were taken from the interior of the ship and wrapped around this to hold it together and create a flat surface. It was more an open fireplace than a stove. The men cooked by holding the pots over the flames on rods.

Captain von Mücke selected a cook and several assistants and gave them the keys to the storerooms. They had plenty of tinned foods and sacks of rice, so they would not go hungry.

The water problem was more serious. The 150 gallons he had brought from the island was not drinking water but contaminated fresh water used by the islanders only for their machinery. A few days out, von Mücke discovered that their fresh water supply was gone. He had several cases of bottled soda water on board, but did not wish to use that save in an emergency, particularly if they had to abandon the *Ayesha* and go back into the cutters. But on this first day von Mücke did not worry about water. He had the water, he thought, safe in four iron tanks. He was more concerned about seawater coming in than fresh water going out. He remembered now the words of the captain that the *Ayesha* was rotten and he went below to investigate. Sure enough, when he plunged his knife into her planking it came out red and covered with long rotten fibers. She was pulpy and leaky both, and soon the water began to rise in her. He checked the pump, but it would not work, and he set men to dismantling it. The leather packing was dried and rotten, so it was replaced with rags soaked in oil and then worked serviceably.

On that first day the ship's company was divided into two watches, and the men were taught to man a sailing vessel. Most of them knew nothing about sailing ships, but von Mücke had trained in them as a cadet, and some of his crew came from North Sea fishing families, so the cadre was there and they could whip the others into shape. They learned to set sails, and—more important— to mend them. The *Ayesha*'s canvas was old and rotten, and von Mücke was afraid to put much strain on it, so they traveled slowly and conservatively.

On the fourth day out from Direction Island they discovered the water problem, but it bothered them only for a few hours. The tanks were cleaned out and a sail was spread on deck, horizontally across the main hatch with a hole in the middle. Below the hole in the hold stood a five-gallon petroleum can. That afternoon the tropical rain came with its usual quick ferocity. Men went below and formed a chain gang, passing the petroleum cans as they filled, dumping them into the tanks, and returning them beneath the sail for refill. The roof of the deckhouse was also made into a rain catcher by fastening molding around the sides and making gutters that ran into petroleum cans. The men of the *Ayesha* did not suffer for lack of drinking water.

Washing was another matter. Salt-water baths are not very comfortable; soap does not lather and the bather emerges with a sticky feeling of needing a bath. There was not enough fresh water to provide for baths, but every time it rained the men had one anyhow; they stopped up the scuppers on the decks and let the water accumulate to a depth of four or five inches. As the ship rolled, they rolled on the deck and were quite effectively covered and cleansed by the rainwater.

The men had come aboard in their summer white uniforms and with only such extra clothing as they had been able to beg from the men of Direction Island. In a few days their clothes were in tatters; to save what remained the men worked the ship in their underwear and sometimes in no clothes at all.

Just how rotten their ship was the captain and crew discovered a few days out of port. The cutters were towed on long lines. In the wake and the heavy swell, they danced this way and that and were saved from collision by being fastened to the separate sides of the ship and towed on ropes of different lengths. The cutter on the short rope fouled the ship one day in the heavy swell, coming up just under the overhanging stern and burying its stem in a plank above the water line. A sound plank would have bumped or broken the boat's stem, but the *Ayesha*'s planking was so far from sound that it crumbled away. So the first cutter was set adrift, to save the ship, and a few days later the second cutter broke away, carrying off a large piece of the rotten bulwarks.

The crew shared one comb and one razor. The comb was used daily by nearly everyone, the razor by very few, and it soon grew rusty and hardly usable at all. A light watch was kept at night, but most of the men slept nights and arose at six o'clock in the morning to begin the day's work of keeping the ship fit and clean.

They doused the decks in salt water by hauling pails up over the side in the traditional manner of sailing-ship sailors. One watch went to work on the pumps, pulling out the water that had leaked into the hold overnight. There was tea in the morning for breakfast, with rice, and gooseberry wine with lunch and coffee in the evening, again with rice.

Since the ship was built for a five-man crew, and could be handled quite easily by that number, most of the crew had very little to do all day long. Some of the men learned sailing-ship seamanship—steering, rigging, and navigation. Others sat on the deck and dreamed of the future. They were bound for Padang in the Dutch East Indies, and they wondered what fate would have in store for them there. They would at least learn what had happened to the *Emden*.

All day long the men amused themselves. Some of them fished, although they had no bait and none of them ever caught anything. They ate in relays because there were not enough eating utensils to go around. They played cards and slept and smoked and told tales.

In the evenings they sang old German songs, sentimental and sad ones for the most part, but happy ones, too. There was a marked absence of military songs on these occasions. The war seemed far off as they lay on the deck of the silent schooner, listening to the sounds of the sea and watching the moon and stars that are so much brighter in the southern skies than in the north.

As the days went on, and they were unmolested, even von Mücke relaxed a bit. The watch then consisted of two men, the forward lookout and the man at the wheel. The *Ayesha* carried no lights, since she did not want to be discovered, and she depended on the acute sensitivity to sounds of sailing-ship men to protect her.

The one fear the men had now was not that they might be detected but the age-old fear of the elements. Sailing a rotten ship through the monsoon seas is no joke. The thunderstorms that brought them fresh water also brought high winds that threatened the sails and the masts. Captain von Mücke did not know how much strain those masts would take, and he had no desire to discover the breaking point, so as they rode into a storm and the black clouds came up from the horizon the captain ordered his hands aloft to furl the sails and they lay to, head of the ship into the wind, until the storm had passed. One day, when they waited too long to take in sail, the wind caught the mizzen topsail and flung it like a sheet of paper into the air. It caught on the mizzen gaff, the spar that held the sail at an angle to the mast, flung across it and fouled in the stays of the mizzenmast just above the point where the two spars of the mast were bound. The threat to the sail did not bother von Mücke; he had plenty of canvas aboard. But if the mizzenmast should go, the whole ship was endangered, and it swayed and crackled in the storm.

This was also the worst storm they had encountered, a real typhoon. The lightning flashed and the thunder crashed all about them; when the eye passed over them the wind stopped suddenly but the seas grew even higher, swirled by the wind on all sides of the ship. Then the *Ayesha* caught the other side of the storm, which was nearly as bad as the beginning, and the *Ayesha* bounced like a cork in the violent heaving of the seas.

Finally the storm ended, to be followed by dead calm, and this was nearly as uncomfortable as the storm, although not nearly so dangerous to the ship. The *Ayesha* rolled dreadfully in the swell when there was no wind, the sails flapped and the booms swung back and forth. Usually the men furled the sails in calm as well as storm, to make sure that the flapping of the sails did not drive the booms across the ship so hard as to tear the masts out of her.

One day the men of the *Ayesha* were becalmed when they saw a smoke cloud on the horizon. The steamer traveled along the horizon for several hours before disappearing, giving the crew of the sailing ship much anxiety, for they did not know whether it would be friend or foe, and they were nearly defenseless on their tiny sailing vessel.

The matter of defense was all in how one looked at it. As far as defense against civilians and savages were concerned, the *Ayesha* was strong. Captain von Mücke had mounted the four machineguns on deck and had cut holes through the solid rail of the main deck so the guns could be trained at a ninety-degree angle of coverage. Against unarmed men or men armed only with rifles this was a formidable show of force. Against even a patrol boat with a single small cannon it was no force at all. Von Mücke knew this and knew that his one chance of reaching a neutral port and safety was to avoid all shipping at all costs. His greatest fear was a Japanese or English patrol boat, because this was the type of vessel that was most likely to take an interest in the schooner.

At ten o'clock in the morning on November 23, when the

Ayesha had been at sea for two weeks, land came into sight. Von Mücke had been navigating with a large map of the Eastern hemisphere, which represented the eight hundred miles from the Cocos Islands to Sumatra as about the breadth of a hand. He was not quite certain if he had even managed to hit Sumatra, or the Dutch East Indies for that matter. One tiny island gave place to the next as the *Ayesha* threaded her way through the shallow water. At four o'clock in the afternoon some of those who were more familiar with the South Seas than von Mücke realized where they were and said they were just outside Seaflower Channel, about eighty miles from Padang.

The Germans knew nothing about Seaflower Channel except that it was dangerous, full of reefs and shallows. Von Mücke had not come so far to pile the *Ayesha* up on a reef in sight of his objective, so the sails of the schooner were furled and she drifted toward the sea as evening came on. In the morning they would try to move through the channel into Padang.

That night, as the eight-hundreth mile of their voyage registered on the taffrail log, Von Mücke distributed the soda water he had brought from the island's stores, and the men drank it with the reverence usually offered only to champagne. The supply of tobacco and cigarettes was gone, but the men smoked tea leaves in their stead, and some of them claimed they actually liked them.

There are certain disadvantages to reliance on sail alone, and now Captain von Mücke discovered one of them. The breeze that night and the next morning was blowing offshore, and it was a light breeze. The *Ayesha* made practically no progress all day long, although the men could plainly see the mountains and forests of Sumatra. The wind slackened several times almost to dead calm, the heat grew oppressive, and finally they were forced to bring up a spare sail and spread it above the deck as an awning. That night they saw Padang light, but they also saw that they were passing it at a great distance. The breeze continued offshore and light, there was no chance to tack, and by morning they discovered that they were five miles farther from Sumatra than they had been on the night before.

Worse, they were lying in the central roadway for passenger ships, which would also be the lane used by patrolling warships. Since they wished to meet no one before they came into Padang, Captain von Mücke lowered the two boats, one carrying two men and the other three, and set the men to the oars to pull the schooner along where the wind would not. He also lashed together the oars of the *Emden's* cutters, which had been saved, and rowed the *Ayesha* thus like some primitive galley of Roman times.

On November 25, finally, the wind came up and began to blow onshore for a change. In the distance the crew of the *Ayesha* could see steamers moving in and out of the harbor at Padang. One of them seemed to be lying very still, and then suddenly, belching great black clouds of smoke, she headed straight for the sailing vessel at high speed. Captain von Müller, familiar with the ways of small ships, would have spotted her immediately as a patrol boat from her smoke, but the crew of the *Ayesha* were unsure until she came very close, and then they could, with relief, see that she bore the flag of the Netherlands at her masthead.

Chapter 22

PADANG

THE SHIP that bore down on them so quickly might have been called a destroyer or might have been called a torpedo boat. She was both. Since Captain von Mücke had no desire to explain his presence in the waters to any captain until he was actually inside the harbor at Padang under the protection of the German consulate, he sent all but one of his men below decks. First the crew hurriedly pulled the machineguns out of their improvised ports and cleared the decks of rifles and pistols. As the Dutch ship pulled alongside, to within fifty yards, all that could be seen on the deck of the *Ayesha* was Captain von Mücke in cutoff trousers and a singlet, and one wild-looking sailor with a luxuriant beard, dressed even more scantily. They looked like anything but sailors of His Imperial Majesty's navy.

As the Dutch ship came by Captain von Mücke identified her as the destroyer *Lynx*. The compliment was hardly returned, because the Dutch could not read the *Ayesha's* name through the heavy coat of paint, and none of the officers aboard her was familiar enough with the ship to identify her by her shape or the bowsprit figure. All the officers of the *Lynx* crowded onto the ship's little bridge and every man of them trained field glasses on the strange white schooner. The destroyer passed alongside and then swept around the *Ayesha*, the officers talking with animation all the while. About five thousand yards astern the *Lynx* turned and lay to, which meant she was prepared to keep a watch on the slow sailing vessel.

She stayed for several hours, and then ran off into Padang, leaving the *Ayesha* without coming alongside and without asking her to show her colors. The danger to the *Ayesha* was not what the Dutch might do offshore, but the interest that might be taken outside the three-mile limit in the *Ayesha* by enemy ships. She was still fair game until she came within three miles of an East Indies coast.

That night the *Ayesha* came to the mouth of the harbor of Padang and was picked up there again by the *Lynx*, which followed the schooner into harbor, staying not farther than a hundred yards astern of her all the way.

Captain von Mücke did not like being followed—it made him nervous. He brought a white bulls-eye lantern and one of the signalmen used it to send a message in Morse code. First in English the *Ayesha* asked the *Lynx*:

"Why are you following me?"

The signal was acknowledged by flashes of the warship's signaling lamps, but there was no answer. Half an hour later, the *Lynx* still trailing her, the *Ayesha* sent the same signal in German. Again the signal was acknowledged, but again there was no reply. Still, the dual signaling had some effect: In a short time the *Lynx* turned and sped away.

Getting rid of the *Lynx* was not an unmixed blessing. As long as she was following close behind, with her deeper draft, the men of the *Ayesha* knew they were making their way safely through the shoal water. When she left, they were on their own again. But for the next twenty-four hours they were never very much alone. The *Lynx* kept reappearing at odd moments, satisfied herself that the *Ayesha* was doing what she apparently wished or expected, and sped away again on her various missions.

On November 27 the *Ayesha* finally came within Dutch territorial waters, and she ran up her German war ensign when Captain von Mücke was certain she was inside the three-mile limit. The *Lynx* saw and understood. She did not again draw near to the *Emden,* but stood off several thousand yards, still shadowing.

Around noon it became doubtful, at least in Captain von Mücke's mind, if they could manage to navigate their way through the shallow and dangerous channel without help. Fortunately they were approached by a Malay sailing dhow and were able to negotiate with the men aboard to take one of them on as a pilot. The Malays were quite pleased to have the work and readily accepted the promise of payment by the German consulate. It was fortunate that von Mücke did not have to haggle. The men of the *Emden* had gone to Direction Island without money, and all they had now was a little more than a shilling, which had been found in an old wallet that belonged to Captain Partridge.

After the pilot was taken aboard, under the sharp eyes of the *Lynx,* the Dutch destroyer came dashing up toward the *Ayesha.* Von Mücke decided the time had come for a show of independence, and he presented his beam to the destroyer, ordering his men, now in their uniforms, to come up, stand at attention on the deck and salute as the other warship came past. The *Lynx* turned and returned the courtesy.

They approached the mouth of the harbor, and von Mücke decided it was time to settle with the commander of this Dutch ship and discover just where he stood. He signaled the *Lynx* that he was coming aboard and stepped into one of the *Ayesha's* tiny boats, wearing his landing suit, which he had been careful to preserve for the past three weeks.

The captain of the destroyer greeted von Mücke formally at the gangway and escorted him into the ship's tiny wardroom, questions written on his face. Von Mücke opened the conversation.

He felt very much flattered at the interest shown by the *Lynx* in their little schooner the past few days, he said.

The captain said he was ordered to accompany them.

Von Mücke identified himself as the commander of the landing party from the *Emden,* and the commander of the destroyer indicated he knew as much. (The cable and wireless station at Direction Island had been back on the air, communicating with Singapore, on the very day that the *Ayesha* sailed out of the harbor. Von Mücke's men had been thorough, but in the anticipation of a visit from the *Emden,* weeks earlier the superintendent had caused emergency equipment to be hidden on the island. The world knew of the escape of the *Emden's* landing party, and the Dutch were half expecting them.)

Von Mücke said that he and his party were on their way to Padang with his Imperial Majesty's ship *Ayesha.* At Padang they wished to repair damage to the ship, replenish stores and their water supply. Was there any reason the *Ayesha* should not enter the harbor, he asked.

The destroyer captain said there was nothing to prevent the *Ayesha* from going into the harbor but that she might not be able to come out. The British were making strong representations about the piracy of the ship. The matter would be decided, he said, by the Dutch civil authorities.

Von Mücke set his firm jaw and warned the Dutch captain that the *Ayesha* was a German warship and no one was going to stop him from leaving the harbor when he was ready.

That was the end of the interview. Von Mücke closed the meeting with a joke. He hoped he did not have a fight with the destroyer when he ran the *Ayesha* out of Pedang, he said. The Dutchman did not think the remark was particularly funny.

Captain von Mücke had returned to his ship but had not been aboard long when the harbormaster came out in a steam tug to show the schooner where she might anchor. He indicated a place far out in the harbor, on the usual precept that a sailing ship found it more comfortable to be outside, where she did not have to worry about maneuvering among the steamers. Von Mücke had spotted a number of ships flying the German and Austro-Hungarian flags, however, and he had other ideas. He told the harbormaster he wanted more shelter for his ship than was available in the far space, and that his anchor chain was too short for the deep water. As they talked, the *Ayesha* kept moving inshore, and soon the harbormaster became insistent that von Mücke anchor. Just then the topsails on the mainmast and mizzenmast stuck and for some minutes they firmly refused to come down. Von Mücke's sailors kept working at them, but not very hard, and by the time they were brought down he had reached the point he wanted for an anchorage.

After the *Ayesha* had sent about a sixth of her anchor chain out to reach the bottom of the harbor, and all was made secure, von Mücke sent Lieutenant Schmidt ashore to report their arrival to the Dutch port authorities officially and to pay a call on the German consul and request that he come to the ship. Other than port officials and government officials, no one was to be allowed on board the *Ayesha* and no one was to be allowed off except on official business.

Within an hour the identity of the newcomer was known all over the harbor, and soon the boats of three German ships were in the water, bringing greetings, gifts and newspapers from home to the men of the *Ayesha*, who had not seen a German newspaper since July. The newspapers were six weeks old, but what did that matter? For the first time the crew felt they had some contact with the war in Europe. What they had read about it in the English newspapers and the Indian newspapers meant very little, and they did not believe most of what the enemy said. Now they learned of the marvelous German victories and the predictions that the war would be over by Christmas.

None of the Germans from these other ships came aboard the *Ayesha*, but they threw their gifts up to the deck. It would have been a breach of international law for them to have gone any further in making contact in a neutral port.

Captain von Mücke was having enough trouble with the law and the Dutch interpretation of it as matters already stood, without courting trouble. Goaded by the British representatives in Padang, the Dutch authorities first took the position that the *Ayesha* was a prize of war and that she could not be sailed out of the harbor but must be interned or sold in Padang.

Captain von Mücke replied that the *Ayesha* was a German warship and any affront to her was an affront to the Kaiser and the Imperial German government. He said he would account only to his superiors in the navy for his right to command the *Ayesha*. He demanded permission to take on water, provisions, charts and equipment. The German consul began making arrangements for the purchase and shipment of the supplies to the harbor. The legal complications might take some time but the supplies must be made available in any case.

The Dutch officer in charge of enforcement of the neutrality laws telegraphed Batavia for instructions. He was under heavy pressure from British and Japanese officials to intern the crew of the *Ayesha* as men of the *Emden* and to return the *Ayesha* to the British.

All day long the argument raged. By late afternoon von Mücke felt that he was losing it, so he approached the harbormaster and demanded that he be given his supplies, since he must leave the harbor twenty-four hours after he entered it. The harbormaster was faced with a dilemma; this certainly was the law, and it must be obeyed. On the other hand, the *Ayesha* was a strange kind of fighting ship, and the conditions here were not foreseen by those in the Hague who had enacted the law.

As they argued the provisions began to come alongside, and the harbormaster was mute when asked if they might be loaded. His lack of response was taken to be assent and the tins of food and other supplies came aboard, along with ten live pigs who milled around on the deck near the anchor housing.

At seven o'clock that night the neutrality officer of Padang returned, apparently burdened with his instructions from Batavia. He did everything he could to persuade the Germans to accept voluntary internment as refugees from the wrecked *Emden*. Von Mücke brought his two officers into the conversation, and the three German officers were unanimous in demanding that they be allowed to sail out of port in their schooner of war.

The neutrality officer argued that they could not possibly escape, that British and Japanese warships lay outside the harbor waiting for them and would blow them out of the water. He said the government would not allow the *Ayesha* to take out nautical charts or handbooks of navigation (which might give star charts and tables of logarithms), nor could they have any war materials such as toothbrushes, soap, and combs, which would "increase their fighting strength." They could not have any clothing either.

Von Mücke shrugged. They would go without such niceties, but they would go. He insisted. He would sail without charts, without provisions, without water if need be, but he would sail, and if the authorities prevented him from sailing, His Majesty's government would not be pleased, and the Hague would hear about it within a few hours.

The neutrality officer gave up, finally, and gave them permission to leave the harbor. He was nearly as much trouble to the men of the *Ayesha* as their pork on the hoof. The pigs held up matters for some time because they absolutely refused to move from the foredeck and allow the crewmen to heave in the anchor.

Chapter 23

THE END OF THE AYESHA

As THE *Ayesha's* crew unfurled her topsails and the schooner began to move out of the harbor, Kapitänleutnant von Mücke of the Imperial German Navy led the fifty men in singing the Fatherland song: *"Es braust ein Ruf wie Donnerall"*—"There roars a call, a thunderous sound"—and in martial vigor the most unlikely ship of His Majesty's navy passed out to sea.

Outside the harbor they were hailed, in German, from a small boat, and alongside came a pair of volunteers from Sumatra: a reserve officer, Leutnant Wellman, and an enlisted man. Both were members of the reserve and both now insisted on being taken into active service. They were welcomed, although the new officer, in particular, created problems, since the only place for him to sleep was under the mess table in the tiny third cabin.

Back in Seaflower Channel the *Ayesha* was shadowed by the Dutch cruiser *De Zeven Provincien*. All that first night as the Germans cruised through Dutch waters the ship followed them. They were concerned lest it be a British or Japanese warship, so they remained very close to the islands. They were relieved the following morning when the cruiser came close alongside and they saw that she was Dutch.

The neutrality officer in Padang harbor had quite convinced Captain von Mücke that his enemies would be lurking everywhere. He had made a few tentative plans of his own, however. It was quite impossible for the German consul to get word in confidence to any of the German captains in the harbor, and everyone connected with the *Ayesha* was watched closely and suspiciously all the time the ship was in port. But when the German boats came alongside, even the authorities could not help but countenance feelings of comradely good will, and in the shouting of greetings, Captain von Mücke had made it a point to let it be known that he was going to follow a certain course, and be at a certain place at a certain time. He expected at least one of the German merchant captains to respond to this invitation to help the *Ayesha*. In fact he had come as close as possible to making direct arrangements with the *Choising*, one of those merchantmen, to meet him in the Indian Ocean.

The *Ayesha* sailed and drifted in the calm for three weeks. Her rolling in the calm was matched by her pitching in rough weather. The pigs, in particular, were discomfited. Since they had taken so great a liking to the capstan and the bows, Von Mücke had a pigpen constructed around them. As the weather grew rough he had to send men up forward to nail slats to the deck so the poor creatures were not forever sliding back and forth.

In the three weeks that they waited, the men of the *Ayesha* had two bad frights, both from English ships. One passed close by but after looking them over turned away and increased its speed, as if to shrug them off. The second, which von Mücke took to be an auxiliary cruiser, took entirely too great an interest in the little *Ayesha* for some time and began finally to move purposefully toward her. The normal expectation, then, was that the big English ship would come alongside, hail the sailing ship and demand to see her flag. If there was any suspicion about her, the English ship would send a boarding crew to examine the ship's papers and speak to the captain. Under such circumstances, of course, it would never come to that. Von Mücke would proudly run up his German battle flag and either start shooting or scuttle the *Ayesha*. In either event a gesture would be made, but no victory could be won, and the whole purpose of the voyage would be lost. Von Mücke did not want to make any useless gestures. He wanted to return the landing party of the *Emden* to fight again. So he used guile rather than making a brave show.

As the English ship turned toward him, he turned the *Ayesha* directly toward her, as if he wanted nothing more than to seek her presence and conversation. While far away from hailing distance he had his signalmen ask for the geographical position. This was a common request of sailing captains, or of some sailing captains, when they met a steam merchantman. It was an annoyance to the steamers, and the captains usually cursed or joked about the idiot sailors who could not navigate their own ships. In this case, von Mücke's request established a definite relationship between his ship and the Englishman; he was now regarded as a poor, stupid island captain, sailing an old schooner with ragged, patched sails.

Yet the Englishman's suspicions were not totally allayed. From the big ship came the information, but also the embarrassing question:

"What ship are you?"

Von Mücke knew how to deal with this in a fashion to suit the character he had assumed. He took four signal flags that were close at hand, arranged them one above the other, tied knots in the two top flags so no one could tell what they were, and then hoisted the signal up the mainmast so it was half hidden by the sails.

The English ship seemed to watch for some time, puzzling over the strange reply. Then she ran up the signal: "I have seen your signal but I cannot make it out."

Captain von Mücke blithely ignored all this and kept flying his spurious signal all the while, making no attempt to move away from the steamer. It was easy to imagine the reactions of the captain of that ship: He became certain that he was dealing either with imbeciles or lunatics, and he had no desire for any more of the *Ayesha*'s company. He turned and moved majestically away.

A few days after this incident, on December 14, the *Ayesha* was sailing in the area where she hoped to meet the *Choising* when

that ship suddenly loomed ahead through the thick rain and fog of
the day. The *Ayesha* had been sailing back and forth, east and west,
for some days, searching. Now, sailing west, they saw that the other
ship was sailing east, which meant that she was bound on some mission other than making way between two ports. In this part of the
Indian Ocean ships did not sail east and west to make port. From
the moment of sighting, von Mücke sensed that this was his country-
man. The problem was not to be careful and check her, but to attract her attention. Even at four thousand yards there was grave
danger that the merchantman might miss her in this soupy weather,
and the chance of escape from the Indian Ocean would be gone.
Von Mücke had no illusions about his hopes of sailing the *Ayesha*
across the Indian Ocean, through the Red Sea, the Mediterranean,
under the guns of Gibraltar and then to Germany. His hope from
Padang had been to encounter a German ship and transfer his crew
to that vessel, taking charge of it in the name of the Imperial Navy.
Here was his chance.

The *Ayesha* began signaling to the *Choising* and for once
put on all the sail the little ship would carry, desperately hoping to
close with her and show herself before the other passed in the fog.
The signalman produced the signaling pistol and they fired their
precious supply of red and white fireballs, a half dozen shots.

At last these attracted the attention of someone on the
Choising's bridge, and the merchant ship turned and headed back
toward the schooner. Immediately the *Ayesha* ran up flags and
streamers which identified her as a German warship. The *Choising*
hoisted her German ensign, too. Most of the fifty men aboard the
Ayesha clambered into the shrouds, cheering and shouting, mother-
naked, many of them, looking like so many wild men.

Von Mücke took charge at once. He saw that the seas were
too rough to board the *Choising* safely, so he signaled the merchant
ship to follow him and turned south, where he expected to find
better weather.

Contrarily, the weather turned worse instead of better. The
next day the *Ayesha* was taking heavy seas, but she rode them well
and her rigging seemed to withstand the tortures of the storm. The
Choising captain became very nervous and signaled that he must
get out of this weather and the shoal water into which they were

heading. A new rendezvous was arranged and the *Ayesha* was again left alone.

The night of December 15 was the worst the men of the *Ayesha* spent aboard their little ship. The storm was so severe that they could see nothing, and the tossing of their schooner so severe that they were wet and miserable and afraid all night long. They were being blown onto some small islands of the East Indies chain; both current and wind were carrying them toward the reefs, and so it was necessary to keep canvas on the ship to stand away from the land. Closely reefed as the sails were, they were not strong enough to stand the storm. First the foresail and the staysail tore away. The foresail was scarcely gone when the fore staysail went, too. It was impossible to rig new canvas, and so the ship sailed with her after sails alone, and with hope that these would keep her off the beach.

They did. The wind died down, and the next morning the crew bent new sails and headed toward the second rendezvous, arriving at nine o'clock in the morning, in the bright sunshine, with the welcome sight of the *Choising* steaming down on them from the distance. Even when the wind died and the sails began to flap no one aboard the *Ayesha* cared. In a few hours, the men knew, they would be out of their cramped and damp quarters, and free still, again aboard a proper German ship.

Von Mücke signaled the *Choising* to take the sailing ship into tow in the calm and to make for the lee of one of the small islands nearby. There the men of the *Emden* would leave their little vessel.

In the interim, as the sailing ship was under tow, the navy men began to unrig their ship. All the arms were brought on deck, all the provisions were brought up to be taken along. The figure-head was taken down and the wheel was taken off its post; both would be carried along by the men of the *Emden* as souvenirs of their voyage and given to the navy in Berlin.

In the lee of the tiny island the job of destruction was begun. The *Ayesha*'s shrouds were cut through and holes were bored in the hull. At four o'clock in the afternoon the transfer was completed and the *Choising* started her engines, moving away, planning to leave the sailing ship. But the *Ayesha* followed, and a few moments later, as if angered by her treatment, she fouled the ship of those who had betrayed her, carrying away much of the gangway ladder. The *Choising* was stopped then, and von Mücke and his men watched the little schooner sink. It took her fifty-eight minutes to go down, her decks slowly sinking below the water, the bow rising, and falling and rising again. Finally the pigs of iron below must have shifted forward, because she turned her bowsprit under and went down like a porpoise diving, the cheers of her last crew ringing above her grave.

<hr>

Chapter 24

DESTINATION: ARABIA

CAPTAIN MINKIEWITZ of the *Choising* was a loyal German officer and a forbearing man; even so it was difficult for him to place himself under the orders of the brusque Captain von Mücke, who now took charge of the *Choising* without apology. Yet Captain Minkiewitz behaved nobly from the beginning; he had known what was in store for him when he responded to the command call of the German officer back in Padang.

Von Mücke wasted no time in making preparations to move in secrecy and as swiftly as the seven-and-a-half-knot speed of the *Choising* would allow. She did not even make that speed most of the time, because she was carrying an inferior grade of coal. At one time, the *Choising* had been designated as collier for the *Emden;* this was one reason that Captain Minkiewitz was so quick to respond to von Mücke's call. She was one of those ships for which the *Emden* had searched at the beginning of her voyage and had not found. In the *Choicing's* case there was no mystery about it: while waiting for the *Emden* her cargo of Australian and Indian coal had been fired by spontaneous combustion and she had left the rendezvous to put out her fires.

The fires had been extinguished, and now the survivors of the *Emden* made their beds in the coal storage. This time they had mattresses and plenty of blankets, however, and the quarters were far more comfortable than those they had just left atop the *Ayesha's* pig iron. The new captain and his officers took over the bridge and the choice accommodations, and the captain of the *Choising* yielded, in effect, his command.

The next problem, which must be decided immediately, was a course. Where did the men of the *Emden* propose to go?

In the beginning, when the *Ayesha* reached Padang, von Mücke had hoped to sail the little ship to Tsingtao. His hopes were dashed when he learned in the Indies of the attack on the colony by the Japanese. Governor Meyer-Waldeck had known, even as the *Emden* steamed out of Tsingtao, that war was sure to come. The next day he had declared martial law in Kiaochow. Private vehicles were requisitioned, coolies were impressed into military service, and railroad travel was put under military rule. On August 15 the Japanese had issued an ultimatum, demanding possession of Kiaochow to be handed over to Japan not later than September 15.

On August 22 the Kaiser had sent a farewell message to the Germans in Tsingtao. "God will protect you, while you fight bravely," he had cabled. "I trust in you." In other words, the Tsingtao garrison was doomed to fight to the death.

On August 25, Admiral Kato had blockaded the port. There had been heavy fighting, the naval forces had acquitted themselves handsomely, the little gunboats had accounted for several Japanese ships in the battle, and the land forts had resisted vigorously, but two days before the *Emden* fell before the guns of the *Sydney,* her home base had fallen to the Japanese. The news was complete and well digested by the time von Mücke and the survivors of the *Emden* had arrived at Padang.

As he sailed out of Padang to meet the *Choising,* von Mücke had formulated another plan. He would take his men to German East Africa to join the cruiser *Königsberg* and fight again in the manner they knew best.

Aboard the *Choising* Kapitänleutnant von Mücke was in for a shock. When he mentioned the *Königsberg,* Captain Minkiewitz shook his head. She was either sunk or she was bottled up in the Rufiji River, he said. He had received two reports, he did not know which was true.

It made no difference to von Mücke. Either report spelled the end to his plan. (The *Königsberg* was actually bottled up in the Rufiji River and eventually was scuttled there.)

Von Mücke's next plan was to take his troops to German East Africa to fight on land, but he abandoned this idea when he considered the logistics and the cost. General von Lettow-Vorbeck had won a victory at the Battle of Tanga in November, but the British were pushing him hard and he was forced to retreat into the interior. Von Mücke did not know the country, his men had no provisions, no tropical clothing, no proper weapons, no medical supplies, no guides, no knowledge of the languages, and no maps. He gave up the plan as hopelessly naive.

The one plan left, then, was to make his way home to Germany to fight again. (He never considered anything less than fighting again.) This presented some serious problems. Should he try to provision the ship somewhere and steam around the Cape of Good Hope, and then make his way through the English Channel and to the North Sea? All the way he would be in danger of running afoul of British warships.

A newspaper he found aboard the *Choising* gave von Mücke hope that another course would be possible. He saw a report of a battle between Turkish and British troops at Sheikh Said, near Perim, an island in the Strait of Bab el Mandeb. This was a definite indication that Turkey was in the war, although he had not seen or heard of any declaration. Searching, then, among the old newspapers on the *Choising,* von Mücke found the declaration of war of November 5, which followed the raid on the Russian Black Sea coast by Turkish warships and the German cruisers *Goeben* and *Breslau,* masked as Turkish vessels. He also learned that nine days later the sultan had declared a holy war on the Triple Entente, which gave von Mücke hope that he would find friendly Arabs in the Arabian peninsula. So, he evolved a plan in a very few hours. The *Choising* would take the men of the *Emden* to the Arabian peninsula and they would disembark to make their way overland to Turkey and fight again for the Kaiser.

Now, an end in mind, Captain von Mücke looked over his new command. She was a German Lloyd steamer, and like all of that line, she wore the company uniform: black hull, white bulwarks, and ocher trim. This must be remedied, and it was. She was painted over, a single drab color. Then she looked like a Dutchman, but this was unsatisfactory, because the British were bound to take an inordinate interest in a neutral ship. Looking over the shipping lists in Captain Minkiewitz's cabin, von Mücke discovered that a 1,700-ton vessel named the *Shenir* had recently been transferred from British to Italian registry. Since the Italians were still vacillating about their entry into the war (and would until late 1915), von Mücke chose to masquerade the *Choising* as an Italian ship, with the thought that the British would not harry an Italian. The *Shenir* was exactly the size of the *Choising*, so on the stern of the Lloyd steamer was painted the wording: "*Shenir*, Genoa." All that was needful, von Mücke hoped, was that the Chinese crew of the *Choising* be kept out of sight when British ships were in the vicinity.

There was one other need, an Italian flag. There was none aboard the *Choising*, so one was manufactured. A green window curtain was sewed to a strip of red cloth and a strip of white cloth, and a volunteer artist from among the men of the *Emden* set about painting the coat of arms of the Italian kingdom on the white strip. The green window curtain was not the right color, so it had to be stripped off. Then the artist mixed blue and yellow paint to obtain the correct shade and dipped the curtain into it. When it was dry he sewed the curtain back onto the red and white and had a very presentable Italian flag, as long as it did not rain.

While the artist worked over the flag, Captain von Mücke set a course westward to cross the Indian Ocean slightly south of its center, avoiding the steamer lanes always and keeping out of the typhoon region. There was only one real task for the men of the *Emden*, and that was to keep sharp lookout all around the horizon. Discovery in their case meant instant capture, and so they crept through the Indian Ocean hoping they would be unseen.

~~~~~~

Chapter 25

THE LANDING

THE VOYAGE ACROSS the Indian Ocean was totally without incident. The *Choising* made the trip in twenty-two days, an excellent
time considering the slowness of the ship and the out-of-the-way
route she followed. They were not stopped by any steamers and had
no difficulties. There was no shortage of food or drink or any other
trouble. Christmas was celebrated as a religious holiday, but on New
Year's Eve they broke out the beer and wine and finished up the
entire supply on the ship. Then all was quiet until they arrived at
the Strait of Bab el Mandeb, the southern gateway to the Red Sea,
on January 7, 1915.

Since they had no charts of the area, von Mücke arrived at
the strait in the middle of the day, which did not suit him at all;
he wanted no observers as he sailed around Perim island and into the
narrow sea where the British might track him easily if they but knew
who he was and what he was trying to do. Coming in past Socotra
island, he then turned back and steamed slowly back and forth, waiting for the daylight hours to fade away. There was one alert, when a
large steamer from Jibuti came toward them, and they feared she
might be a cruiser. The ship turned out to be a French mail steamer,
however, and they confused her, as they had confused other ships,
simply by setting an apparent course for the African coast, then re-
setting their course when the French ship had vanished.

They were nearing the point of danger, as they approached
the straits, and von Mücke knew it. He had his men prepare to land.
Their weapons were oiled and their provisions were stacked in the
four longboats of the *Choising*. The longboats were run out on their
davits after night fell and lowered to the bulwarks. Now that he had

four officers, including himself, von Mücke could put an officer in charge of each boat. He checked the supplies as they were loaded; there was food and water calculated to last them for eight weeks.

At this danger point in the straits, von Mücke had two plans. If discovered, as he half expected, by a patrol boat, he intended to beach the ship and abandon the crew. They would be interned as noncombatants, but he and his warriors from the *Emden* would be free to continue the fight against the enemy. If they were taken on the southern, or African, side, they would flee. If they were taken on the northern, or Arabian, side, they would seek the telegraph station that stood in that vicinity and attack it.

They approached the strait on the African side, without lights. Von Mücke had debated with himself about the question of carrying lights; a small steamer carrying lights and moving into the Red Sea would scarcely be questioned, for what German would be so foolhardy as to sail into waters completely dominated by his enemies? Yet he wanted to take no chance of detection, so the lights were extinguished, and his officers and petty officers patrolled the ship to be sure the Chinese crew members did not show a light in carelessness.

Von Mücke ordered the helmsman to steer very close to the African shore, hoping to be hidden there against the dark horizon. The revolving light on Perim island nearly undid him, for regularly its beam fell on the ship like a searchlight. He could see two English warships lying just off the island, signaling to one another in Morse with their lights.

The *Choising* inched past, von Mücke certain that they must be discovered at any moment. The inching took half an hour, and astonishingly to von Mücke they were not seen. Outside the perimeter of the light they were still in danger for another hour, but the seas blew up and ran high, which helped protect them and helped keep the minds of others on seamanship.

All night long the men of the *Emden* kept worried lookout, even when outside the straits. The next day they watched the horizon anxiously, even when they were in the broad Red Sea. They did their best, again, to avoid detection by staying well away from the steamer lanes.

Captain von Mücke decided to land Kapitänleutnant von Mücke and the fighting men of the *Emden* near Hodeida and try to reach that Arab city. The best information he possessed, which came from an old guidebook, told him that Hodeida was a large commercial city and that a dozen years earlier, when the book was published, the Hejaz railway was being built to connect Hodeida with a number of other points in Arabia. Leutnant Wellman recalled that a number of years earlier he had met a French engineer who had worked on the railroad. So, as far as von Mücke knew, there was a railroad, and it should lead him eventually to Constantinople and thus to Berlin. He did not put aside the contingency that the railroad might not be operating, however. If there was no road, the side trip was still valuable, for at Hodeida they could find charts of the Red Sea and would learn what was happening in the war.

The four boats were ready to go over the side, and the men of the *Emden* were ready to move. Dr. Lang, the ship's physician on the *Choising*, was persuaded to accompany the men of the *Emden*, so now they had their own doctor and some medicines.

As they came near to the area where they expected to find Hodeida, von Mücke saw from the bridge that the town was brightly lighted.

At least the port was. This gave him hope that the railroad would be running and that in two weeks they would be on the North Sea, assigned to another powerful German warship.

As they neared the lights, these began to move, to change position relative to the shore. Port lights do not do that, so von Mücke took alarm. The engines of the *Choising* were stopped and soundings were made. He calculated that they were in twenty fathoms of water and that the port must be several thousand yards away, but the lights were very close. Abruptly he had the feeling that he had best get away from those lights, so he took the ship sixteen miles north, before the boats were put into the water.

The order was given for the men to get into the boats, and this time it was not countermanded. When the men of the *Emden* were aboard, the fourteen-foot boats were heavily laden. Three of them were rigged in German fashion, and a fourth was rigged as a sampan, which would certainly cause some raised eyebrows if sighted by knowledgeable seagoing men along the coast.

Von Mücke gave some last instructions from the bridge. The captain of the *Choising* was handed his written orders, to spend the next two days in the vicinity of a given point outside the steamship routes, and on the next few nights to return each night to the point of departure and wait. If the men did not return after a week he was to proceed to Massawa, a port in Italian Somaliland.

Von Mücke was operating totally in the dark. He did not know who was in control of Hodeida or the area into which he was piercing. If his enemies were in control he intended to hide in the desert during the daylight hours and make his way back to the sea at night.

He had considered every eventuality, it seemed. If there was danger to the *Choising* the shore party would send rocket signals, and these would mean the captain of the ship was to break off and proceed immediately to Massawa. By this von Mücke meant unusual danger. There was danger to the ship and its crew every moment they spent in these waters that were dominated by the French and English.

The crews of the four boats raised their sails and the men began to bail. All the boats leaked, since they had not been in the water for a long time. That is how the night was spent, sailing and bailing, until the sun popped up over the flat horizon and the day's heat began. Early in the morning, before the shimmering heat haze set in, von Mücke could see for a long distance, and he saw that the "port" he had observed the night before was actually a French heavy cruiser, the *Desaix*, anchored beside the Italian ship *Juliana*.

As the light came up, Kapitänleutnant von Mücke brought his boats to anchor and the rigging was stripped down. It would never do to have questions asked about the Chinese rig on one of them. It was best to appear as fishermen, and they could do this with bare masts showing, but hardly otherwise. They could not remain long, however, because they would be seen and undoubtedly investigated by that cruiser. So they pulled for shore.

Near the shoreline they encountered an Arab fishing boat whose occupant was all smiles at seeing so many men in small boats. He grinned and gesticulated happily, and spoke to them in his native tongue. Von Mücke and the others tried a succession of languages on him, but the fisherman understood nothing. He seemed to understand the words *français* and *Franzose*, and by conversing loudly and in vigorous sign language plus German, von Mücke was able to gather that indeed the French did occupy Hodeida, thank you very much.

His heart fell, and he was only slightly consoled when the four boats all managed to make the far side of the surf without swamping or capsizing.

The shore was long and sloping. They were through the surf and on the beach, and yet were half a mile from land. They made rafts of the oars and masts and some lifebelts and floated their guns and supplies into shore.

On the shore they encountered two Arabs, who ran away from the landing party in spite of von Mücke's gestures of friendship. Then up came an armed man riding a camel. He was dressed in a red-and-blue uniform, with a headcloth of the Arab style. Von Mücke did not know whether he was a French soldier or of what army, but since the man sat on his camel, pointing a cocked gun in their general direction, he gathered that here was a soldier. He approached the man on the camel alone and without guns, starting from the point about six hundred yards away from the group where the soldier had stopped his camel.

Von Mücke took a few steps forward. The soldier raised his gun. Von Mücke stopped. The soldier lowered his gun. Von Mücke started forward, hopefully. The soldier raised his gun. Von Mücke stopped, and the gun went down; he moved again, and the gun went up. This ballet continued until he reached a point fifty yards from the soldier, where the gun stayed up when he stopped. He went no farther, but began to try to make conversation, an effort as futile as talking with his fisherman acquaintance back in the boat.

After von Mücke had exhausted his knowledge of communication without language, and without the slightest effect, the soldier indicated by a gesture that the party was to remain where it was, and wheeled off.

In the distance von Mücke could see the white houses of Hodeida. What was to be done now?

Kapitänleutnant von Mücke proposed to take his men to hide in the dunes around them and then to send an officer into Hodeida at night to seek information. If the French were truly there, then the next night they would return to the sea and reembark on the *Choising*, making an alternate plan when they could.

He was making ready for a brief march when from behind the sandhills came a swarm of Bedouins, around a hundred strong, all armed with rifles. They formed a skirmish line and dropped down to the ground. The Germans picked up their guns and made ready for a fight. They dropped to the ground, and formed themselves into a loose semicircle, facing the land. Von Mücke waited for the first shot.

Instead of a shot, from the hills came a dozen men, unarmed, who were making gestures that seemed to be peaceful and seemed to call for a meeting. Von Mücke put down his sword and pistol and walked to meet them. Then began the parley.

Von Mücke spoke in German, French, and English. The Bedouins spoke in gibberish as far as he was concerned. He had his German flag brought to the meeting and explained what it was. The Bedouins looked at it, fingered it and nodded understandingly. They had not the slightest idea what it might be.

He pointed to the French cruiser off shore and shook his fist, shouting "boom, boom, boom" as he did so. The Bedouins grinned at his lively act.

The Bedouin leaders then had their turn. One held his head with his hand, as though he had a terrible ache in both temples, and wagged his head violently from side to side to relieve the pain. Another, whom the Germans though might be suffering from neuralgia, passed two fingers up and down his face. A third rubbed his two extended forefingers together.

This last sign was quite clear to von Mücke. He was certain that it meant enemies, because the rubbing was friction. And he pointed to the rubbing and said it was not true. The Arabs knew he did not understand, then, because all these signs were signs of friendship, and this tall, blonde, stupid man was telling them they were not friends but enemies.

Von Mücke's officers had come forward by this time, trying to lend a hand. Leutnant Wellman spoke to the Arabs in Malay. It was as effective as von Mücke's German. In despair, Leutnant Schmidt reached into his pocket and pulled forth a gold piece. He pointed to the head of the Kaiser on it.

"*Aleman! Aleman!*" shouted the Bedouins in instant comprehension, fingering the gold piece.

Immediately the beach became a shambles. The Arabs stacked their guns and then came flying down the dunes, their white and gray and black robes trailing behind them and the sand flying in spurts from beneath their feet. They embraced the Germans, danced wildly around them, shouted words that must mean friendship, and insisted on carrying the Germans' guns and gear. First, however, they insisted on looking into it. The sailors gave them some soap, which sent their new friends into ecstasy, and soon the bundles were shouldered and a certain amount of order was restored to the gathering.

They moved towards Hodeida. The desert seemed grim and empty, but as they came by heads began popping up and soon another hundred armed men and boys joined the procession.

If the French were in possession of Hodeida, they would certainly know that something was coming.

But the French were not in possession. Hodeida was safely in Turkish hands, courtesy of the Arabs. Half an hour after they began, before they reached the city, still another two hundred Bedouins appeared, guns at the ready, wanting to find out what all the shouting was about. They too, joined the throng when they learned about the marvelous gold piece.

Before they reached Hodeida, the German landing party had gathered a crowd of about eight hundred Arabs about them, all armed, all shooting their guns into the air enthusiastically, and most of them dancing about the desert as they went.

An armed party of Turkish soldiers appeared well before they came to the city, cautiously scouting this unknown menace. The Bedouins were able to make themselves understood above the shouting, and the Turks came down from the heights on which they sat, gingerly riding in among the mob. One of the Turkish officers spoke German. After a few words he turned in his saddle and barked a stream of Turkish at a soldier, who dashed off on his horse.

What was that all about, von Mücke wanted to know.

The soldier was going back to the garrison, the officer said. The entire force had been alerted and the artillery was being brought out to repel this landing. The word had come that a large force of British or French had made its way ashore and the entire garrison was on its way to fight.

Now, as they approached the city, von Mücke ordered his men into a military unit, the German war flags flying and their guns carried in military fashion. They stepped smartly as they came into the city, surrounded by Turkish troops and the undisciplined Arabs, and they sang one German marching song after another to keep cadence. From the windows and the streetcorners veiled women and bearded men and naked children and skulking dogs stared at them, and here and there came the clapping of hands and shouts of wonder at the sight of the Germans who had come to help the Turks win the war.

In Hodeida tent houses were quickly put up for the men of the *Emden*. The officers were given a house overlooking the town, from which they could see the French heavy cruiser offshore, making its very effective blockade of the port of Hodeida.

∿∿∿∿∿∿∿∿∿∿∿∿∿∿∿∿∿∿∿∿∿∿∿

Chapter 26

IN THE ABSENCE OF A RAILROAD

THE FIRST FEW HOURS of the German stay in Hodeida were sheer bedlam. It was necessary that they be examined by all in the city with special attention from the city fathers, because it was not often that the Turks had the opportunity to impress the unruly Arabs with the might of their association with the German Empire across the sea.

The men were taken sight-seeing that day. They walked through the narrow streets, staring and being stared at, visiting the local marketplace, buying souvenirs, avoiding dogs and children, and taking off their shoes as they went inside the mosques.

For several days they rested and saw the sights. The Turks would not hear of their leaving immediately and there was no opportunity to send messengers back to the *Choising*'s point of rendezvous. Von Mücke stood on the roof of his borrowed house on the second night and fired three shells from his signaling pistol, the agreed signal that there was grave danger in these waters and that the *Choising* must depart immediately for the neutral port of Massawa. With a heart that must have been much lightened to be away from the demands of the *Emden* party, Captain Minkiewitz steamed away, and eventually he reached the port of Massawa and safety from the enemies who overran those waters.

The Germans were the center of attention for several days. A pasha invited them to a feast, and the entire crew came to his establishment, sat on rich carpets and watched Turkish and Arab dancing girls in their nakedness, smoked water pipes, and ate sheep's eyes.

Von Mücke endured these celebrations stoically. His mind was fixed on their departure, the trip that would take them back to Germany. He consulted with the High Sherif of Hodeida and the colonel in charge of the Turkish regiment. The railroad, alas, existed only in the guidebook.

There were two possible routes to safety. One involved movement through the Red Sea, which, von Mücke learned, was even more heavily infested with British and French warships than he had been given to expect. Daily he could watch some of them move back and forth in the waters beyond his window. Actually, he and the *Choising* had been extremely fortunate, because the allies maintained a blockade north of Hodeida. Had they gone any farther they most certainly would have been stopped and captured. There were adequate supplies for them in Hodeida, and they could have charts of the entire stretch of water that would lead them to Constantinople.

The second possibility involved a trek overland. The Turks advocated this second course and assured Kapitänleutnant von Mücke that all Arabia was quiet and under effective Turkish rule. They would supply the Germans with mules and horses and even more arms than they had brought with them into Hodeida. The only difficulty about the land route was the distance and the slowness of travel through the desert. They could not expect to reach the railhead for about two months.

Von Mücke had already seen that the sea route was extremely dangerous, and he allowed himself to be persuaded that the land route would not entail too much difficulty.

Yet almost immediately he began to encounter some difficulties.

The first problem was the health of the men. On the sea, no matter how hot it became there was a cooling breeze and there was at some time an end to the heat. In Hodeida there was no end to it.

The Germans slept in the garrison and must live in much the same fashion as the Turkish troops if there was not to be friction on every level. The Turkish troops had never heard of sanitation. They slept side by side on a divan constructed of cushions stuffed with straw. They drank unboiled water, and had never heard of malaria prevention. Von Mücke had to inaugurate an entirely new set of regulations and sanitation rules for his men, and some, such as the boiling of water, were difficult to enforce. He ordered every man to keep taking quinine constantly.

Yet a week had not gone by before cases of dysentery and malaria began to break out among the landing party. Von Mücke discovered that there was an alternative: while waiting for the supplies for his caravan he could go to Sana, the chief city of Yemen. Arabs and Turks alike recommended this as a healthful place, high in the mountains, excellent for Europeans who were not used to the warm climate.

The journey overland would take them through Sana anyhow, so von Mücke decided that they would go there immediately, and the supplies and animals would be brought to them at that place. He outfitted his men in new uniforms. He did not have German naval stores at his disposal, but there was plenty of khaki drill cloth and there were enough Turkish tailors in Hodeida to do the job. The men wore khaki trousers and khaki shirts. Their distinguishing mark was a broad-brimmed felt hat which sported a cockade of red, white, and black. It was not a naval uniform, but it was a uniform of sorts, and it was very impressive to the Turks and Arabs, as it was meant to be.

They left Hodeida on the Kaiser's birthday, but only after a celebration of the birthday and their honored presence. German and Turkish soldiers all formed in the middle of the town square, the Germans surrounded by Turks. Kapitänleutnant von Mücke and the Turkish colonel reviewed the troops, and then von Mücke made a speech in German in honor of the Kaiser, and the German and Turkish troops all cheered. The Turkish colonel called for three cheers for the sultan, and the Germans and the Turks all cheered again.

The troops paraded and bands played, and all the men then marched back to the Turkish barracks for a feast of mutton and rice while the officers went to the palace of the mayor of Hodeida for a feast—mutton and rice. At five o'clock in the afternoon the party set out, the Germans all on horses and mules, their baggage carried by donkeys and camels.

Five o'clock was the proper hour. They would travel at night and sleep in the daytime under canvas. It was quite impossible to travel in the heat of the day. The Germans mounted their animals and the Turkish garrison formed a lane down which they passed, the bands playing again as they rode out toward the mountains of Yemen on a journey that would last three weeks.

An hour after leaving Hodeida the caravan was in the heart of the desert. There was no road, not even a trail; occasionally they saw the signs of a previous caravan, but as often as not these were covered by the blowing, drifting sand. All around them was sand, white and yellow sand, with a bit of dry grass tufting here and there.

In the beginning there were many stops, because the sailors kept falling from their mounts, or were thrown in a battle of wits with horse or mule. The officers could ride, for they had the benefit of the gentle life in Tsingtao behind them, but the men could not, and the officers spent much of that first evening chasing riderless animals and resaddling others. From this developed an unusual form for the caravan: The officers rode in the rear, reassembling the troops who had fallen and forming them into a rear guard. All the way this became the pattern.

It was wild and fierce country. The nights were clear and bright and sometimes cold, since the land did not hold the heat of the day. The caravan rode all night every night, stopping only two or three times for half an hour's rest.

No one had told them in Hodeida, for it was common knowledge and not a fig was given for it, that the region through which they must pass was the haunt of robbers and murderers. At the end of the first night of travel they had passed enough skeletons of animals *and men* so that they knew what their fate might be. On the second night out they had another reminder. Suddenly in the moonlight on the side of the road there appeared a dozen heavily armed men, bandoliers of ammunition about their shoulders, mounted on swift riding camels. The Turkish police who accompanied and guided the German war party said these were robbers, and the police advised the men to stop and bring up their arms. This was not difficult since every German was now armed to the teeth. The animals were stopped and the long noses of rifles began to train toward the sides of the ravine that formed a road at that point. The robbers saw that they had a band of heavily armed men to deal with, and they vanished among the dunes.

On the third night out the caravan left the flat desert country and moved into the mountains. These mountains rise almost straight out of the desert to eight thousand feet and more, and now the route was upward. As they rose they moved through narrow twisting ravines and tumbling rocks in streambeds that were quite dry. But eventually they came out of this arid land and into farmland, fruited valleys and forested mountainsides, often topped by stone castles where the sheikhs lived in protection against the marauding bands of robbers.

The farther they traveled the more difficult the trip became. In the last few days before they reached the town of Menakha they crossed by a tortuous mountain trail, with sheer cliff on one side and sheer drop on the other, so steep that the men dismounted often and led their pack animals.

The mess squad and one officer traveled always ahead of the main party, starting a little before them in the evening and arriving at a camping point a few hours earlier, so that when the main body arrived the major meal of the day was ready for them to eat. Then they wriggled off to roll up in blankets and sleep.

Most of the stops were made at caravanserais prepared by the Turkish army for the use of troops. Once in a while a camp was made elsewhere, but it was safest and most comfortable to use these official stopping points, and they were located one day's journey apart.

Menakha represented the attainment of the peaks to the Germans. Several hours before they reached the town they came upon the Turkish garrison, which had marched out to meet and greet them and accompany them in glory into the town. The people cheered and danced and chanted as they came by, and a crowd of white-cloaked civilians bounded ahead of them all the way.

In Menakha the barracks were made of stone, and inside the Turkish soldiers had prepared a feast. Flowers covered the tables and cigarettes and fresh water stood beside dishes of sweets and meats. The town even boasted a hotel, the only one von Mücke saw in all Arabia, and there the officers were quartered in rooms that had real beds. Before they had slept on beds made of wood with rope matting for springs and straw in pallets for mattresses.

The Germans spent two days in this mountaintop resort, and then began their trip downward. Now, wonder of wonders, there was a road, a real road and a broad one that could be compared with a European highway. The long nights in the saddle had made the men of the *Emden* into riders, and they could maintain a formation. They rode easily along the road, looking at the camels grazing along the roadsides and in the distance seeing bands of wild gazellelike creatures and sometimes baboons on the sides of the mountain passes.

Several days of travel brought them to a point where they could see Sana, the capital of Yemen, on the plain below them. Turkish troops rode out to the edge of the plateau when they saw the dust of their visitors. They had been apprised of the coming of the Germans, and they brought a horde of civilians and the garrison band, which had been practicing and played a fair rendition of *Deutschland über alles* to warm the hearts of their guests.

The Germans paraded proudly through the city in company with the Turkish troops, and bands of men and women stood on the sides of the road waving. Even the French consul, who was being detained by the Turks, stepped out on his balcony to watch the Germans pass and listen to the band playing German patriotic songs.

The welcome of the people and the Turkish troops was all that von Mücke could have hoped for, but the welcome of the country itself was not up to his expectations. He had been misled by the exuberance of his hosts in Hodeida, or the miserable climate of that place had done its work already, and the hard trip had helped with the job. Less than a week after their arrival in Sana eighty percent of von Mücke's men were down with fever. Had he been a hygienist, he would have known that the fever must have been contracted elsewhere, and his doctor should have known.

That was not the worst of it. Soon those whose fever was brought under control with quinine came down with colds or with stomach cramps from the rapid changes in temperature and the water.

For two weeks the party rested in Sana. Von Mücke took the time to learn something about the countryside and the city. He discovered that the city, divided into Turkish, Arab, and Jewish quarters, was built as a fortress, with the streets located so they could be swept by gunfire. Yemen was a wild and forbidding place, and only a decade before no Turks were allowed in Sana. They had laid siege to this city and starved it into submission then. They had not starved the countryside into surrender, however, and there were many Arabs outside Sana who would shoot at the sight of a fez or a Turkish uniform.

Von Mücke learned in his two weeks in Sana just how difficult the journey overland would be. They would be surrounded all the way by Bedouin tribes who could not be guaranteed to be friendly. The commander of the Turkish garrison here was much more forthright with his German ally than had been the colonel in Hodeida. The land was not pacified. Their safety could not be guaranteed, although if they wished to proceed the Turks would send troops with them on the journey.

The illness of his men and the dangers from climate and sickness as well as wild enemies were enough to bring pause to any man. The men continued to be sick, and that convinced von Mücke that it would not do to attempt the difficult overland journey. His men were sailors. He told the Turks to stop the preparations for the overland caravan. He would return to Hodeida, and he and his little force would take their chances of travel in the manner they knew best; they would go home by sea.

Chapter 27

PERILOUS VOYAGE

THERE WERE NO garlands of flowers and no hosts of capering villagers to greet the men of the *Emden* as they turned back to Hodeida. The villagers were friendly, but the amusement value of the foreigners had been exhausted, and the Germans were allowed to go their way quietly back to the seacoast. This was a blessing to von Mücke; unhindered by the needs to impress and follow protocol he could now move ahead of the slow caravan and arrive in Hodeida before his officers and men. He took a small party and, mounted on fast horses, they traveled rapidly in the night, reaching Hodeida a day and a half ahead of the others.

The commander of the German party then was able to make plans while his men were still on the road. Having sent the *Choising* away, he had no choice but to find other vessels for travel. It was as well, he knew, because the *Choising* was too large and too much out of character for that region to stand much chance of making her way through the Red Sea unmolested. He must use local transportation.

Von Mücke searched the waterfront at Hodeida, under the nose of the French warship there, and discovered two small sailing boats, each about forty feet long and twelve feet wide, of the variety called zambuks along the Arabian shore. He purchased these in behalf of the German navy with a chit, and had them sent north to the bay of Yabana. It would never do to try to embark from Hodeida. He had been warned that spies must already have told the allies of the presence of a German war party in the area. Von Mücke listened to his informants and carefully made it public that he planned to sail from Isa bay, a few miles away, on March 13. He intended no such thing. The day before he set watch on Isa bay. It was not easy because there was no house or tree or brush to shelter men from the sand. But it *was* easy for von Mücke to observe the antics of the British gunboat which suddenly came into Isa bay that evening, hunting up and down the shore by searchlight for Germans who were supposed to be encamped there waiting for the dawn.

Two days later, March 14, at five o'clock in the evening, Commodore von Mücke set sail from Yabana with his two-ship fleet. They had only one German war flag with them, and this was flown from the masthead of his "flagship." The sick were all aboard the second zambuk, and there were several of them, suffering from malaria, dysentery, and typhus.

Von Mücke had learned something about the manner in which the British were conducting their blockade of the Red Sea. Two gunboats and the auxiliary cruiser *Empress of Russia* were entrusted with carrying out the blockade. Two zambuks might arouse their attention sailing day or night, while one would certainly not. The Red Sea was the home of these vessels and the British could not stop every one of them.

The war party, for that was what one might call von Mücke's boat, as opposed to the sick party in the other, found itself becalmed a few hours after sailing, and the current carried it into the line of search usually followed by the blockaders. Fortunately it was a weekend—von Mücke believed he was unmolested because the British did not ever do anything on weekends, even make war. They drifted until the end of the second day when the wind came up, and they began to make their way north.

Von Mücke chose a difficult course, quite purposefully; he steered along inside the Farsan bank, which runs along the shore of the Arabian peninsula for 350 miles. No oceangoing vessel would come near the bank, because it is guarded on the outside by a series of coral reefs, and even inside the waters are treacherous and filled with shallows. But here was safety of a sort, and here was the place where the zambuks met again, then continued in company.

Now the force numbered seventy men, including German-speaking Arabs who could translate for them, and the crews of the zambuks who were valuable to work the boats and also to appear when necessary to show the enemies of the Germans that these were Arab sailing craft. Each of the forty-foot vessels, then, carried thirty-five men crowded together. The days were extremely trying, and the men of the *Emden* stretched blankets across the ships from the bulwarks, in order to have some shade. They cooked at an open fireplace lined with tin, eating rice and mutton day after day. Occasionally they anchored at night, and one night they were given lodging by a pasha known to some of the Arabs of their crew. But at daybreak they were up again and in the boats, journeying northward.

The trip was extremely slow. The flat-bottomed boats made little headway, and the sails spilled much of the wind without getting full motive power from it. Worst of all was the frequency with which calms settled on the waters close inshore.

In the boats life was as uncomfortable as the men could remember. The Arabs brought lice and bedbugs and fleas and cockroaches with them. The lice were worst: one day a sailor from the *Emden* counted seventy-four of the insects in his shirt.

On March 17, Commodore von Mücke decided to anchor for the night, and to follow that practice thereafter. They were entering an area only vaguely charted on their maps, and the crews of their zambuks did not know the waters. It would not be safe to travel more in the darkness.

That evening they came near the island of Marka, von Mücke's zambuk leading and the other two hundred yards astern. Suddenly the lead boat struck a reef, pounded once, then again, but fell away. Von Mücke ordered the anchor dropped at once and began to examine the craft for damage. Fortunately it was not seriously hurt. Then he tried to signal the men in the second boat to sheer away from the reefs, and the captain of the second zambuk did avoid the reef they had struck, only to impale his boat on another. A flag was run up the masthead, showing that something was wrong, and in a moment von Mücke saw what was the matter. The second zambuk slowly disappeared from sight until only its masthead was showing.

It was just after six o'clock, but it was almost sundown, and near the equator the sun drops and night sets in within a few moments. Nor was there a moon to help them that night, so if they were to save boat or crew they must work quickly.

The anchor was hoisted, the sail was put up, and they moved back through the dangerous water to try to find their comrades. They had no small boats to send out—only a single dugout canoe, and now the sea was running high and the wind was brisker than they liked.

It grew dark suddenly, and von Mücke tried to light the single lantern his zambuk carried. He could not light it; each time he touched a match to the wick the wind blew it out. He had with him a few torches, and he called for them, but they would not light either; they had grown too damp in the months since they had been taken from the stores of the *Emden* for the fateful adventure on Direction Island.

Suddenly, although they were not quite sure where they were at that moment, they heard voices behind them, and discovered that the survivors from the zambuk had reached them and then swum past. Von Mücke shouted back. He was very worried, because this water was known to be heavily infested by sharks. He was worried, too, about the sick aboard the other boat. Had they been able to save themselves or had their comrades saved them?

No light could be made. Finally von Mücke piled firewood in the bottom of the boat, poured gasoline over it, and lighted a bonfire. This was a beacon; it also helped dry their torches until they would burn. He sent off some shots from his signaling pistol, even though these would be visible to any ship within two miles. The chance had to be taken if the party was to be kept together.

His little dugout was sent out, and soon it returned, followed by the dugout of the other zambuk. The men were found, clinging to the wreck or floundering in the water. Swimmers began to arrive alongside and to clamber in or be pulled in, thrashing in their life vests. Before long there were fifty people in the zambuk, and it was apparent that no more could climb in. But more men had to be brought in, almost twenty more. So the crew began jettisoning their belongings; provisions and water and personal treasures were thrown over the side until all that was left were the guns, ammunition and enough food and water for only three days.

The lights lasted just long enough for the last officer to be rescued, then they were left in darkness.

Aboard the flagship, Leutnant Schmidt and the others told their story. Their ship had been holed and had settled rapidly, but not so deeply that they could not remain aboard. They sounded around her and discovered that they lay on the edge of a reef, with a sharp dropoff into which their boat might fall given any twist of current or heavy wind. For the moment, however, they were safe until the flagship could rescue them.

Their plight had been noticed by another zambuk which had come into the lee of Marka island, and a small boat had come to their rescue. Or so it seemed. The small boat had come alongside, and some rapid questions had been shouted in Arabic. Then the men in the boat had seen Dr. Lang's topee and had shouted questions about the nationality of these people. The Arab crew had been forced to admit that these were Europeans, and the owners of the other zambuk swore that the infidel dogs could drown and turned away. They were members of the Idriss tribe, which hated Turks but hated Europeans more.

The next morning von Mücke sent an interpreter to the other zambuk offering a fortune if the captain would sell or even let them rent his ship for a few days. The captain spat and sent the interpreter back with a harsh message. Even if the Germans offered them a hundred thousand English pounds they would do nothing for them. They were infidel dogs and deserved to die.

Von Mücke considered the obvious course, which was to take the zambuk by force, but as he made those plans, dawn broke and with it came a following wind from the south. He could sail, even with his overloaded ship, in this weather, and it would be best not to arouse the Arabs by attacking some of their number if it could be avoided.

The men of the *Emden* moved to the wrecked zambuk, which had tilted off into deeper water but had not yet fallen down the steep side of the reef. They dived and recovered the two machine-guns that had been aboard her and some pistols, rifles and ammunition. But their clothing and, most important, their medical supplies were lost beneath the tilted boat and could not be recovered.

The one blessing was the weather. In one afternoon they made as much mileage as they had made in the previous six days, and that very evening they arrived at the town of Kunfuda, a point almost halfway up the Arabian peninsula. They rested for a few days at Kunfuda, entertained by local officials with feasts night after night. Von Mücke was fortunate enough to be introduced to a traveling Turkish official and his wife. They were seeking passage back to Constantinople and they were glad to join this band of armed men, for they were afraid of robbers and Bedouin tribesmen both on land

and on sea. The official agreed to help von Mücke find another boat and to translate for him if they could come along. It was an admirable arrangement for all concerned.

Through the Turkish official's intervention, they were able to charter a large zambuk, one almost twice as large as their flagship, and they abandoned the old boat and took to the new, the entire landing party, with the Turkish official and his wife. Now they seemed to be out of difficulty. This ship sailed like a ship, and it had decent accommodations, at least for the officers and the civilians. There seemed to be no reason why they could not sail on and safely arrive at some port where they could take transportation to Constantinople.

All went well as far as El Lith, a few miles north of Kunfuda. There they stopped for provisions and to learn the news. From this point on they would go into the open sea, for here was the end of the Farsan bank that kept the foreign ships away from the Arab shore. It was fortunate that they stopped, for through the Turkish official they came into possession of a letter from a merchant in Jidda, the port to which they were next bound. The merchant wrote that Jidda was blockaded by the British and that no ship, not even a zambuk, was allowed to enter the harbor until after it was inspected by a British naval boarding party.

That was the end of the voyage of the men of the *Emden* in the Red Sea. Now Kapitänleutnant von Mücke knew he had no recourse but to travel overland, and he began looking for the animals and supplies he would need to take a camel caravan across the desert. He had never led a camel caravan before, and he had never crossed a long expanse of desert before, but what difference did that make to an officer of His Imperial Majesty's Navy who must take his landing party back to duty?

Chapter 28

THE CARAVAN

IN A WORLD seeking rules of conduct for a new kind of war, the exploits of the *Emden* had come already under more than the usual attention. The *Emden* would have become legendary anytime anywhere, for the concept of a single vessel invading the heartland of its enemy and scourging the seas for weeks on end would always appeal to human beings. In the twentieth century, when men were being ringed by government, and group action was infringing steadily on the individual, such an effort was bound to appeal to men on every level of society in every civilized land. As Kapitänleutnant von Mücke guided his zambuk into El Lith the world was still buzzing with the story of the *Emden*, and he found that it had penetrated even to this outpost of Turkish civilization. On the sinking of the *Emden* the Kaiser had telegraphed the people of Emden town, promising a newer, larger *Emden* "on whose bows the Iron Cross will be affixed in memory of the fame of the old *Emden*." The press in Germany, Austria and the neutral countries expressed the greatest admiration for Captain von Müller's "valor and initiative." Even in England the London *Daily News* wrote that von Müller was "a gallant man, full of resource and chivalry." The *Times* said, "If all the Germans had fought as well as the captain of the *Emden*, the German people would not today be reviled by the world."

That was the point. The Germans were proud of von Müller's remarkable exploits as a warrior. Germany's enemies were comforted by his chivalry and regard for the rights of noncombatants. The performance of the *Emden* was in glaring contrast to the "total war" theory of the German general staff, which led to the massacre of thousands of Belgian civilians because of the resistance of others to the German occupation. The story of the *Emden* spread everywhere in the world, and although it was encouraged by German propagandists it need not have been; people everywhere recognized it as one of the epics of the sea.

When von Mücke's little ship entered El Lith harbor, four months and seventeen days had passed since the morning on which the landing party of the *Emden* stepped into the cutters and the steam pinnance to leave their ship forever. Von Mücke did not know it, but from one source and another little bits of his odyssey were beginning to trickle out to the world. There was the report of the civilians of Direction Island in the first place. They told of the encounter with von Mücke and his men. Two and a half weeks later came the report that the *Ayesha* had sailed into, and out of, Padang in the Dutch East Indies. Then there was nothing until the *Choising* made her way into Massawa in January, then again the silence closed in until the spies reported to the British that a German war party was lurking near Hodeida.

In Germany there was much misinformation and speculation about the fate of these men of the *Emden*; it was believed that they had sailed the *Ayesha* all the way across the Indian Ocean and halfway through the Red Sea. In the Indian Ocean even in the winter months of 1915 captains kept reporting that they had sighted the schooner, armed to the teeth, continuing depredations against shipping.

So the continuing interest in Germany and in the neutral countries caused the newspapers to keep the story of the *Emden* quite alive all these months.

The one valuable asset this publicity gave the men of the *Emden* was to make their credit unquestioned; otherwise the story of their travels might have ended at El Lith, for now they must equip a camel caravan and set forth across the wide desert.

Von Mücke was as indefatigable as usual. He was first up in the morning and last to bed at night, attending to a thousand details. The saddest was the funeral of Seaman Keil, who died at three o'clock on the morning of March 27, as they lay in El Lith harbor. He was not yet twenty years old and with his natural vigor he might have survived even the attack of typhus that had brought him down in Hodeida, but the wetting of the shipwreck and the loss of all the party's medicines had been too much. Early on the morning of

March 27 the others sewed his body into canvas, weighted it with stones, and after a brief religious service rowed the body out to sea and tilted the bier against the side of the boat, and the shrouded figure sank into the Red Sea. Von Mücke led the services and took the boat out to deep water. Then he came ashore to make the men ready for departure.

It was not easy to find camels in El Lith, so he took his Turkish friend and went to call on the sheikh. They drank innumerable cups of strong, sweet coffee and ate from the carcass of a whole roast sheep which was torn to pieces by servants before them.

In two days von Mücke rounded up ninety camels. He purchased straw mats and food and water for the journey. He supervised the boiling of the water and the loading of the camels. He knew nothing about camels, but he made it his affair to learn, and in those two days he acquired a very fair knowledge of the art of loading and goading a recalcitrant ship of the desert.

On March 28 the men of the *Emden* set forth with their ninety camels and the promise that twenty more laden with supplies would meet them within a few days. The officers rode on free camels, but the riding camels of the men were fastened together by ropes, the muzzle of one camel tied to a rope four yards long that was then tied to the tail of the camel in front. This was slow going, but safe, for if the men had difficulty in learning to ride horses, they would have met tragedy in coping with riding camels in the heat of the desert.

The caravan route they followed wound along the sand hills quite close to the sea. It was regarded as the least dangerous of all the routes; this was one area later scourged by the rebel Arabs led by T. E. Lawrence, the British officer who was to create as vigorous a legend as the men of the *Emden*. The coastal route was supposed to be safe, but the men of the *Emden* kept their rifles oiled and loaded and at hand on the backs of their camels.

The march was long each day. It began at four o'clock in the afternoon and lasted until nine or ten the following morning, when the heat became too intense for further travel. They stopped then, when they reached an oasis, or a well.

The travelers could not possibly take with them enough water for the journey, so they were forced to depend as did the Arabs of the desert on these wells and the brackish dirty water they contained. At every stop one of the first moves was to build fires, draw up the water in leather buckets, and boil the water. Von Mücke was insistent on this practice, and he and his officers patrolled the camp to make sure there were no violations of the rule.

In the beginning, from El Lith, the party was accompanied by a Turkish police officer and seven of his men. The sheikh was also with them, following the Turkish custom of taking as hostage the chief law-enforcement official of the region when important government officers or visitors were traveling. This was the Turkish concept of control in Arabia in 1915.

Four days out from El Lith, the party arrived at a well which was said to be just one day's march from Jidda, the party's next objective. Here the Turks from El Lith left them, along with the sheikh of El Lith, and they were greeted by an officer and seventeen Turkish policemen from Jidda—but no sheikh. The entire party lay down on straw mats and woolen blankets, pushing in as far as possible among the thorny desert plants to find protection from the blazing sun. Von Mücke and his officers supervised the cooking of the usual rice and mutton; he, now sporting a pink turban, walked smartly among the campfires, encouraging his men with a word or a pat on the shoulder here and there. He had grown more slender than ever and seemed taller and younger than his thirty-three years, in spite of the yellow beard that covered his brown face. The sharpness that had been part of his job as first officer of the *Emden* seemed to have disappeared; even with the added responsibility of command, he was making a better impression on his men as captain than he had as first officer. He was gentler, for one thing, made so by the sickness and death and the knowledge that these men—boys, most of them—were being asked to undertake the impossible.

He was determined to take them back to Germany. This idea dominated his thinking every moment, and it left no room for petty emotions or unfair judgments of the men. The men sensed von Mücke's purpose, his dedication and his superiority. They were awed by his ability to do anything: bargain with a pasha or saddle a camel. He had shown them that he could navigate across an ocean without a chart; he had done it twice, once in an unfamiliar sailing ship and once in a steamer. The men would now go anywhere he asked and do anything he wished without question. There was no more of the talk of him as a Prussian that had been heard by the British on Direction Island.

When von Mücke saw the Turkish party that had come to meet them he was ready to relax. He had been told that this was a danger spot, because this area around Jidda was the home of a tribe which claimed direct descent from the prophet and called itself Father of the Wolf. But if eighteen men could come out from Jidda unmolested, then he was quite sure that they and the fifty of his party could reach Jidda now without incident. He lay down to rest for a few hours with a sense of relief.

At four o'clock in the afternoon the party struggled out of the sand and began to move ahead. The route now took them away from the Red Sea, inland among sand hills that undulated across the horizon, cutting visibility in any direction to around four hundred yards. The hills were covered with rough desert grass which grew here about two feet high.

Darkness came and the caravan continued to move forward. The moon came up and reflected brightly on the sand. Not long afterward there suddenly appeared a dozen Bedouins on horseback, who came out from behind a hill on the right and vanished down the trail which the caravan had just vacated. The police officers took tight hold of their guns. These were robbers, the Turkish commander told von Mücke, probably part of a band of about forty who had been terrorizing caravans in the area during recent weeks.

Von Mücke did not become too concerned about forty bandits, since his party consisted of nearly seventy armed men, including the police. Still, he was careful. He divided his camels into two lines of fifty, and he and his officers examined every man's gun and warned each man against going to sleep on his camel.

All was quiet that night, except for the soft clopping of the camels in the sand as they moved at their jolting trot across the desert. At dawn von Mücke began to relax again; it was common knowledge that the Bedouins never attacked in the daytime. He slung his rifle across his saddle, took the heavy cartridge belt off his waist, and began to ride back down the line from the front to check his men.

Suddenly, as he reached the midpoint of the caravan, he heard a loud whistle, a signal, followed immediately by a volley of rifle fire that came from all directions. They were ambushed, caught between the dunes on the left and ahead, and the foothills of a range of mountains on the right. From cover on every side the Arab bandits were firing down on the caravan.

Von Mücke leaped off his camel, grabbing his rifle as he ran, and shouted for his men to follow him to the head of the caravan, where the firing seemed heaviest. As he moved up he could see that the enemy was about eighty yards away. He could see very little more but he was comforted because neither could the raiders. The men were on the ground; the bandits were firing at flashes and at the silhouettes of the camels.

Von Mücke now began to dispose his force. Some men were sent back to reinforce the rear guard. The important task, however, was to bring out the machineguns, which would give the caravan an infinite superiority of firepower. Two of these guns were strapped to the backs of camels at the head of the column and two were at the rear. In a few minutes all four guns were out and trained. In the front, von Mücke ordered his gunners to fire a few bursts and when this was done suddenly the desert became quiet. The raiders had not expected their victims to be so heavily armed.

During the lull of the next few minutes von Mücke and his officers brought the men into a concentration at the left front, where the fire had been heaviest and where he supposed the most of the raiders were hidden. The camels were pulled in and made to lie down so they would not provide such outstanding targets. The officers were assigned to small details of men.

Von Mücke was fortunate in having the officers he did. When he left the *Choising* he had been joined by one of that ship's mates, Leutnant Gerdts. He had been invaluable in the sea voyage aboard the zambuks, for he was an experienced seaman. Leutnant Wellman had been a fine source of information all the way from Sumatra. Dr. Lang's function was obvious. Now von Mücke was to see the particular abilities of his two young lieutenants who had come with him all the way from the *Emden*. These were Leutnant Schmidt and Leutnant Gyssling, both barely promoted from ensign, both in their very early twenties. Leutnant Schmidt came from a naval family of some renown; his father was admiral in charge of the naval facilities at Kiel. Both young lieutenants were originally assigned to the *Gneisenau* but were attached to the *Emden* when it became apparent that the *Emden* would need men familiar with infantry tactics and officers capable of leading boarding and landing parties. Both were well trained in hand-to-hand fighting.

When the men of the *Emden* had set forth in their zambuks they had been heavily armed. But the sinking of the second zambuk had cost them much of their armament. Now they counted up the weapons. They had the four machineguns, and three modern Turkish rifles von Mücke had acquired in El Lith, but of the old *Emden* rifles only thirteen had been saved from the shipwreck. They also had ten old Turkish rifles which were neither reliable nor accurate.

The three modern Turkish rifles were given to the three best shots among the officers, and the other guns were shared out among the men. Beside this firepower the party had twenty-four pistols which could be used at short range.

The sailors, as soon as the rifles were handed to them, fixed bayonets on them, and in a few minutes all the rifles were so equipped, although von Mücke had not issued any such order.

As the sun began to come over the horizon, they could see their enemy. The sand hills were dotted with black and gray figures; von Mücke estimated that there must be at least three hundred Arabs around them.

They waited uncomfortably. One young sailor on the right asked permission to ask a question. Von Mücke assented. The sailor wanted to know how soon they were going to charge the enemy with their bayonets.

Von Mücke did not hesitate. Under the cover of the machineguns, the men with rifles charged out, first to the left, then to the right. The Bedouins faded away before them, falling back rather than engaging in hand-to-hand combat.

Another charge and they had enlarged the circle of their perimeter to about 1,200 yards. This was more comfortable. The machine guns were spread out, each to cover a section of the perimeter, and the party sat down to wait. The enemy had backed away and firing had stopped again completely.

Von Mücke stopped to count noses. Only one German sailor was wounded, but all the policemen had vanished except seven, and among their Arab camel drivers, nearly all were either dead or wounded. The wounds were uniformly in the legs and buttocks. Von Mücke puzzled over this for a few minutes, but the answer came.

The camel drivers had taken refuge among the camels when the shooting began, and had thus put themselves directly into the line of fire. The Bedouins, used to such evasion, had fired beneath the standing camels and between their legs and had thus taken the heavy toll of the drivers.

Looking around, outside their perimeter, they found fifteen dead Bedouins but were able to recover only one enemy rifle, a British gun of the most modern type.

The Arabs had moved off to distant sand hills out of respect for the machineguns and bayonets, but they were still there in force, waiting in the sun. The heat of day was approaching, and the caravan could not remain long in the sun without shelter. Von Mücke decided to move.

A third of the camels were dead or injured. They were stripped of necessities, and the sound camels were loaded with only necessities. Von Mücke abandoned the camel caravan route and turned left to find the sea, intending to follow its shores so that at least he would have flank protection on one side.

The caravan was now divided into six lines of camels which traveled abreast. The wounded Arabs and the one German sailor were strapped to camels so that they hung on the inside flanks of the beasts and were protected from bullets by the animals. Two camels bearing machine guns were put at the head of the column and two brought up the rear. Now twenty men were detached from the column. Ten, under officers, were sent out forward on their camels as skirmishers, and ten dropped back 150 yards to form a rear guard.

Except for nine men, this disposition exhausted the supply of rifles. The nine were split, five on one side and four on the other, and they became flank guards. The pistols were allocated to the other men, who would ride in the main body of the caravan. They would not carry far but they would be valuable in close combat. Leutnant Gerdts took the advance guard, Leutnant Schmidt took the rear guard, Leutnant Gyssling was in charge of the flankers, and Leutnant Wellman and the doctor remained with the caravan itself. Von Mücke prowled back and forth, watching every side and every motion.

The caravan set forth again, this time flying the German flag and banner. If there were any mistake on the part of the attackers, this was their opportunity to remedy it. There was no mistake. Ten minutes later the fire began again. The Arabs were riding on all sides of them, out of sight, and stopping to ascend a sand mound and fire off a few harrying shots. The shots came from every direction, but they were concentrated in the rear. From Leutnant Schmidt's area came constant sounds of fire, and on going back, Von Mücke learned that Schmidt and his men were forced to stop every few hundred yards to return the enemy fire. When they did so, the enemy faded away, only to reappear in another position in five minutes.

Von Mücke was investigating this rear-guard problem when the enemy increased their activity suddenly. One of the machine-gun camels fell, and Leutnant Schmidt stopped the rear guard to protect the gun while it was taken off the dead camel and repacked on a live one. Just then von Mücke was called to the front, where Leutnant Gerdts was in trouble. The whole area ahead was dotted with figures, and the rate of fire was increasing. The attack was being launched again.

Von Mücke arrived at the front, pursued by a sailor, who reported the events in the rear guard. Firing had increased there, too.

Von Mücke could hear it. From the rear the two machineguns were firing. He gave the signal to stop the caravan. Now all the Arab drivers who could move ran away to join the Bedouins and the other camel drivers, and the Germans and their few police companions were left alone. It was not easy to stop the caravan and force the camels to lie down, but the officers had seen von Mücke do it, and they now pushed and pulled to bring the caravan to some kind of unity in a protected position.

Von Mücke moved to the rear guard to see what was happening, afoot now, having forced his camel to lie on the ground. He found one seaman, Rademacher, dead on the ground, and Leutnant Schmidt shot through the chest and through the abdomen. Either wound was fatal. He was lying, conscious and gasping, on the ground.

As von Mücke looked around the perimeter, Leutnant Wellman came up with two camels to retrieve the machineguns, and he was placed in charge of the rear guard.

Suddenly the firing stopped and von Mücke looked up to see two of their remaining Arab policemen running toward the Bedouins, carrying large white flags. Another, one of the few now remaining, said they had gone to parley with the enemy.

Von Mücke realized now that it was an enemy, and not robbers as he had believed. He had no faith in talk, but the knowledge
that this was an organized force changed his course of action. He
decided to fortify his position as best he could and remain where he
was, awaiting help. Thus the machineguns could be used for protection. It was simply a question of how long they could hold out and
how long it would be before a relieving force arrived, bringing water,
food, and ammunition.

The Turkish official, one of those wounded in the leg, took
his wife and went to join the police in the parley with the Arabs.

The men were put to work digging in the sand. The camels
were unsaddled and moved to a central point, to become the hub of
the defense. The saddles were filled with sand and dotted about the
perimeter to make a rampart. Between them sacks of rice and coffee
and other provisions were piled, and sand was heaped around to make
a wall. The bottles containing the precious water were buried in the
sand where they would be as safe as possible from gunfire. Inside
the perimeter another rampart was made, about four feet high, constructed of empty petroleum cans filled with sand. This was to be
the hospital. Leutnant Schmidt could be carried there to join the
wounded German soldier and the wounded Arabs. Dr. Lang presided
over this makeshift infirmary.

The lull lasted for some time. There was time to bury seaman
Rademacher and to make a stretcher to transport Leutnant Schmidt.
The four machineguns were set up at the edges of the perimeter,
and the riflemen were scattered between them.

The preparations were all made when the Arab policemen
returned from their parley with the Bedouin leaders, bearing conditions for a truce. The Germans were to give up all their arms and
ammunition, to surrender their camels and their food and water. If
they would sign a note on their government to pay eleven thousand
gold pounds to the Bedouins, then they would be allowed to go in
peace. The Turkish official did not return.

Von Mücke was quite certain that if they gave up their arms
they would be massacred, or at the very least imprisoned and held for
ransom. He had no intention of surrendering, and he said so, whereupon the firing began again.

Chapter 29

THE SIEGE

KAPITÄNLEUTNANT VON MÜCKE knew that the German position was extremely perilous. They were short of ammunition, and even shorter of dependable ammunition. When the firing began again he broke into some of the extra ammunition that had been carried on the second zambuk, had been sunk, and had been rescued. Several riflemen reported that some of the cartridges would not fire. Von Mücke gathered up the good ammunition then and distributed it carefully among the machineguns. A rifleman could eject a bad cartridge and replace it quickly. The jamming of a machinegun at this point might be fatal.

From the sand hills the Bedouins continued firing, sometimes heavily, sometimes lightly, until darkness. They made no attempt to rush the German position, warned away by the ugly snouts of the Maxim guns.

Inside the perimeter, von Mücke and his men prepared to resist a night attack. The firing had not caused any more casualties, except among the camels, and von Mücke was not concerned about them; a dead camel was probably better protection against gunfire than a live one, until the decay set in.

All day the Germans kept flat behind their ramparts. If a man raised his head he drew fire. Under these circumstances there was little movement; only von Mücke crawled about the sand, checking his defenses and speaking to his men.

The logical time for an enemy charge was the few minutes after sunset before the moon began to rise. Then darkness was so black that the defenders could scarcely see their ramparts and nothing beyond them was visible. They were ready and waiting nervously for the whistle's sound, the shots, and the yells of charging tribesmen, but out in the blackness nothing stirred.

When the moon came up, von Mücke could see some three hundred yards outside their position. Lookouts were posted so they would not be surprised, and then he set the men to work to improve the tiny fortress. First the dead camels had to be removed. In the heat of the day they had already begun to stink, and by the next day they would be unbearable. They were dragged out to the south of the perimeter, since the prevailing wind at this season was from the north. The Arab attackers, and not the defenders, would have the benefit of the odor. The carcasses had already swelled and the entrails had burst through. The flies had come.

Water was served out in careful rations and hardtack was broken out from one of the cases and given out to the men. Now trenches were made around the perimeter so the men could move a little and would not be forced to crawl along the ground.

At nine o'clock, Leutnant Schmidt died. Von Mücke ordered the men to dig a grave as deep as possible in the center of the perimeter, and he and the other officers carried their comrade to it. There was no sewing in a sack, no burial service, no volley of fire over the grave. They could not waste their ammunition on the dead.

By midnight the trenches had been deepened, the perimeter strengthened, and the wounded cared for. It should have been time for rest. But not for Kapitänleutnant von Mücke. He made his way slowly around the camp, checking each man's gun and helping clean and test it. The machineguns were gone over. The men wrapped their handkerchiefs around the firing mechanisms and stuffed cloth into the muzzles to keep the sand out. Then he set up watches, as on shipboard. Half the men would sleep while the others stayed on guard. Always at least one officer was awake and touring the perimeter.

The men slept with their guns in their hands that night, but there was no attack. Von Mücke slept hardly at all. Late that night when the moon had gone down, he dispatched a man for assistance. It was not a German, for the chances of a German making his way to Jidda through the lines were so slim as to be negligible. The messenger was an Arab, one von Mücke was inclined to trust because he had served the Germans as interpreter and handyman all the way from Hodeida.

Half an hour before sunrise, von Mücke awakened his men.

If there was to be an attack that morning it would come with dawn. He proposed, if the enemy began to fire, to return it with such vigor that the Arabs would overestimate their supply of ammunition and would remain wary. He estimated that it was about ten hours to Jidda and that if the messenger got through, they should be able to expect relief that night or the next morning. Now it was a problem of holding out. If the messenger had not gotten through, it was still a problem of holding out.

Von Mücke had been correct in his estimate of the enemy's intentions. As dawn broke and the sun came up suddenly behind the hills, a volley of fire broke out all around the camp, and a wave of firing followed it. The Germans fired back at every head that appeared and the machineguns fired a few bursts. If they were short bursts, that information did not seem to mean anything to the Arabs.

The shooting died down quickly, and during the morning shots were fired only when there was movement in the camp.

As the sun rose and began to beat down in its desert ferocity, the men lay in their trenches, seeking what shelter they could from the parapet and shirts thrown up around their heads.

Just before the morning attack each man had a drink of water and was given a handful of hardtack. He would have no other food or water until night fell; there was no way of moving outside the trenches without exposing men to fire. The Germans learned that early in the day when two of the seamen became careless and exposed themselves. Both were wounded in the body, and the officers moved out to rescue them and drag them into the inner enclosure.

That day a camel suddenly raised up on its hindlegs and then its fores and leaped across the parapet, running for the sand dunes to the north. A shot from one of their enemies brought the animal down, very close to the camp. By midafternoon the camel's hide had split and the noxious stench of rotting flesh was coursing across the perimeter.

That afternoon, as the men of the *Emden* lay in the heat, fighting sand and black beetles that overran their camp in search of food and camel dung, von Mücke could look across to the sea and watch peculiar activity there. He saw two zambuks pulled in to shore and from them an unending stream of Arabs carrying provisions back and forth. Far out in the desert he could also see camels grazing. So some of his enemies had come by sea and some by land, and they were prepared for a long siege. He estimated the enemy force now at eight hundred men.

He was not prepared for siege. The wounded were suffering terribly. All the medicines of the party had gone down in that second zambuk; all that remained were the emergency dressings the men carried in their kits and a few bottles of brandy for anesthetic.

The heat was sapping and dangerous. The men burned their hands on the barrels of their rifles. They could not wear the head-cloths they had adopted from the Arabs, because the colors were bright and would bring enemy fire. Von Mücke took off his pink turban, and his head ached and his eyes swam in the sun.

It grew so hot that the grease-soaked camel saddles around the perimeter began to smoke and threatened to burst into flame before the men doused them with hot sand.

The sand drifted in the wind and the men were put to work repairing the trenches. The sand got into their eyes and made them red from weeping. It caked their nostrils and cracked their lips and rubbed their faces raw. The sweat got into the cracks and their lips and faces swelled and turned red and gray.

All afternoon vultures circled the camp, attracted by the smell from the rotting camel meat. Their presence was unnerving, but they did not dare to land.

As darkness fell and the expected attack again did not materialize in the dangerous hour after sunset, von Mücke's confidence wavered. What if the messenger he had sent had defected to the enemy? He dispatched two more Arabs—two of the remaining police, who tore up their uniforms and managed to look as much like Bedouins as possible. He counted the hours. Ten hours to Jidda, ten hours back, and half a day to prepare for the fight. If the man had gotten through, relief could be expected that night.

No relief came. The men slept and guarded in shifts. At midnight the sleepers were aroused by shots, and von Mücke crept to the guard post from which they had come.

"Where are they?" he said.

"Straight ahead," said the guard. "There goes one now,"

He fired at a slinking shape about forty yards from the perimeter. Von Mücke strained his eyes in the night. Soon he could see that the shape had four legs and a tail. It was a jackal, making a meal from one of the camels.

That night one of the wounded died.

As dawn broke the next morning, von Mücke took stock. This would be the last day. By nightfall they would have exhausted their strength, and any amount of rationing of water and food could only spell disaster after that. They faced an enemy who was well supplied from the sea, who obviously had plenty of water and food and ammunition. They had only two chances. The relief column would come, or they must fight their way out and try to make it to Jidda by night.

He moved among the officers and the men giving his instructions. They were to stay in the position all day, conserving their strength and ammunition. When darkness fell, they were to force their way through to Jidda. The sick and wounded would have to be deserted; only thus could any of them hope to survive.

Around noon of this third day an Arab appeared on the hill before them waving a white flag and von Mücke beckoned him in. The Bedouin leaders had reduced their demands, the messenger said. They would settle now for promise of payment of twenty-two thousand pounds in gold. The Germans could keep their arms and ammunition and food and water.

Although his arms were few, his ammunition nearly exhausted, his water gone except for a drink for each man that evening, and his food reduced to rice and hardtack, von Mücke pretended that the caravan could hold out for weeks. He pointed to a stack of empty cans and said he was indicating part of their water supply. As for ammunition, it was only because of Christian charity that they had not descended on the Arabs with the machineguns and wiped them out. No, he said, they would not accept the offer. The Arabs could go back and fight some more.

Von Mücke reasoned that the Arabs would not be coming to him if they did not know something was happening. He hoped the word had gotten through to Jidda and that the relief column was on its way. He could not tell.

So von Mücke stalled.

The emissary went back with his high-flown statements, to return in half an hour and repeat the original offer. Von Mücke said he wanted to talk to their leader. The envoy returned to the Arab lines and came back a second time to report that if the Germans did not agree at once to the terms there would be plenty of fighting. Von

Mücke said there had already been plenty of fighting and the dispirited negotiator went away.

In a few moments the camp rang with shots. The Arab fire
was heavier than it had been at any time since the beginning of the
siege. Then, suddenly, it stopped. A quarter of an hour passed and
there was not a sound. Another fifteen minutes went by, and von
Mücke cautiously raised his head. The horizon was empty. The zambuks were gone. No camels stood grazing on the hills; there were no
camels about at all except their few mangy live ones and the evil-
smelling dead ones around the perimeter.

Soon he arose cautiously. There was no fire. The others arose.
Still the air was silent. They sent out searchers. The Arabs were gone,
every camel, every robe, every gun of them.

The men were anxious to be off, even on foot, with the camels
left to carry the wounded, but von Mücke would not move by day.
It might be a ruse, and the enemy might be lurking beyond the next
hill. In any event he would not travel until nightfall.

An hour went by, then in the distance two figures on camel-
back appeared, carrying a white flag. They dismounted and identified
themselves as representatives of the emir of Mecca, who had heard
of the attack on the Germans and had sent troops to relieve them.

Von Mücke scarcely believed them. He had approached the
parley with cocked pistol and drawn sword and he did not put them
down. The Arabs seemed to understand his disbelief, but quite comfortably they reassured him. Abdullah, second son of the emir, would
soon appear leading the relief and they would see. It was true; in half
an hour along came a troop of some seventy camel-borne soldiers,
carrying a red banner marked in Arabic. It bore verses from the Koran,
the interpreter said. The Arabs were chanting and some of them were
beating on drums as they came.

Prince Abdullah rode up to the gathering and presented his
father's greeting and apologies for the attack by the Bedouins. Now
they could go to Jidda in peace, and Abdullah and his troops would
accompany them.

It took the Europeans some time, with the help of the Meccan
soldiers, to round up the camels, saddle them, and get the caravan's
supplies loaded again. Many supplies had to be left behind, because
forty of the camels had been shot.

Late in the afternoon they were ready to go, and they began to march, accompanied by Abdullah and his men. At evening they came to an oasis and there they stopped. Von Mücke wanted his men to wash and clean up before appearing in Jidda. They camped at the oasis, and the next morning they rode in dignity into the city.

~~~~~~

Chapter 30

THE LAST LAP

AT JIDDA the wounded were placed in a clean Turkish military hospital and Kapitänleutnant von Mücke rested with his men for a few days, considering again the best manner in which they might make their way to the railroad. In spite of the strenuous adventures of the last week, they had come only a few miles and were nearly as far as ever away from the railroad to Constantinople and Berlin.

For the moment, he had enough of travel by camel caravan. Their diminished number and diminished supply of ammunition was an important factor in the making of this decision, but von Mücke, the seaman, again preferred to entrust his fortunes to the sea, even when he could gaze down from the window of the house in which he stayed and see the British destroyers and patrol boats coursing up and down the waters off the port. It would never do to allow the British to believe that he would brave the sea again, so von Mücke carefully planted the story that he was traveling overland again. He met, once again, with the Turkish official and his wife who had deserted the caravan when it was under siege, and he told them this story as well.

At the same time he purchased a new large zambuk in the name of His Imperial Majesty and hired an experienced pilot and crew.

He borrowed a motor launch and each day scoured the harbor, trying to ascertain the pattern followed by the British in their blockade. On the night of April 8 the wounded were taken from the hospital, with the assurance of Dr. Lang that they were fit for travel, at least by ship, and the zambuk was loaded and set to sea. The wind held steady all night long and by daybreak they were well away from the coast of Jidda, hugging the shoreline far north, creeping behind the reefs.

The party stopped frequently at little towns, partly because this gave them a leisurely air and partly to obtain news about the movement of the British in the waters offshore and to buy provisions for the voyage. They could not buy mountains of provisions in Jidda without ruining von Mücke's cover story. They anchored every night, as did every other zambuk in the Red Sea, running in close to shore and planting their anchors in the coral reefs just below the surface of the water. At the next large port, Sherm Rabigh, they changed zambuks, because the one they had chosen at Jidda was too small. This occasioned some refitting and supply, but did not delay them long; in a few days they were on the sea again.

It was a most uneventful voyage. They passed a few fishing boats and some coastal zambuks traveling southward, but saw no British ship or other sign of Europeans, and on April 28 they arrived at Sherm Munnaiburra, a tiny bay south of El Wegh, the town inland where they would head by camel caravan toward the railroad at El Ala. This decision was made almost on a moment's notice: von Mücke somehow felt uneasy about continuing the sea voyage, and, leaving their provisions aboard the zambuk, they found camels and began the overland trip.

On April 29 they found enough camels in El Wegh to begin the trek to the railroad. They bathed in El Wegh, and changed their clothing, dressing more or less as they would out of sheer need. Most of them had lost their campaign hats with the red, white and black cockades. Their shirts and trousers had been torn and wrecked in the shipwreck and the siege. They found other clothing; some wore fezzes, some wore Arab headcloths, and von Mücke retained his pink turban.

On May 2, 1915, at eight o'clock in the morning, the men of the *Emden* boarded their camels and set forth for the railhead. Before them had gone the news that they were coming, and in Germany this had created a sensation. The important biographer and man of letters Emil Ludwig was commissioned by a number of newspapers to rush to Constantinople and to Damascus to greet them.

The men were familiar enough now with camels that they could safely follow the custom of this northern country and guide their own mounts without being tied together in caravan. The sheikh of El Wegh accompanied them, not because he was a hostage but because he was honored to join these men about whom the Turkish world was talking. They traveled through desert again, and then moved into the mountains, where it was possible to travel by day and sleep at night. The Arabs were surprised that first night and thereafter to see the Germans build revetments and trenches before going to sleep. The results of the siege were lasting, and von Mücke did not trust anyone at this point. There was one more point of uneasiness. To travel to El Ala they must cross the domain of another sheikh, who was at odds with Suleiman Pasha and was angry because although he had sent emissaries when he knew the foreigners were coming, they had not agreed to dismount from Sulieman Pasha's camels and rent camels from him for the last four hours of their trip to the railway. Their sheikh friend indicated that they might well have to fight their way through those last few miles, and he gathered a considerable force of his adherents around the caravan, prepared to do so.

Fortunately the unfriendly one turned out to be engaged in some other unpleasant enterprise north of their route, and the men of the *Emden* and their large escort passed through his territory unhindered. When the news came that all was well, von Mücke rode on ahead of the caravan to reach the station at El Ala and order a train for his men. They arrived at noon to find a special train waiting, along with Emil Ludwig, another German, and several Turkish officials, who had traveled for fifty hours from Damascus to greet the returning heroes. There were letters, there was news, and there were the comforts of civilization: a bath, a glass of Rhine wine, and some conversation in civilized German with some civilized people.

When the men arrived a few hours later, von Mücke formed

them on the edge of the village into a marching unit and they came smartly, their battle flags flying, up to the train. In a few moments it started, and began carrying them homeward at the rate of twenty miles an hour.

By rail they traveled to Damascus and Aleppo, then across Asia Minor to Constantinople. The train stopped often and there were many gifts. There were new naval uniforms, sent from His Majesty's ship *Breslau*; there were presents and messages, including word from the Kaiser himself that they had been awarded the Iron Cross. Von Mücke was given the Iron Cross first class for his exploits, plus the Saxon Johanniter order and the Bavarian Cross. He blushed in pleasure as he read the formal notices. Leutnant Gyssling, too, received the Bavarian Cross.

Von Mücke sent telegrams along the way. His first was to the German high naval command, asking for a new ship so he could fight against the enemy. His second was to his mother and father in Saxony, announcing his safe arrival in friendly lands.

On the train that first night, the officers and men celebrated with champagne and brandy, and before they were finished, late in the night, not a bottle was left unopened. In the small hours of the morning, Emil Ludwig walked through the train, seeing the men sleeping wherever there was a place to lie, and he wondered at how young and unprotected they all appeared, not a man over thirty years of age except von Mücke, thirty-three.

The train trip to Constantinople took seventeen days. Every day there were stops and the local officials came out to greet the heroes and pay them homage. They changed from a Turkish to a German train at Damascus, which meant they had sleeping cars and sheets.

It was pomp and circumstance all the way, from a military parade during the changing of the trains at Damascus to receptions by the governors of the various Turkish provinces through which they passed. All the way von Mücke continued to shepherd his charges, although it was no longer strictly necessary. He made sure they were all on the train before he would allow it to move. He brought them newspapers and watched their health. Once he pulled the emergency cord and stopped the train so one of his sailors could retrieve a fez that had rolled into the ditch. He continued his chalk talks, giving his men the news of the war, and in Baalbek he took the men on a tour of the Roman ruins and guided them like an expert. In Aleppo, when the official mail was received, he announced that all of them had the Iron Cross, and he read aloud to all of them the various messages of praise and endearment received from the fatherland.

Finally the train reached Haidar Pasha, the end of the railway, and there the men of the *Emden* were greeted by the first German naval officers they had seen since leaving their ship at Direction Island. Admiral Souchon, chief of the Mediterranean division for the Imperial Navy, was there with his staff in their blue-and-gold uniforms, waiting at the station. The men of the *Emden* stepped off their train in their shining new uniforms and lined up briskly. Kapitänleutnant Hellmuth von Mücke stepped out in front of them and ordered a salute; on the right flank the flags of a German warship flew. He called his crew to attention, gave the salute, and lowered his sword, stepping toward his smiling admiral, and spoke, huskily.

"I report the landing squad from the *Emden*, five officers, seven petty officers, and thirty men strong."

BIBLIOGRAPHY, NOTES AND ACKNOWLEDGMENTS

PARTS OF THE STORY of the last cruise of the *Emden* and the fate of its men have been told many times, but the only comprehensive attempt was made by Kapitänleutnant Hellmuth von Mücke after his return home from the long trip in the *Ayesha* and *Choising* and the zambuks. He treated the story in two books, *The Emden* and *The Ayesha*. Both are invaluable, but neither is complete, and, since both were written at the height of World War I, they suffer from von Mücke's patriotic zeal. Indeed, *The Emden* is most inaccurate, because von Mücke obviously took pains to conceal dates, times, places, and other facts and figures lest they give aid and comfort to his country's enemies. His tale of the cruise on the *Ayesha* suffers less in this regard, although it is purposely misleading in some respects, such as the heroic account he gives of a day-long battle between the *Emden* and the *Sydney*, when it actually took the *Sydney* only forty minutes to wreck the smaller ship.

Much more has been written about the *Emden* than about the *Ayesha*. I used the following works: von Mücke's *The Emden*, Ritter and Company, Boston, 1917, translated by Helene S. White; *Der Kommandant der Emden, Das Leben des Kapitäns von Müller*, by Karl Bartz, Im Deutschen Verlag, Berlin, 1939; *Unsere Emden, Erlebnisse auf den Kaperfahrten im Jahre 1914*, by R. Witthoeft, Verlag von Reimar Hobbing in Berlin, 1926; *Das Buch von der Emden*, by Hermann Ottiger, K. Thienemanns Verlag, Stuttgart, 1936; *Emden, My Experiences in S.M.S. Emden*, by Franz Joseph, Prince of Hohenzollern, Oberleutnant z. S. a. D., G. Howard Watt, New York, 1928, translated from the German; *Lauterbach of the China Sea, the Escapes and Adventures of a Seagoing Falstaff*, by Lowell Thomas, Doubleday, Doran and Company, Garden City, 1930; *L'Emden, Ses Croisières et sa Fin*, by Paul Ardoin, Librairie Maritime et Coloniale, Paris, 1920; *L'Emden, croiseur-corsaire,* by Jean Feuga, Librairie Alphonse Lemerre, Paris, 1931; *Auf der Emden und Ayesha, Erlebnisse eines Teilnehmers, Nach den Aufzeichnungen aus seinem Tagebuche,* geschildert von Hermann Oesterwitz, Wallmanns Verlag und Buchdruckerei, Berlin.

Other books used for specific and self-evident portions of this work were: *Tsingtau Under Three Flags,* by Wilson Leon Goodshall, The Commercial Press, Ltd., Shanghai, China, 1929; *The Guns of August,* by Barbara W. Tuchman, Macmillan, New York, 1962; *The War in Outline, 1914–1918,* by Liddell Hart, Random House, 1936; *Der Krieg zur See 1914–18, Kämpfe in den Kolonien* (Berantwortlicher Leiter der Bearbeitung Kurt Ussmann, Konteradmiral a.D.), Verlag von E. S. Mittlev & Sohn, Berlin, 1935.

The story of von Mücke's adventures aboard the *Ayesha* and afterward was dealt with in *The Ayesha, A Great Adventure,* by Hellmuth von Mücke, Philip Allan & Co., Ltd., London, 1930. There have been other English editions of this work, notably one published in the United States in 1917; this Allan edition is far more valuable because it contains a foreword by J. G. Lockhart which sums up the British knowledge of the *Emden* and *Ayesha* and an afterword by Phil Andere, published first in *Zodiac* magazine, which gives a British eyewitness account of the German landing on Direction Island.

A number of newspapers and magazines were consulted in preparing this work, particularly *The New York Times* for 1914 and 1915 and the *Times* of London, both of which contained several articles dealing with the *Emden* and its men. Emil Ludwig, the German biographer, was dispatched to Damascus to meet the heroes of the *Emden* and the *Ayesha,* and he wrote a journalistic account which was published in paperback in 1915 and widely distributed throughout Germany. It is useful largely to give the emotional impact of this entire adventure on the German people, since the facts are scanty and often inaccurate.

I am indebted to a number of people for information about the *Emden* and its crew: to Professor Carl Dolmetsch of the John F. Kennedy Institut für Amerikastudien, Berlin; to K. von Kutzleben of the Marine-Offizier-Hilfe in Essen, West Germany; to Kapitän-zur-See Helmut Schmoeckel, Naval Attaché of the Federal Republic of Germany's embassy in Washington; and to Kapitän-zur-See Bidlingmaier, director of the Militärgeschichtliches Forschungsamt in Berlin.

I am also greatly indebted to Elfriede Gruhzit and to Olga Hoyt for translations from the German and to E. W. Harrison, circulation director of Yale University's Sterling Library, for the lengthy use of certain books and documents.

Edwin P. Hoyt
Bomoseen, Vermont
September 1, 1965

INDEX